Electronic Publishing:
Politics and Pragmatics

New Technologies in Medieval and Renaissance Studies
Volume 2

ITER

MEDIEVAL AND RENAISSANCE TEXTS AND STUDIES
VOLUME 401

Electronic Publishing: Politics and Pragmatics

Edited by
Gabriel Egan, Loughborough University

NTMRS Series Editors
William R. Bowen and Raymond G. Siemens

Iter Inc.
in collaboration with
ACMRS
(Arizona Center for Medieval and Renaissance Studies)
Tempe, Arizona
2010

The publication of this volume has been supported by grants
from the Senate of Victoria University in the University of Toronto
and the Renaissance Society of America.

Published by Iter, Inc. and
ACMRS (Arizona Center for Medieval and Renaissance Studies)
Tempe, Arizona

Library of Congress Cataloging-in-Publication Data

Electronic publishing : politics and pragmatics / edited by Gabriel Egan.
    p. cm. -- (New technologies in medieval and Renaissance studies ; v. 2)
(Medieval and Renaissance texts and studies ; v. 401)
  Includes bibliographical references.
  ISBN 978-0-86698-449-2 (alk. paper)
  1. Scholarly electronic publishing. 2. Communication in learning and
scholarship--Technological innovations. 3. Humanities--Digital libraries.
4. Library materials--Digitization. 5. Criticism, Textual--Data processing.
6. Transmission of texts. I. Egan, Gabriel.
  Z286.E43E4385 2010
  070.5'797--dc22
                                                          2010043523

ISBN 978-0-86698-021-0 (online)

∞
This book is made to last.
It was typeset in SIL Gentium at the
Institute for Research in Classical Philosophy and Science (Princeton).
It is smyth-sewn and printed on acid-free paper to library specifications.
Printed in the United States of America

Contents

Editor's Acknowledgements

My largest debt is to the contributors to this volume, who allowed me to put my name on the cover of something containing their work. The little I did in shaping the collection was less than adequate recompense for that honour. The contributors and I are jointly in the debt of the three anonymous peer reviewers who read, approved, and often improved every contribution. Aside from the general editors of the book series, Ray Siemens and Bill Bowen, who had the excellent idea of suggesting the topic to me and guided the collection at every stage from suggestion to completion, I would like to thank a couple of institutions for organizing events at which its content took form in my mind and in the minds of several of the contributors. At De Montfort University's Centre for Textual Scholarship in 2007–8, Peter Shillingsburg organized a series of one-day meetings to discuss in general terms the future of scholarly editions in the digital age and in particular certain thorny issues such as the purpose and extent of editorial annotation and explication. At Sheffield Hallam University, Lisa Hopkins runs an ongoing series of Digital Humanities days, which recently enabled several of the contributors to meet and develop plans for this volume. I am grateful not only to Peter and Lisa for these fruitful meetings, but also the funding organizations (most especially their universities) that had the foresight to support them.

Stratford-upon-Avon, January 2010

Introduction

Gabriel Egan
Loughborough University
mail@gabrielegan.com

The technologies, economics, and politics of scholarly publication in the humanities look set to change rapidly in the near future. Even if the market for print publication were to remain relatively buoyant, national governments (the main direct and indirect funders of research) are increasingly questioning the efficiency and cost of traditional means of dissemination. The academic humanities book market is an unusual sector in publishing because the producers, the academic authors, comprise also the largest sector of the consumers, either directly or through their institutional libraries. From the perspective of those who pay for research, publishers appear to have created and plugged themselves into a circuit of knowledge dissemination (from academics to publishers and back again) to which they do not contribute as much value as they extract. With new electronic publication technologies that do not require large investments of capital (printing presses, warehouses, transport), there are powerful forces directing academic authors away from traditional print publication.

This book brings together a group of academics with experience in this new field in order to explore not only the practical matters of electronic publication but also to have them reflect on the politics of the vastly changed knowledge landscape that is likely to exist soon. As well as eliciting their accounts of how such matters as intellectual property rights (IPR) and coding standards figured in their projects, the book draws from the contributors their wider visions of the future of the knowledge economy and how the humanities disciplines will fare in a world that increasingly entrusts its cultural heritage to magnetism and laser optics rather than inks and paper. The essays are grouped into two categories, concerning the creation of digital projects and their dissemination. There is always a necessary connection between writing and reading—acts of production presume their own subsequent consumption—but in this topic the linkage is especially close because the technology tends to narrow the gap between "making" and "getting." That is to say, in print publication the author or editor uses creative tools (paper, typewriters, computers) that are nothing like the tools for dissemination (presses and binding machines, trucks/boats/aeroplanes, warehouses, and retail outlets). In electronic publishing, however, the author or editor may create very nearly the final object and the act of distribution alters it little or not at all.

Whereas in print publication the author may leave the final choices of mediation (paper quality, binding, pagination, image reproduction) to someone else, in electronic publishing the creator is obliged to consider closely how the reader will experience the content. Contributors who have made digital content have pertinent things to say about how their close involvement in the dissemination shaped their creations. This narrowing of the gap between producer and consumer is also crucial in regard to the adoption of standards since creators must ensure their output will work with the computers available to consumers: there is no point planning a project whose outputs are a LaserDisc with accompanying 8-track audiobook.

Part One of this collection is concerned with the creation of texts and, in particular, the tools, standards, and skills needed. The recent past of electronic publication is littered with projects that have become unusable because of rapid changes in the standards of computer hardware and software. The BBC's 1980s project to create a new digital Domesday Book recorded life in the United Kingdom 900 years after the original book. The many thousands of items assembled for this project are now lost because the hardware platform, a LaserDisc attached to an Acorn/BBC microcomputer, is incompatible with standard computers today. The 900-year-old first (paper) edition of the book remains readable and the second (digital) version is useless. The widespread adoption of computer standards ratified by the International Standards Organization (ISO) ameliorates but does not eliminate this problem.

In the digitization of writing, the Text Encoding Initiative (TEI) aims to provide a standard set of tags for marking up literary works, and in all disciplines eXtensible Markup Language (XML) is touted as the means to ensure that intellectual content can be migrated across the ever-changing future hardware and software standards of the computer marketplace. Nonetheless, debates continue about the philosophical underpinnings of such standards and, in the case of TEI, whether creators should tag only the logical structures of writing (line, stanza, chapter, and so on) and not its visual appearance (boldface, italic, whitespace). Despite the widespread acceptance of TEI, the tools needed to produce an electronic edition are considerably more complex and fragile than those needed to produce a print edition (for which Microsoft Word is ubiquitous), and within certain learned societies the discipline of tagging is considered solely the young scholars' province because it is so technically difficult. One school of thought maintains that careful human tagging of old texts will turn out to be wasted effort because computers will eventually be able to make sense of texts as readers do, inferring structure and meaning from content.

In the first essay in this collection, Peter Shillingsburg considers how computers have changed the art of scholarly editing, looking at the fundamental nature of electronic text as opposed to paper-based text and the problems, as well as the opportunities, it creates for the editor who wants to record the historicity of the art she is attempting to mediate to new readers. His is an established textual scholar's-eye-view of the print/e-publishing differences, and it starts with the pertinent observation that we do not make electronic scholarly editions in order to solve problems of conservation: paper is already very good at that, and the electronic medium very poor. Print editions are expensive to get into first appearance but have little ongoing costs, whereas electronic editions are relatively cheap to get into first appearance but have large ongoing costs for upkeep. When we compare the two media, the new one defamiliarizes the old and makes us reconsider the print medium and in particular how its materiality—its quality of embodying abstract thought in tangible objects—conditions its capacity to carry meaning.

For Shillingsburg, the materiality of the medium in which literary texts from the past first appeared so fundamentally affected what was written that new electronic editions of the works must find ways to preserve traces of that materiality. He contrasts the print medium and the electronic medium, showing the advantages and disadvantages of each, but is careful to insist on the materiality of both. Just as Matthew Kirschenbaum argues in his book *Mechanisms*, Shillingsburg sees the exploration of the social nature of textuality—the fact that writing is always done in a specific historical context and using specific technical means—to apply as much to the new media as to the old (Kirschenbaum 2008).

Shillingsburg ends by surveying particular online projects in the light of his own desiderata; all are archival rather than editorial projects: they do not attempt to provide a critically edited text. This, Shillingsburg suggests, is an effect of the reaction against the mid-twentieth-century editorial school of W. W. Greg and Fredson Bowers, now widely decried as overly Platonic in its distinction of the medium from the message of writing, or in G. Thomas Tanselle's terms the distinction between *text* and *work* (Tanselle 1989). Perhaps those such as Margreta de Grazia who critique this distinction have thrown the baby out with the bathwater: just because we can, by electronic means, make comprehensive archives it seems natural to reject the critical-editing approach of Greg-Bowers (De Grazia 1993). Shillingsburg argues for synthesis of the best of both traditions, based on the principle that we can recover a particular kind of authorial intention. We cannot know what the author wanted the text to mean but we can get a pretty good idea what the author wanted the text to be, which words in what order.

Robert Whalen reports on these matters from the coalface, or if you prefer, the front line. He shows what has been achieved with an electronic edition of George Herbert's poetry and how it supports certain kinds of literary analysis that a print edition could not. To achieve this has meant tackling the limitations of current technical means for representing the particularities of Herbert's manuscripts and the *mise en page* of early print editions, and in the process Whalen has found himself disagreeing with the choices of the poet's recent scholarly editors, F. E. Hutchinson and Helen Wilcox (Herbert 1941; Herbert 2007). Digitization allows copious documentation and presentation of the archive, and digital delivery obviates the arcane codes used when variants are presented in print: we can just show the different versions of a poem together on screen. Whalen explores some of the interpretative consequences of the differences in particular poems, showing how agencies other than the author's are embodied in the resulting artefacts and thus supporting the approaches pioneered by theorists of the social text (McGann 1991).

Some material characteristics (such as the famous typographical layout in the poem "Easter Wings") are particularly difficult to encode in an electronic text. Worse, the most commonly used standards for text encoding, the TEI's P5 guidelines, require a division of the work in hierarchical units that do not seem to accommodate Herbert's poetry very well. (This matter is taken up also in Ian Lancashire's contribution.) Whalen illustrates how the project aids literary-critical work on the poetry, especially in relation to poetical self-censorship. He concludes that despite limitations, there is plenty that can be done in an electronic edition that cannot be done in a print edition, and done to the considerable benefit of modern readers. Moreover, the creation of the digital archive will enable its exploitation using tools as yet undeveloped or in their infancy, a point explored at length in Martin Mueller's contribution.

Whether the final output will be an electronic text or a printed book or both (as with the present collection), virtually all new professional writing is done by typing on a computer keyboard. The software that turns those keystrokes into a digital file will, in almost every case, be Microsoft Word. Jeff Smith makes a powerful argument for the unsuitability of this and every other authoring tool currently available to creative writers. Interface designers need to think in new ways about the nature of textuality so that they can produce tools that are better suited to creative work than the clumsy ones we use now. Smith gives concrete examples of tools he has created to this end. By thinking about the principles underlying authorial creativity, for example Mihaly Csikszentmihalyi's notion of "flow" as a state of mind (1990) and Denis Alamargot and Lucile Chanquoy's work on iterative development of ideas (2001), Smith shows that current writing tools are too constraining and offer entirely inappropriate options. What novelist, he asks, wants to set the pagination of her book before she has even worked out her characters' motivations? She needs not a word processor but an ideas processor, a device that acknowledges that we have prelinguistic notions and will want to manipulate those. Because writers are in a sense literary critics too—they are, after all, the first to critique the work as it takes shape—the kinds of materials the two disciplines generate are much alike, and the same tools can help both.

This collection of essays surveys the interchanges between humanities scholarship on the one hand and computer technologies on the other, and inevitably this brings into view C. P. Snow's argument that the relationship is asymmetrical: humanists know less about the work of technologists than vice versa (Snow 1959). Taking an opposing line to Peter Robinson, who thinks the production of electronic scholarly editions has been stifled by the requirement for sophisticated technical knowledge on the part of editors, Alan Galey argues that gaining this knowledge is good for editors and their editions. He argues along the same lines as William J. Turkel and Alan MacEachern in *The Programming Historian* when he insists that editors should be competent programmers because only then can they bend the machines to their wills (Turkel and MacEachern 2007). But more than this, the discipline of writing a Document Type Definition (DTD) or XML Schema—the technical specification that defines the elements that make up the edition and how they may be combined—forces the editor of a literary text to think hard about the object in hand and her approach to digitizing it. Galey looks back to the transformation of "the human record" that came about because of the Gutenberg press, which he takes as an analogue for the digital transformation currently underway. It is noticeable that humanists have traditionally been in the vanguard of new textual technologies: we are the ones who know how to use them to organize knowledge.

How should editors get the technical skills they need? One way is through best-practice training provided by institutions such as Modern Language Association (MLA), but Galey is sceptical of this because the best reconceptualizations of the processes of editing in the last thirty years have come from outside of the big institutions and in contestation with their orthodoxies. Galey thinks the digital editor must, to some extent, go it alone and he offers a sketch of certain fields of technical knowledge that he thinks are both essential and within the otherwise non-technical editor's grasp. Galey's focus is as much on the generic skills as the technical ones, and the need to develop a kind of platform-independence of mind even while learning about particular technologies that are necessary to produce results today. Delegation of the technical matters is not, according to Galey, a wise option. Collaboration is the current buzzword with funding agencies—get the technologists over here to apply their skills to the humanists' projects over there—but it can actually strengthen the divisions between disciplines. Better for humanists to learn the technical skills themselves, for what is at stake here is the power to harness the technologies.

At the middle of this book there is a historical intermezzo comprising a paper from Ian Lancashire written at the end of the last millennium and a reply to it freshly written by Murray McGillivray. In 1994 C. M. Sperberg-McQueen and Lou Burnard published *Guidelines for Electronic Text Encoding and Interchange, P3*, a highly influential set of guidelines for the tagging of literary works, and it is to these that Lancashire directly responds. But the import of his argument goes beyond the specifics of that standard and concerns any tagging system derived from Standard Generalized Markup Language (SGML) that requires the editor to decide upon matters that properly are the province of the reader/critic. The orderliness of the hierarchical-content model just is not appropriate for literary writing. Despite being an ISO standard that specifies no tags, just a syntax, SGML embodies a theory of text to which researchers in the humanities may not willingly assent. The TEI guidelines not only accept the highly debatable theory of text implicit within SGML but also superimpose upon it a tagset expressing a semantics of textual objects that further narrows the acceptability of the TEI document architecture.

Just as Jeff Smith's essay argues that current tools for creative writing tend to straitjacket the creative mind, Lancashire's shows that anyone who uses the TEI SGML-conformant tagset is forced to work within a positivist paradigm: a theory and a semantics of text at odds with the majority of literary theories of the past thirty years. This paradigm results in a text packaged not just with the editor-annotator's judgments, but also with theoretical axioms and decisions about meaning that others—most of them anonymous—have built into the encoding terminology and the DTD. This paradigm misrepresents the complexities of text by underestimating the powers of both the author and the reader, the two muses, in determining and undetermining textual semantics and structures. We do not need to establish one-size-fits-all tag-sets before working on texts: we can, as Lancashire illustrates, do analysis that lets the tags emerge from the text itself. TEI's attempt to codify once and for all (in the temporal and spatial senses) the structure of text is a mistake.

McGillivray starts his response to Lancashire's critique by observing its reliance on the notion that tags can, as it were, lie: the object being tagged is not the kind of object that the tag's name seems to imply, as would be the case with "<address> Gabriel Egan</address>." As McGillivray points out, our habit of giving tags names that suggest their purpose is misleading here, and meaning in fact inheres not in the names of tags—the names are arbitrary—but in the relationships between them and the uses to which we put them. Lancashire himself makes a distinction between "characters and spaces" that are truly language and the other elements of the tagged file that are really only part of the technology of language storage. McGillivray objects to this distinction: a materialist approach to language entails acknowledging that we cannot separate the medium and the message quite so neatly as this. Moreover, McGillivray reminds us that it was by answering the question "What Is Text, Really?" that Steven J. DeRose and his co-authors convinced many in the humanities that SGML and its derivatives were the correct way forward (DeRose et al. 1990).

Certainly, McGillivray acknowledges, there is a kind of Platonic idealism in the TEI guidelines, an assumption that one can separate language from the media that convey it, but he finds the more recent versions of the guidelines to be less guilty of this fault; they are coming around to the materialist position. Maybe TEI will never be good enough for those who want to take a document-centred approach to writing, but distancing himself from Lancashire's characterization of the first of his "muses," the author, McGillivray sees merit in the way the TEI standard forces attention upon features of the text rather than the person who wrote it. To achieve the kinds of interpretative ends Lancashire wants, we really need machines to be much smarter readers, able to work out the lemma for any particular inflection or conjugation, and to identify parts-of-speech. Martin Mueller's paper in the second half of this collection describes just how far machines have come at doing these tricks that readers perform so easily.

The second half of this book is concerned with the politics and pragmatics of dissemination, or, as we used to call it, publication. Just as there are projects that failed because computer standards moved on, there are projects that failed because too few buyers were willing to pay for the product on sale. At several thousands of dollars apiece, almost no one bought the Arden Shakespeare CD-ROM and the Thomson Gale English Short Title Catalogue (ESTC) on CD-ROM. The print version of the *Encyclopaedia Britannica* costs about that much and has remained just about marketable, while the CD-ROM version of the same content has settled at around $50. Unusually in this sector, the *Oxford English Dictionary* appeals to a large non-specialist market and has been able to keep its price relatively high at around $500. By contrast, the market for the specialist research book is small and the price-per-unit is fairly high (around $100–200). This market may not be sustainable if academics and research-library buyers cease to support it, as seems distinctly possible.

The papers in this half of the book survey the recent history of electronic publication and suggest its possible futures, both in relation to the technical particularities of how users engage with electronic editions and the economic models that will emerge as our cultural heritage goes fully online. Peter Robinson looks at the development of electronic methods for editing and publishing literary works over the last twenty years, focusing especially on his own role and the achievements and failures of the projects he has led. Robinson mounts an attack upon the institutional structures that have grown up to support this kind of work and argues that lack of interest from lone scholars in producing new digital editions is a damning indictment of current methods of e-publishing. As can be seen from collections of essays such as Susan Hockey and Nancy Ide's *Research in Humanities Computing 4* (1996), around fifteen years ago SGML seemed like a godsend, but we had forgotten about software for practical implementations. Then came XML and the Web, and Robinson tried to produce his own software, Anastasia, that would enable anyone working essentially alone to make digital editions. This failed, and these days digital editions are made only within large institutions with considerable technical infrastructures.

Robinson thinks that the concentration of resources in a few centres of specialist technical excellence is a bad thing: many scholars who could make new editions of important literary works are put off doing so because they do not have access to these centres and are unwilling to learn the gory details of XML. Institutional projects are also regressive in that they tend to encourage editorial teams to design an interface, which we now know is a mistake. The central lesson to be drawn from the recent explosion of the interactive Web is that editors should provide well-described data that users are able to bring together within their own, home-brewed interfaces or mash-ups. Robinson describes early explorations he has made into the solution of simply exposing to the world one's set of scholarly digital materials (digital facsimiles and transcriptions) with attached metadata that is sufficient to enable creative users to employ them in new configurations as they please.

Since the Budapest Open Access Initiative in 2002, the Bethesda Statement on Open Access Publishing in 2003, and the Berlin Declaration on Open Access to Knowledge in the Sciences and Humanities in 2003, the idea that the results of scholarly research should be given away freely over the Internet—the Open Access (OA) principle—has gained many adherents. The United Kingdom government's Science and Technology Committee has declared itself in favour of OA and endorsed three routes. The first is the creation of Institutional Repositories (IRs) to hold and preserve research outputs from particular institutions, primarily universities. This process is already well advanced. The second method is self-archiving (Web-based dissemination) by individual academics, and the third is author-pays publishing as opposed to reader-pays as at present; these have scarcely begun. OA has been driven by the journal-centric sciences, but the humanities disciplines place at least as much importance on the book as the journal article. There may be book-specific barriers to OA, and although major academic publishers (such as Elsevier and Taylor & Francis) have declared their acceptance of some OA principles in respect of journal articles (limited dissemination and deposit of preprint articles) the picture with monographs and critical editions is far from clear.

Shawn Martin's contribution is primarily concerned with the economics of digitization projects, and he advocates an abandonment of a simple binary logic that contrasts Open and Closed Access models. While accepting the arguments about models for revenue generation in an influential report by Kevin Guthrie, Rebecca Griffiths, and Nancy Maron (2008), Martin's survey finds that there is in fact a greater variety of arrangements currently in place between universities and publishers. To get important work done requires creative invention in the fashioning of these relationships, and Martin details the remarkable Text Creation Partnership (TCP) that makes transcriptions of books from the image-only Early English Books Online (EEBO) database. By bringing commercial and academic institutions into partnership, TCP is able to fund the creation of fully searchable, highly consistent electronic texts that would not be a viable proposition for any commercial or academic institutions on their own, or even several of them working together. Martin's analysis of the economics makes a powerful argument for rethinking how academia engages with commercial publishers of electronic text.

Because the World Wide Web contains many unreliable sources in humanities disciplines, the electronic medium has suffered a credibility gap in comparison with print. The new kinds of collective authority that the interactive Web has fostered—manifested most obviously in the largely reliable Wikipedia database and in sites where hotel guests review the hotels they have stayed in—have so far gained little purchase upon the academic mind. Andrew Keen's book *The Cult of the Amateur: How Today's Internet Is Killing Our Culture and Assaulting Our Economy* argues that the new interactive Web encourages an anti-intellectual narcissism amongst users, who are encouraged to suppose that their amateur efforts (at writing, film-making, or commentating) are as valid as the professionals' (2007). Paul Vetch finds Keen's argument elitist and specious, and his contribution to this collection approaches the question via a consideration of the ways that interfaces for digital editions have been developed, leading to his conclusion that principles of user-interactivity might improve the interfaces for future projects in ways equally useful to professional and non-professional readers. Speaking from personal experience as a designer, Vetch charts recent technical developments, starting with the explosion of client-side JavaScript that makes web pages look and behave much like applications.

The trouble is, Vetch points out, that we do not have agreed standards for the ways in which Web-delivered applications do things; indeed, there has been little research into how users react to the things that designers put on the screen. What research there is seems contradicted by recent developments: the social networking website Facebook breaks most of the accepted rules of usability and yet is perceived by its users as a highly intuitive and easily navigated interface. Clearly our self-imposed rules for what users need and want are not keeping up with their real needs and wants. Vetch details the ways that these problems were handled on one project he was involved in, which was particularly concerned with how user-generated content (including annotations of the project's materials) could be included while managing scholarly fear of the Wikipedia syndrome, where bad information devalues the credibility of the good.

When the information scientist S. R. Ranganathan published his *Five Laws of Library Science* (1931) he included the principle that collections must grow, and in his essay Martin Mueller reads this to mean not only grow in size but also grow in what are now called affordances, the things we can do with texts. Like Vetch, Mueller sees value in user-generated and user-maintained content, and he describes how a richly marked-up large corpus of electronic texts of literary works might be produced from existing resources and with minimal investment by exploitation of collaborative-working tools. Using examples of what can be achieved now in literary-critical work with the relatively modest corpora already in existence, Mueller gives tantalizing glimpses of what he thinks we might be able to do with datasets covering most of the literary works in existence. The new kinds of literary analysis that Franco Moretti introduces in his book *Graphs, Maps, Trees* (2005) could be greatly extended if more literary texts were available in digital form with a minimal quantity of tagging.

Taking as his model GenBank, the publicly available set of DNA sequences of thousands of living organisms, Mueller determines that we need a repository of around 10,000 texts from the world of letters that have been sufficiently normalized—with part-of-speech tagging and encoding to show structure— that they may function as "intereditions" that can be used collectively in a variety of computer-automated comparisons. This repository would need "textkeepers," a user community of people curating the material. Project Gutenberg's network of proofreaders has demonstrated that a community of interested amateurs is more than sufficient to do the distributed collaborative work that Mueller envisages "textkeepers" undertaking. The places for these repositories to be housed are university libraries, which do not need to redefine their core role in conserving the human record in order to take over this function.

With such a dataset in place, the kinds of analysis across many different works that only linguists have formerly been interested in become of interest to literary scholars. The technical difficulty of raising a lot of texts to the relatively low plateau of commonality needed for such a "Book of English," as Mueller calls it, is not great, and he has some ideas about how it may be achieved as an extension of existing projects. Implicitly disagreeing with Ian Lancashire, Mueller reckons that so long as a very minimal set of features is captured—ignoring much that makes a literary text interesting to literary scholars—the view of the canon provided by "distant reading" (Moretti's term) would more than make up for the loss of local detail about particular works.

It is clear that the contributors to this collection are not unanimous on the procedures and infrastructures that are needed for the transition to an essentially online approach to the humanities. Indeed, the editor of the collection found himself in considerable disagreement with the ideas present in the abstracts for several of the essays when they were first submitted. Upon reading the full versions of the essays, these disagreements did not entirely evaporate and there remains here much that he would want to argue over if it were presented in debate following from oral presentation. This should be understood as healthy disagreement, since what is at stake—if we grant that our primary modes of access to intellectual resources will soon be digital—is the future of humanities scholarship itself. The vibrantly sketched differences of opinion presented in this collection are testament to the importance we place upon the details of how that scholarship is to develop and grow.

WORKS CITED

Alamargot, Denis, and Lucile Chanquoy. 2001. *Through the Models of Writing.* Studies in writing v. 9. Dordrecht: Kluwer Academic.

Csikszentmihalyi, Mihaly. 1990. *Flow: The Psychology of Optimal Experience.* New York: Harper & Row.

De Grazia, Margreta. 1993. What is a Work? What is a Document? In *New Ways of Looking at Old Texts: Papers of the Renaissance English Text Society, 1985-1991,* ed. W. Speed Hill, 199–207. Medieval and Renaissance Texts and Studies 107. Binghamton NY: Center for Medieval and Early Renaissance Studies at the State University of New York.

DeRose, Steven J., David G. Durand, Elli Mylonas, and Allen H. Renear. 1990. What is Text, Really? *Journal of Computing in Higher Education* 1, no. 2 (Winter): 3–26.

Guthrie, Kevin, Rebecca Griffiths, and Nancy Maron. 2008. Sustainability and Revenue Models for Online Academic Resources. May. http://www.jisc.ac.uk/media/documents/themes/eresources/sca_ithaka_sustainability_report-final.pdf.

Herbert, George. 1941. *The Works.* Oxford: Clarendon Press.

————— 2007. *The English Poems of George Herbert.* Cambridge: Cambridge University Press.

Hockey, Susan, and Nancy Ide, eds. 1996. *Research in Humanities Computing 4: Selected papers from the Association for Literary and Linguistic Computing-*

Association for Computing in the Humanities (ALLC-ACH) Conference at Christ Church College Oxford, April 1992. Oxford: Clarendon Press.

Keen, Andrew. 2007. *The Cult of the Amateur: How Today's Internet Is Killing Our Culture and Assaulting Our Economy.* London: Nicholas Brealey.

Kirschenbaum, Matthew G. 2008. *Mechanisms: New Media and the Forensic Imagination.* Cambridge, MA: Massachusetts Institute of Technology Press.

McGann, Jerome J. 1991. *The Textual Condition.* Princeton, NJ: Princeton University Press.

Moretti, Franco. 2005. *Graphs, Maps, Trees: Abstract Models for a Literary History.* London: Verso.

Ranganathan, S. R. 1931. *The Five Laws of Library Science.* Madras: Madras Library Association. http://dlist.sir.arizona.edu/1220/.

Snow, C. P. 1959. *The Two Cultures and the Scientific Revolution: The Rede Lecture, 1959.* Cambridge: Cambridge University Press.

Tanselle, G. Thomas. 1989. *A Rationale of Textual Criticism.* Philadelphia: University of Pennsylvania Press.

Turkel, William J, and Alan MacEachern. 2007. The Programming Historian. http://niche.uwo.ca/programming-historian.

PART ONE
CREATING ELECTRONIC PUBLICATIONS:
THE POLITICS AND PRAGMATICS OF TOOLS,
STANDARDS, AND SKILLS

The Impact of Computers on the Art of Scholarly Editing

Peter Shillingsburg

Loyola University Chicago

pshillingsburg@luc.edu

This essay has three parts: an introductory general assessment of the issues; a five-point approach to the idea of the impact of computers on scholarly editing; and a brief analysis of electronic editions assessing their successes and failures in meeting the challenge of electronic scholarly editing: preserving and re-presenting historical texts in an alien medium with demands and potentials not foreseen by their authors and publishers.

The issues

There are two proven characteristics of paper/print books that are impossible for electronic books to replicate: print books are capable of being read with the naked eye and they continue to be readable without change or intervention (except careful storage) for centuries. There is no known plan to store electronic texts in a medium that itself can be read with the naked eye or that will last centuries. Therefore, the purposes for creating electronic scholarly editions have nothing to do with being able to read them or to make them last. The purposes for the use of computers in scholarly editing are completely other.

Some scholarly editors are in a state of denial, having yet to realize these truths. The fact that files written to hard disks cannot easily be erased or destroyed beyond the capacity of heroic efforts to rescue data is notwithstanding for the ordinary editor, whose electronic edition will become unreadable to any ordinary reader within ten to thirty years of completion unless regular maintenance and porting to new media is conducted (Kirschenbaum 2008). This might not be true of editions rendered as Adobe Acrobat Portable Document Format (PDF) files or image files of fixed pages, but adopting those formats would virtually defeat many of the singular advantages of electronic over paper editions.

ISBN 978-0-86698-021-0 (online)   ISBN 978-0-86698-449-2 (print)

New Technologies in Medieval and Renaissance Studies 2 (2010) 17–29

For clarity, creating scholarly editions should be distinguished from other editing done by and for scholars. It consists of preparing new texts of canonical (or would-be canonical) works (of literary or other historical significance) according to standards that almost always include the collection and detailed comparison of all extant authoritative historical texts of the work from manuscripts to most revised edition and providing some detailed report of the results, the selection of a base text to reproduce as a reading text (possibly emended) of the work, an account of the composition, revision, publication, dissemination, and reception of the work, and an account of the editor's principles and methods for preparing the edition.

The purposes for scholarly editing include providing a standard or specifically identified text of the work, ensuring that it is free of errors and of interpolations other than those deliberately accepted by the editor and reported, providing a history of the genesis and development, corruption or censorship of the work, and placing the work in historical and bibliographical contexts.

The uses of scholarly editions include engaging with a text of known characteristics and history, understanding the work in a declared historical set of contexts, understanding how the text under immediate scrutiny relates to its alternative versions, and understanding how the work functioned for readers historically, through the introductions, commentaries, and notes usually attached to scholarly editions.

All of these elements of scholarly editing were developed in the manuscript and print eras. The two questions before us now are, why should this complex and time-consuming scholarly work be published in an ephemeral, vulnerable form requiring special equipment to access—electronically? And, in what ways have the capabilities of electronic publishing affected the scholar's notion of what a scholarly edition should be or can be?

Some answers to these two questions are especially relevant to editors because of how editions are constructed; others relate more to readers because of the way scholarly editions are used. Editors use electronic equipment in preparing texts for print as well as for electronic publication, and so the two modes of publication follow parallel paths during much of the research, compilation, and editing phases of the work. Also, editors, because of their intimate and extensive familiarity with the materials, may see more quickly than others that print requires a very high degree of selectivity in what is produced, whereas the electronic medium allows a more generous representation of source materials. Readers, on the other hand, might prefer the simplicity and familiarity of print and yet see that electronic search tools work faster than print indexes and that increased amounts of visual material in electronic form offer greater access to the physical appearance of original material forms of the work than is possible in printed editions.

Some things can, of course, be done equally well with a print book or an electronic one and, therefore, do not constitute by themselves reasons for producing electronic texts. But frequently these things are done in very different ways. For example, it is obviously easier for an editor to generate an index electronically with a computer than manually on paper index cards, though the former is often merely a mechanical process responding to predicted circumstances defined by a program and the latter is a conceptual one capable of nuanced responses to unexpected situations because a human mind is the engine of process. Further, it is nearly as easy to use a printed index as it is to conduct a search of an electronic text for on-the-fly links to specific words in the text. And print indexes are sometimes subject indexes, not available to merely mechanical retrieval. However, given enough forethought, an electronic text can be marked up with subject tags making searches equal to the advantages of subject indexes. Incidentally, that markup process in the preparation of scholarly edition texts is still manual and shares much of the tedium of card indexing. What is gained by electronic processes often entails some kind of loss. The question is, are the gains worth the losses and can the losses be recouped by better technology or in some other way?

There are, however, other things that a computer can do with a text that cannot be done as well, if at all, in book form. Therefore, there are many reasons to construct electronic scholarly editions, though it remains true that paper scholarly editions will last longer and be useful even when electricity fails. Nevertheless, electronic editions are attractive because scholars can provide more materials and more functions in them than publishers allow in print ones. It follows that it takes more effort to construct an electronic scholarly edition than a print one. For electronic scholarly editing, a greater number of documents must be brought to publishable standards, more parts of the edition are created and must be coordinated, more things can go wrong and are vulnerable to inadvertent change, and there are more complex intellectual property rights (IPR) to respect and to assert. Thus, there is more proofreading and checking to be done. Print editions benefit from a five-hundred-year tradition of craft, skill, equipment, design, production, marketing, and dissemination, all with entailed personnel and infrastructure in place to bolster the scholarly effort. In the electronic world, on the other hand, the experience and knowledge is all new, routines are not yet established, designs have not yet stood the test of time, and marketing and dissemination are largely in the hands of electronic publishing bandits who know very well how to entice scholars into binding contracts but seem to care little about the quality of the goods.

These considerations lie behind priorities for the use of computers and electronic publishing in scholarly editing, which require re-examination. They are: to encourage preference for archive construction over critical editing, to focus attention on form over content, to encourage reliance on mechanical means for ensuring quality, and to raise expectations among users who all too frequently come away from electronic resources with the same sad looks with which they turned away from print scholarly editions to return to their beloved paperbacks.

Some effects of computers

In scholarly editing, electronic environments have changed the ways we think about dissemination, searchability, cost, the nature of print, and imagining the possible.

The first is the most obvious. Physical books are material objects and are, therefore, limited in number by print runs and are distributed, until the supply is exhausted, by carts, trains, boats, trucks, and planes. Electronic editions are digital, electronic entities and are, therefore, almost instantly iterable and potentially almost unlimited in number. Electronic copies are made and stored on relatively inexpensive hard disks or other storage devices and are distributed at low cost by wire, wirelessly, or on recorded surfaces. Thus, dissemination (apart from considerations of cost, copyright, and permissions) can be virtually free, easy, global, and nearly instantaneous.

The second consideration, searchability, has become so well known it is hardly worth mentioning except to repeat the observation that all texts, print or electronic, are searchable, though the process is faster electronically and thus more people are willing to do it (Tanselle 2006). The price paid for this speed is that electronic searches (even fuzzy ones) are mechanical and when conducted, as they frequently are, on the unproofed results of Optical Character Recognition (OCR) scanning provide irrelevant hits and miss relevant ones at rates that could only be determined accurately by redoing the searches the old-fashioned way, manually, using the material originals. I am not the first to note these limitations, and efforts are underway to mitigate them, as other essays in this collection demonstrate. However, unless work-

ing with well-prepared and proofed text files, search engines will continue to
have these limitations.

The third consideration, cost, is a moveable feast. Construction costs for
a scholarly edition are initially identical for print and electronic editing,
involving, as they both do, locating, collecting, analyzing, and proofreading materials up to the point when decisions are made about what has to
be and what can be done in the final production. At that point, usually, the
electronic project begins costing more than the print one because the aims,
limits, and design of print editions are established and known, whereas editors aiming for electronic publication usually operate from the notion that,
in comparison to print, more primary textual materials, more commentary,
and more ancillary historical material can be presented. The cost of bringing
the extra material to publication standards is high, and design standards are
still developmental. However, once the research and editorial decisions are
completed and the material is turned over to design and production specialists, it is likely that print production again overtakes the cost of electronic
production. The cost of paper, ink, pressing, binding, advertising, and distribution for ponderous scholarly print editions usually equals or surpasses
the cost of electronic design and mounting on the Internet or pressing to
Compact Disc (CD) or Digital Versatile Disc (DVD) for sale and distribution.
Adding to the electronic side of this balance sheet is the cost of maintaining
an Internet scholarly edition and porting it to new environments in order
to avoid the fate of all content tied to obsolescing equipment and software;
print editions require shelf space in homes, libraries, bookstores, or warehouses but, barring disasters, no personal attention.

None of these first three differences between print and electronic scholarly
editions rises significantly above the level of the practical, but the fourth,
refocusing our attention on the nature of print—how it functions and how
it affects both composition and reading—has philosophical potential. Of
course, electronic editions also have existence in particular ways and forms
that affect their functions and that influence composition and reading in
palpable ways (Kirschenbaum 2008). But it was the idea of porting print to
electronic form that actually raised the question, what is print?; for, after
500 years of print, familiarity tended to render transparent the material and
formal elements of the book for which the "important part" was the conceptual and lexical content. Of course, book designers were always interested in
questions of material and form, but often their great pride was to produce
a book that no one noticed apart from the text it conveyed. Although print
offers designers and publishers a great range of options (paper size, format,

binding, typeface, etc.), most of these options are already so conventional-
ized and familiar that, whatever they signify, they convey for the most part
subliminally.

It is the sharp disparity between printed source texts and their electronic
representations that can shock us into a reappraisal of the source medium.
That is not a universal reaction, for if print practice has in fact developed for
us a transparency of medium, it also helped some readers to reduce the book
to its lexical content, to the stream of signs that subsequently were the only
thing early electronic representations of print works provided. But for some,
the shock of seeing works electronically reduced to a stream of characters,
practically disembodied, since they no longer had a fixed form, emphasized
what was left out and animated attention to print as print. A series of attempts, both satiric and serious, tried to visualize what might be meant by
the electronic virtual book as something more than a stream of characters
in malleable form. The most elegant of these, the British Library Turning the
Pages project, has found many uses as a visual substitute for the real thing
where the original is unique and precious. Its use in the James Joyce and
W. B. Yeats exhibitions in 2004 and 2009 at the National Library of Ireland
rendered it possible for viewers to see multiple pages of books that otherwise
are restricted to one opening in a glass display case. Admittedly not scholarly
editions, these point to the importance, difficulty, and limitations of electronic representations of print works where most of the advantages gained
by electronic representation lie in the analytical and manipulative tools that
can help researchers investigate and repurpose the work. And so, in developing electronic scholarly editions there has been a renewed emphasis on
images, not just transcriptions, of original documents and especially images
that show the full margin and edge of the paper and the endpapers and covers of books to highlight the materiality of the originals and to give sceptical
users something against which to check the accuracy of transcriptions.

The core goal of all scholarly editing (regardless of medium) is to provide
a reliable text of a historical work and allow readers to see or feel or sense
the historical materialities and contexts of the work. This contrasts with
most Internet-available texts from which the materiality of the source book
has been stripped away like a banana peel. And so the question becomes,
how can the historical authenticity of works written for print publication
be represented electronically such that their historicity and materiality will
not be lost and yet the potential of the electronic form can be exploited?
That is the current philosophical and practical question for scholarly editing. A detached (rather than partisan) sense of the importance and enormity

of this question can be had by thinking about works originally composed for oral presentation and now represented in written forms without sound. Or, almost equally traumatic, all those works composed originally for manuscript—in which a single copy carries the whole weight of the work's existence, or serves as a unique source, every manuscript copy of which is also a single unique copy—converted into print for mass reproduction. That is the scale of importance of the question, what is print?; for, it focuses attention on normally subliminal elements of printed books. It makes a conscious issue out of how re-presentation of print in electronic form loses important aspects of the material source text at the same time that it overlays the work with desirable but unintended consequences that affect how people read or otherwise use the work.

The fifth consideration in respect of the differences between print and electronic editing is already inevitably introduced by the fourth: how can one develop the electronic medium for scholarly editorial purposes so that it remains true to the historical, material originals and that also imaginatively takes advantage of what can be accomplished electronically that was not available in print? But it does not follow that scholarly editing in electronic forms must be bound by the thinking about texts and communication that informed 500 successful years of print.

It is likely that each scholarly editor and user of scholarly editions has a unique ideal for electronic scholarly editions. So, no list of mine will represent agreed desiderata for the future of electronic scholarly editing. It is not possible, furthermore, to know which of the present limitations of electronic wizardry will give way to innovation. But from a scholarly reader's perspective, a range of potential desirables for editions can be constructed, leaving the details of design and interface and access to the side for now. Here is a chart with questions pointing to my generalized list of desirable contents for an electronic scholarly edition. To my knowledge no current single electronic scholarly edition responds fully to these questions.

A. The Documents

1. What are the important documentary forms of this work?
2. Can I choose a specific historical document as my reading text?
3. Can I choose a critically edited form of the work as my reading text?
4. Can I see photographic images of any of these forms of the text?

5. As I read any text can I pause at any time to see what the other forms of the text say or look like at that point? i.e., are the differences mapped and linked?

6. As I read any text can I be alerted to the existence of major variant forms or all variant forms?

7. Can I alter any given reading text to represent my own emended version of it?

8. Can I read descriptions of the provenance of each document?

9. Can I access the editor's informed opinion about the relative merits or salient features of each documentary version?

B. The Methodology

10. Can I read the editor's rationale for choosing a historical text as the basis for an edited version and can I find an explanation of the principles for the editor's emendations? Are all emendations noted in some way?

11. Is there an account of the composition, revision, and publication of the work?

12. Is there an argument presented for the consequences of choosing one reading text over another?

13. When variants are being shown, is there editorial commentary available about them?

14. Are ancillary documents such as illustrations, contextual works, letters, personal documents, or news items available either in explanatory annotations or in full text form?

15. How was accuracy in transcription assured?

C. The Contexts

16. Are there bibliographies, letters, biographies, and histories relevant to the composition or the subject of this work or guides to the author's reading?

17. Are there guides to existing interpretive works—from original reviews to recent scholarship and criticism?

18. Are there adaptations in print, film, or other media, abridgments, or censored versions that might be of interest?

D. The Uses

19. Is there a tutorial showing the full capabilities of the electronic edition? Is there a guide for beginners?
20. Are there ways I can do the electronic equivalent of dog-earing, underlining, making marginal notes, cross-referencing, logging quotations for future use? Can I write an essay in the site with links to its parts as full-text documentation and sourcing?
21. What other things can I do with this edition?
(Shillingsburg 2006, 92–93)

Particular editions: Successes and failures

A brief overview of several electronic editions may show how they have succeeded or fallen short in meeting the challenge of electronic scholarly editing: preserving and re-presenting historical texts in an alien medium that entails demands and potentials not foreseen by the authors. Foremost among ambitious electronic scholarly edition/archives are the *Blake Archive*, the *Rossetti Archive*, the *Whitman Archive*, the *Pico della Mirandola Project*, and the *Willa Cather Archive*, and there are a number of others on poets, novelists, philosophers, and mathematicians. These lead the way by combining high-quality images of original documents with transcriptions. One cannot always view the transcription and the page image in the same window, but opening multiple windows can mitigate such shortfalls. Providing high-quality images of the print sources pays tribute to the original formats. Most sites include images of the covers and endpapers and give some sense of the quality of the paper, as well as preserving the typeface and widths of margins. Providing accurate (thoroughly proofread) transcriptions (sometimes enhanced by analytical markup) begins to exploit the advantages of electronic forms by enabling fast and accurate searching. Furthermore, each of these sites offers multiple historical (documentary) versions of each work, representing manuscripts and proofs and editions produced in the author's lifetime or otherwise important editions in the textual history of the work.

Of these, only the Rossetti and the Blake projects can be called comprehensive and (nearly) complete at the moment of this writing. All therefore reflect one important difference between print and electronic scholarly editions: a project may be launched when a significant subset of the work is completed and before the whole project is completed. Published electronic edition/archives can be improved, augmented, and revised at any point; one need not wait for a supplementary volume. Although restricted at the moment to one part of one novel, the *Woolf Online* project is a proof of concept project with texts, images, contexts, and tools for user personalization and collaboration.

The Whitman and Cather archives appear to have been conceived after the Rossetti and Blake, using much of the design of those archives but incorporating new technology and new editorial ideas for text and image presentation and tools for text analysis and manipulation. Yet for design and navigation, no two projects are identical, and each requires that users take enough time to master new formats and navigation procedures in order to get the full benefit of the site.

All these sites also provide introductions, commentaries, guides to textual variation among versions, and a wealth of historical contextual materials. None seems to impose any particular view of the author's work or require or privilege any overt critical approach for understanding the significance of the writer or the work. It is taken for granted, as in most scholarly editions, that the work and the writer are significant and require extensive archival and editorial effort to enhance a range of critical engagements. It would be a shift from the exigencies of print to the potentials of electronic media if these sites embraced more of a collaborative and developmental structure than they now do. It is still seldom the case that users are invited to personalize, appropriate, or contribute to the development of these sites. Print very arbitrarily says to a book purchaser, "Although you can fold down the corners of this book, underline passages, write in the margins, interleave pages of your own, you may not alter what is here set in immoveable paper and ink." Electronic media does not say this by its material form: fixity is not a condition of the medium. Electronic editions still stay aloof and fixed, holding readers at a distance, but only because editors have chosen to carry over to electronic forms the fixity and editorial control afforded them by print.

Furthermore, most of these are primarily archival, not editorial, projects. That is to say, they provide a virtual record of the manuscript and print history in images and transcriptions of existing documents and offer guides to the relationships among the documentary versions, but stop short of providing a critically edited text. This reflects an editorial theory in fashion at the time of the inception and growth of electronic scholarly editing, which coincides with a reaction against the theory and practice known as "eclectic editing" or editing according to the school of W. W. Greg and Fredson Bowers.

It is worth noting the coincidence of the birth of electronic editing and the reaction against the Greg-Bowers form of critical editing, for the response rejects eclecticism and reduces editorial goals to the function of recording or re-representing extant historical forms of works. It is worth separating out the causes for this change of scholarly editorial goals because their fusion has led to the rejection of legitimate critical editing goals without proper examination. Greg and Bowers elaborated the techniques of critical editing that would allow the tracing of authorial actions and achievements through production processes in order to preserve or recover authorial wishes in the face of competing wishes of editors and publishers, as well as to detect and eliminate mere incompetence in the publishing business. The exercise of critical judgment to determine which aspects of the textual record were accidental and which were deliberate, and the critical judgment exercised in distinguishing between the deliberate acts of authors and those of other persons in the production chain, were always both painstaking and debatable tasks. For Bowers, that was why it was called *critical* editing.

But this effort to trace responsibility for specific textual variation back to its agents of change and to discriminate the authority or exercise of power by which these agents acted had two consequences that triggered the reactionary response. The first was that Greg and Bowers (perhaps under the influence of the New Criticism's vesting authors with the status of genius and literary works with a perfect ideal form) advocated a clear reading text that the editors hoped would become the established standard for the work. Extensive historical and critical apparatus notwithstanding, Bowers and his followers became known as advocates of a critically edited single text as the newly established basis for reading and critical responses to a work. Obviously, the critically rendered text no longer agreed with any single historical text. Readers of the newly edited texts would not be responding to the same text that generations of other readers had responded to. And so, it became easier to say that an eclectically edited text distorted the historical record than to say it corrected or restored an authorial text.

The second trigger for negative response was that eclectic critical editions denigrated the social interaction of the economic complex that produced the works in the first place. It has been widely averred that "more authorities sit at the textual table than the author" (Buzzetti and McGann 2006, 56); the changes made by editors, typesetters, and publishers are not interference, the new argument claimed, but necessary parts of the social mechanism that provides the public with reading material. In order to understand the social history of books, this view holds, one must accept the contributions of all agents of textual change contained in the material results of each publication effort and must not be misled by critical editions that sort through the various manuscripts and published versions in a supposedly vain effort to fulfil the intentions of just one agent, the author.

This reaction to eclectic critical editing would have occurred even without the advent of electronic editing, but the confluence of the two is important. Electronic editions can be archives in ways print scholarly editions cannot aspire to be. Electronic access to the unique contents of far-flung archives has made it highly desirable to establish electronically the record of historical and textual materials before beginning to think about critical editions. So, rejection of eclectic editing was highly compatible with the primary objective of electronic archives: to provide at one access point an image and transcriptional record of extant forms of a work and, through added analysis, collation, and commentary, to explain the relationships among extant historical versions.

And yet it is simply not true that there are many authorities at the table for each work. The word "authority" derives from "author," and there is seldom more than one author and therefore seldom more than one authority for the text of a work. We all agree that what the author intended the text to *mean* is inaccessible to us in absolute terms, but there is, for modern works especially, usually a great deal of evidence to indicate what the author wanted the text to *be*—what words, in what forms, and with what punctuation the paper should be imprinted. Interferences, even when meant as ministrations, by other persons are not acts of authority. Editors perform editorial acts, not authorial ones. Copyeditors, publishers, proofreaders, press correctors, and the whole panoply of text manipulators from secretaries to censors act upon the text because they have the power to do so, not because they have the authority to do so. It is true that the resulting texts reflect the confluence of economic and social forces upon the texts, but that is different from saying that the texts so produced represent authoritative forms of the work.

From this point of view, the critical attempt to trace the source of each variant in the history of a text back to its agent of introduction and to distinguish that which is authorial and authoritative from that which is *editorial* or otherwise engendered is an important task that should not be neglected. Nor should such scholarly acts be considered the sole object of editing. Electronic archives will fulfil their editorial functions only when they add truly critical editions to their archives of historical texts and, probably, only when they make it possible for multiple critical editions to be added.

WORKS CITED

Buzzetti, Dino, and Jerome J. McGann. 2006. Critical Editing in a Digital Horizon. In *Electronic Textual Editing*, 53-73. New York: Modern Language Association of America.

Kirschenbaum, Matthew G. 2008. *Mechanisms: New Media and the Forensic Imagination.* Cambridge, MA: Massachusetts Institute of Technology Press.

Shillingsburg, Peter L. 2006. *From Gutenberg to Google.* Cambridge: Cambridge University Press.

Tanselle, G. Thomas. 2006. Foreword. In *Electronic Textual Editing*, ed. Lou Burnard, Katherine O'Brien O'Keeffe, and John Unsworth. New York: Modern Language Association of America.

Digitizing George Herbert's *Temple*

Robert Whalen

Northern Michigan University

rwhalen@nmu.edu

The Digital Temple is a documentary edition of George Herbert's English verse. When complete, it will consist of machine-readable diplomatic and modern-spelling transcriptions of three essential artefacts: Williams manuscript Jones B62 (Dr Williams's Library, London), Bodleian manuscript Tanner 307, and a copy of the first edition of *The Temple: Sacred Poems and Private Ejaculations* printed in Cambridge in 1633. Page breaks in these transcriptions are linked to high-resolution images of the corresponding pages in the sources. No such edition of Herbert's poetry exists. While there are two very good modern print editions with eclectic transcriptions and apparatus, they do not offer the detail and user flexibility that a digital documentary edition can provide.

Some aspects of the relationship among the sources of Herbert's poems are still in dispute, but here are a few general observations. The Williams manuscript, transcribed some time between 1615 and 1625 by an amanuensis and emended by Herbert, contains roughly half the poems found in the later manuscript and first edition, plus several poems that do not appear in either. The Bodleian manuscript was transcribed shortly following Herbert's death in 1633, very likely from a source other than Williams. This later manuscript may have served as the copy text for the first edition—the first page looks very much like the title page of a printed book and includes the names of the licensers at the Cambridge Press—but the manuscript is otherwise unmarked. The first edition of *The Temple* follows the Bodleian manuscript in most substantive matters but also introduces a few features not present in either of the manuscripts.

At present, my principal task as editor is to capture the artefacts' intellectual content through manual transcription and to apply descriptive tags in accordance with the recommendations of the Text Encoding Initiative (TEI) P5 standard. The resulting eXtensible Markup Language (XML) file serves as the basis on which to mount four gateways into the materials that it documents: one for each of the three witnesses separately with a table of contents orga-

ISBN 978–0–86698–021–0 (online)   ISBN 978–0–86698–449–2 (print)

New Technologies in Medieval and Renaissance Studies 2 (2010) 31–61

nized linearly—that is, according to the order proper to each witness—and an additional parallel view that allows the user to compare any two or all three witnesses to any selected poem. The table of contents for this last gateway, the parallel view, is organized alphabetically and includes all poems common to all three witnesses. Here is a section from one of the longer poems, "The Church Porch," in parallel display (Figure 1).

The open-source software adapted and customized here was (at time of writing) the latest stage of the Versioning Machine 4.0, produced by Susan Schreibman and a team of developers that includes this editor. In the left panel is the Williams manuscript labelled #w, in the centre is the Bodleian manuscript labelled #b, and to the right is the first print edition labelled #p. Hyperlinked "note" and "crit" markers indicate textual and critical notes, one of which is displayed. An alternate view gathers all notes in an individual window. One may also choose to display any one or two of the witnesses rather than all three (Figure 2).

Here, each line number indicates the point to which the note is anchored in the source file, even though some notes refer to more than one line. Where there is no witness indicator, the note applies to all three. Where there is no line indicator, the note pertains to the title.

Horizontal lines correspond to page breaks (as yet incompletely recorded), each linked to a discrete image file. Here is a sample, again from "The Church Porch," displaying a high-resolution image of the Williams manuscript Jones B62 showing stanzas 60–62 (Figure 3). The image, which can be moved any-where on the screen, is placed just above the three transcriptions of stanza 62.

This brief showcasing begins to demonstrate the advantages of a digital edition. Pretty pictures are certainly one: the sheer aesthetic value of the sources digitally captured is obvious. But the expense and effort of pro-ducing The Digital Temple are justified on other grounds. The following offers this justification and explores some of the pitfalls associated with the effort.

Witness #w (the Williams manuscript)

[53.]
Calmnes is great advantage, hee that lets
Another chafe, may warme him at his fire,
Mark all his wandrings, & enjoy his frets
As cunning fencers ſuffer heat to tire.
Truth dwells not in the clouds: that Bow doth hitt
No more then paſſion when thee talkes of it.

[54.]
Mark what another fays: for many are
ffull of themſelues, & anſweare their owne notio
Take all into thee; then with equall care
Ballance each dramm of reaſon like a potion.
If truth bee wth thy freind, bee wth them both:
Share in ye Conqueſt, & confeſs a truth.

[55.]
Bee vſeful where thou liveſt, that they may
Need & bee glad, & wiſh thy preſence ſtill:
Kindnes, good parts, great places, are yē way
To compaſs this. ffind out mens wants & will
And meet them there. All worldly ioyes goe lefs
To that one ioye of doing kindneſſes.

[56.]
Pitch thy behavior low, thy Projects high
So ſhalt thou humble & magnanimous bee
Sinke not in ſpirit: who aymeth at yē ſky
Shoots higher much then hee that means a tree.
A grain of Glory mixt wth humblenes
Cures both a ffeaver & a Drowsines.

[57.]

Witness #b (the Bodleian manuscript)

53.
Calmnes is great advantage, he yt lets
Another chafe, may warme him at his fire,
Mark all his wandrings, & enjoy his frets;
As cunning Fencers ſuffer heat to tire.
Truth dwells not in ye clouds: ye Bow yts there
Doth often ayme at, neuer hitt ye ſpheere.

54.
Mark what another fayes: For many r
Full of themſelues, & anſwere their owne Noti
Take all into thee; then with equall d
Ballance each dramme of reaſon, like a potion.
If truth be with thy freind, be with ym be
Share in ye conqueſt, & confeſſe a tr

55.
Be veſfull where thou liueſt, yt they r
Both want, & wiſh thy pleaſing preſence ſ
Kindnes, good parts, great places are ye way
To compaſſe this. Find out Mens wants, & will.
And meet them there. All worldly joyes goe le
To ye one joy of doeing kindnes

56.
Pitch thy behavio' low, thy projects hi
So ſhalt thou humble, & magnanimous b
Sink not in ſpirit: who aymeth at ye ſ
Shoots higher much, then he, yt meanes a t
A graine of glory mixt with humbleneſſ
Cures both a Feauer, & Lethargicknes.

Pop-up note

Lines 313-18: The double sense in *bow*—weapon and rainbow—is a fanciful reading of Genesis 9:11-1. God puts up his bow, so to speak, promising to wield but never to use it again. The image here is of a bow poised over and aimed toward the earth: (the *sphere* [*sphære, sphere*] in #b and #p) and either never firing upon it or firing upon it frequently but missing because blinded by the clouds. That is, the bow is to be identified either with the false aimer within the clouds, or the calm truth beyond them—or perhaps both (the referent of *there* being uncertain). Herbert seems playfully to associate the wrathful Yahweh with the rash, less-than-cunning fencer, and the merciful Yahweh of the new covenant with the calm and self-possessed gentleman.

Witness #p (the first print edition)

[53.]
In love I should: but anger is not love,
Nor widdome neither: therefore gently move.
Calmnesse is great advantage: he that lets
Another chafe, may warm him at his fire:
Mark all his wandrings, and enjoy his frets;
As cunning fencers ſuffer heat to tire.
...h dwells not in the clouds: the bow that's there,
Doth often aim at, never hit the ſphere.

[54.]
Mark what another fayes: for many are
ll of themſelves, and anſwer their own notion.
Take all into thee; then with equall care
nce each dramme of reaſon, like a potion.
If truth be with thy friend, be with them both:
Share in the conqueſt, and confeſſe a troth.

[55.]
Be uſefull where thou liveſt, that they may
Both want, and with thy pleaſing preſence fill
neſſe, good parts, great places are the way
paſſe this. Finde out mens wants and will
nd meet them there. All worldly joyes go leſſe
To the one joy of doing kindneſſes.

[56.]
Pitch thy behavior low, thy projects high;
So ſhalt thou humble and magnanimous be:
Sink not in ſpirit: who aimeth at the sky,
Shoots higher much then he that means a tree.
A grain of glorie mixt with humbleneſſe
Cures both a fever and lethargickneſſe.

Figure 1. "The Church Porch" as transcriptions from witnesses #w (the Williams manuscript), #b (the Bodleian manuscript), and #p (the first print edition), with a pop-up note

[The Church Porch] Perirr ʰhanterium	The Church-porch. *Perirrhanterium*	Notes
		In #w and #b, unlike #p, the poem's "title" is actually a running header in the top margin. "Perirrhanterium", apparently a subtitle in #b and #p, is in #w the title of a separate poem. The content of that poem is a version of what in #b and #p is entitled "Superliminare". (Both poems here share the ID #superliminare-bp-perirrhanterium.) Below "Superliminare" in #b and #p is an untitled poem (or perhaps second stanza) that is a version of what in #w is clearly a separate poem entitled "Superliminare". (These latter two poems share the ID #superliminare-untitledbp.)
1.	**[1.]**	
Thou, whose sweet youth, & early hopes inhance [1]	THou, whose sweet youth and early hopes inhance	
Thy rate, & price, & marke thee for a treasure; [2]	Thy rate and price, and mark thee for a treasure;	
Harken vnto a verser, who may chance [3]	Hearken unto a Verser, who may chance	
Rhime thee to good, & make a bait of pleasure. [4]	Ryme thee to good, and make a bait of pleasure.	
A Verse may find him, who a sermon flies, [5]	A verse may finde him, who a sermon flies,	
And turne delight into a sacrifice. [6]	And turn delight into a sacrifice.	*perirrhanterium:* device for sprinkling holy water b p
2.	**[2.]**	**Line number 13**
Beware of Lust: It doth pollute, & foule [7]	Beware of lust: it doth pollute and foul	*wed /wed/:* marry; stake or wager (one's life or money)
Whom God in Baptisme washt wᵗʰ his owne Blood. [8]	Whom God in Baptisme washt with his own blood.	**Line number 17** b p
It blots thy lesson written in thy soule, [9]	It blots thy lesson written in thy foul;	*continence:* self-restraint
The holy Lines cannot be vnderstood. [10]	The holy lines cannot be understood.	**Line number 20** b p
How dare those eies vpon a Bible booke, [11]	How dare those eyes upon a Bible look,	*encloser /inclose/:* one who for private use fences in land otherwise held in common
Much lesse towards God, whose Lust is all their booke . [12]	Much lesse towards God, whose lust is all their book?	
3.	**[3.]**	**Line number 21** b p
Abstaine wholly, or wedd. Thy Bounteous Lord [13]	Abstain wholly, or wed. Thy bounteous Lord	*impaled /impal'd/:* fenced in
Allows yᵉᵉ Chouyse of paths: Take no by-waies; [14]	Allows thee choise of paths: take no by-wayes;	**Line number 24** b
But gladly welcome, what he doth afford; [15]	But gladly welcome what he doth afford	*shifts:* written over an erased (and illegible) word
Not grudging, yᵗ thy lust hath bounds, & staies. [16]	Not grudging, that thy lust hath bounds and staies.	
Continence hath his joy: weigh both, & so, [17]	Continence hath his joy: weigh both; and still	**Line number 27**
If rottennes haue more, let Heauen goe. [18]	If rottennesse have more, let Heaven go.	*list /lift/:* desire
4.	**[4.]**	**Line number 32**
If God had lay'ed all common, certainely [19]	If God had laid all common, certainly	*big /big, bigge/:* pregnant
Man would haue beene thᵉincloser : but since now [20]	Man would have beene th'incloser : but since now	**Line number 48**
God hath impal'd vs, on yᵉ contrary [21]	God hath impal'd us, on the contrarie	*stamp /ftamp, stampe, ftamp/:* image
Man breakes yᵉ fence, & euery ground will plough. [22]	Man breaks the fence, and every ground will plough.	**Line number 60**
O, what were Man, might he himselfe miiplace! [23]	O what were man, might he himself misplace!	*bater:* refrain from
Sure to be crosse he would shift feet, & face. [24]	Sure to be crosse he would shift feet and face.	

Figure 2. Transcriptions from witnesses #b and #p with notes in parallel display

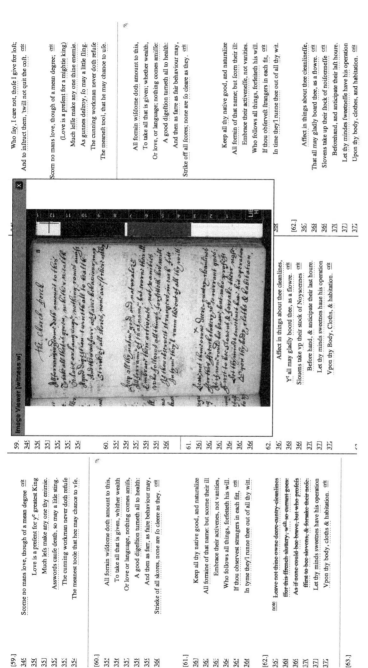

Image Viewer [witness w]

The church porch

[59.]
Scorne no mans love, though of a mean degree crit
Love is a prefent for y^e greatest King
Much lefs make any one thy enimie.
Aswords caufe death, so may a litle sting.
The cunning workman never doth refufe
The meanest toole that hee may chance to vfe.

[60.]
All forrain wifdome doth amount to this,
To take all that is given, whither wealth
Or love or language, nothing comes amifs,
A good digeftion turneth all to health:
And then as farr, as faire behaviour may,
Strieke of all skores, none are fo cleere as they. crit

[61.]
Keep all thy native good, and naturalize
All forraine of that name: but scorne their ill
Embrace their activenefs, not vanities,
Who follows all things, forfeiteth his will.
If thou obfervest strangers in each fit, crit
In tyme they'l runne thee out of all thy witt.

[62.]
note Leave not thine owne deere curry cleanlines
ffor this ffrench sluttery, wth so current goes
As if none could bee brave, but who profefs
ffirst to bee slovens, & forsake their nofe.
Before hand, & anticipate their last houre.
Let thy minds sweetnes have his operation crit
Vpon thy body, cloths & habitation. crit

[63.]

59.
Who fay, I care not, thofe I give for loft;
And to inftruct them, 'twill not quit the coft. crit

Scorn no mans love, though of a mean degree; crit
(Love is a prefent for a mightie king)
Much lefse make any one thine enemie.
As gunnes deftroy, fo may a little fling.
The cunning workman never doth refufe
The meaneft tool, that he may chance to ufe.

60.
All forrain wifdome doth amount to this,
To take all that is given; whether wealth,
Or love, or language; nothing comes amiffe:
A good digeftion turneth all to health:
And then as farre as fair behaviour may,
Strike off all fcores; none are fo cleare as they. crit

61.
Keep all thy native good, and naturalize
All forrain of that name: but fcorn their ill:
Embrace their activeneffe, not vanities.
Who follows all things, forfeiteth his will.
If thou obfervft ftrangers in each fit, crit
In time they'l runne thee out of all thy wit.

62.
Affect in things about thee cleanlineffe,
That all may gladly board thee, as a flowre.
Slovens take vp their flock of noifomneffe
Beforehand, and anticipate their laft houre.
Let thy minde fweetneffe have his operation
Upon thy body, clothes, and habitation. crit

Figure 3. "The Church Porch" stanzas 60–62 as transcriptions and image from witness #w, Williams MS Jones B62, 11r. Used by permission of Dr Williams's Trust.

One advantage of a digital edition is the limitless space available for presenting all relevant materials. Rather than consulting a textual apparatus to reconstruct actual witnesses in the abstract (or, the obverse—to deconstruct an edition's eclectic transcription), parallel viewing simply presents the several versions side-by-side. (The plan, however, is to note and discuss substantive variants in the apparatus too, a kind of built-in redundancy to draw attention to significant differences.) Presenting Herbert's poems in this way is not without theoretical consequence: the method assumes that differences between the witnesses matter and should be in the foreground rather than relegated solely to the apparatus. Look, for example, at the revision in "The Altar," witness #w (Figure 4).

The difference between "thy onely sacrifice" and "thy blessed sacrifice" is pivotal: whereas the former might be an attempt to qualify the poem's Roman Catholic leanings by insisting that the Christian Atonement is in no way replicated in the ritual, the revision removes that hindrance to the poem's ceremonial and material emphases. Such details remind us that, contrary to his reputation as a mild and innocuous pastor, Herbert wrote as a member of an establishment clergy increasingly vexed by sharp religious differences within.

Look at the same display, now including an image of the first edition (Figure 5).

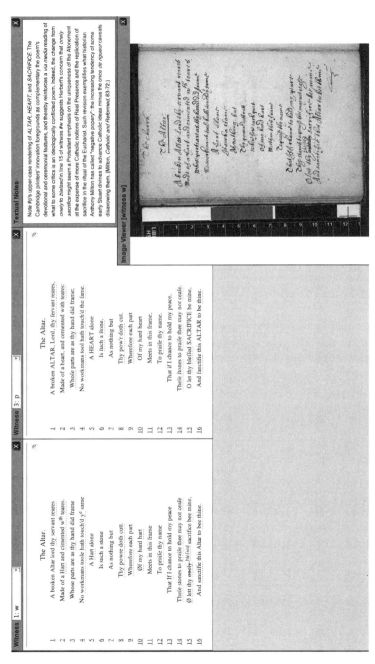

Figure 4. "The Altar," witnesses #w and #p, with #w image (15v) and headnote

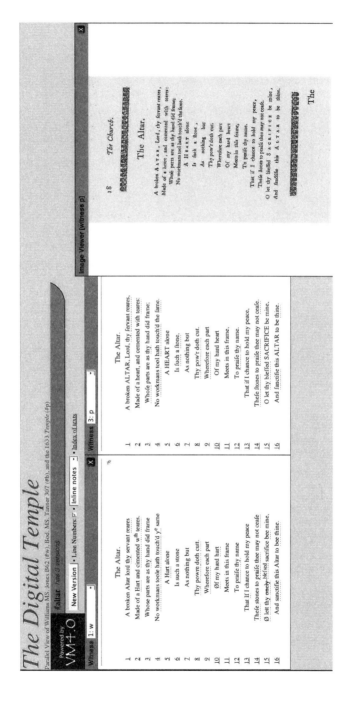

Figure 5. "The Altar" witnesses #w and #p, with #p image (Herbert 1876, 18)

The words HEART, ALTAR, and SACRIFICE have been rendered in upper-case type, despite there being in the manuscripts no authority for doing so. We might suppose, as does Helen Wilcox in her recent edition, that the actual copy text for *The Temple* was not in fact the Bodleian manuscript. It is unlikely, however, that the now lost "little book" mentioned by Izaak Walton—supposedly passed from Herbert on his deathbed to a friend and probably the source from which the Bodleian manuscript is transcribed—contained the novel emphasis that was then simply replicated in some other lost copy and/or in the first edition. Occam's Razor, if nothing else, suggests that the upper-case renderings were introduced by the Cambridge printers, Thomas Buck and Roger Daniel, or by Herbert's close friend, Nicholas Ferrar who, according to Wilcox and others, most likely oversaw the book's production. Like the revised phrase in Williams, the emphasis here matters. Whereas the revision in #w reveals a Herbert sensitive to the often febrile religious atmosphere of the 1620s English church, the printers' renderings of HEART, ALTAR, and SACRIFICE in witness #p emphasize a (happy) convergence of the poem's ceremonial and devotional imperatives. In this they might be said only to have advanced the *via media* piety for which Herbert is often celebrated. But it is their emphasis, not his. And yet Herbert's modern editors, Wilcox and F. E. Hutchinson included, reproduce this printers' typographic feature as though it were Herbert's own (Herbert 1941; Herbert 2007). Indeed, Wilcox includes an image of the #p version only and notes that these "provocative . . . Catholic and Jewish" words are here "used . . . prominently," the passive voice implying but not fully committing to the claim that Herbert—not Buck and Daniel or Ferrar—is responsible for the words' prominence (Herbert 2007, 88–90).

The point here is neither to champion the manuscripts as somehow more authoritative than the first edition, nor to diminish the value of a fine eclectic transcription such as those found in the Wilcox and Hutchinson editions. Indeed, insofar as Herbert's verse is a product of convergence between seventeenth-century manuscript and print cultures, the Daniel/Ferrar edition is of as much interest as the Williams and Bodleian manuscripts. The foregoing critical observations, as an argument about authority, are meant only to show why a digital documentary edition is a useful alternative to the traditional print-based text. For even though a good modern print edition accounts for all variants, its single transcription cannot avoid favouring one authoritative source over another wherever they differ. Parallel display of multiple witnesses in a digital environment foregoes the (perhaps unintentional) rhetorical illusion of a single stable text in favour of an equally rhetorical emphasis on difference and instability. That the manuscript scribes and Cambridge printers are ontologically inseparable from the poems conceived and composed by George Herbert supports Jerome McGann's social-text theory of editing. Drawing a sharp distinction "between a work's bibliographical and its linguistic codes," McGann argues that "as the process of textual transmission expands, whether vertically (over time) or horizontally (in institutional space), the signifying processes of the work become increasingly collaborative and socialized" (McGann 1991, 52, 58). This collaborative process, a kind of social interaction, includes not only readers of texts but those who produce them: authors, amanuenses, printers, publishers, compositors, book designers, etc. One need not embrace Roland Barthes's *mort d'auteur*—his Brechtian vision of the author "diminishing like a figurine at the far end of the literary stage" (Barthes 1977, 145)—to acknowledge that Herbert's poems are not pristine things but artefacts with a history, an ontogeny that can enrich our understanding of their meaning.

A more famous example is the poem "Easter Wings," whose publication history has been exhaustively described by Randall McLeod in his various aliases (McLeod 1993; McLeod 1998). Here is the poem as it appears in the three sources, the Williams manuscript, the Bodleian manuscript, and the 1633 edition (Figures 6–8).

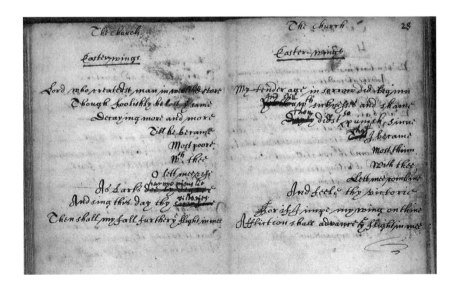

Figure 6. "Easter Wings" #w (27v-28r)

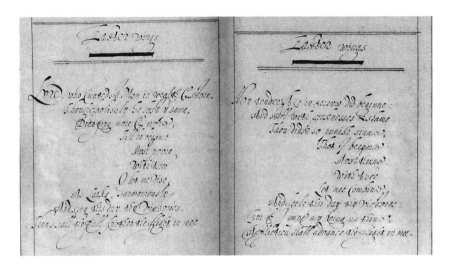

Figure 7. "Easter Wings" #b, (Herbert 1984, 26v–27r)

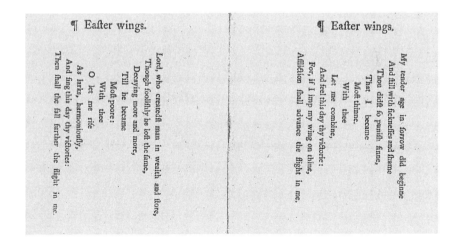

Figure 8. "Easter Wings" #p (pp. 34-35)

F. E. Hutchinson's 1941 Oxford edition, the standard until very recently, retains the manuscripts' horizontal lineation. The new Cambridge edition includes images of #b and #p. There, however, Helen Wilcox's transcription follows the latter's vertical rendering, as well as its slight curvature at the stanzas' top margins and more pronounced curve at the bottoms—which would be respectively the left and right margins if the poem were rendered horizontal. In #b, on the other hand, not only are these curvatures reversed (rendered vertically, the winged stanzas could be said to be flying downward rather than upward—hardly an image of heavenly ascent), but the slighter of the two curvatures is far slighter still. Moreover, in the #w image, which Wilcox does not include, the right-margin alignment is total. To prefer #p is to agree with those who argue for "Herbert's conscious control over his materials," (Herbert 2007, 146) even though the author is unlikely to have had a hand in the novel layout because he died before work on the book began. Of the three artefacts, only #w has evidence of Herbert's hand, and its rendering of "Easter Wings" bears little resemblance to that found in #p.

Notice too that in all three witnesses *both* stanzas are titled. Titles elsewhere in #p appear only at the beginnings of poems; there are no running headers other than those indicating the volume's several sections ("The Church Porch," "The Church," and "The Church Militant"), though the last is also the title of that section's single poem. Similarly in #w and #b, titles are underlined and not reproduced on succeeding pages (except where a second poem with the same title is clearly intended and has been read as such by most editors). Yet, a single title appearing over her transcription (and, albeit, acknowledging the treatment of the titles in all three sources), Wilcox avers that "in the unusual circumstances of this pattern poem spread across two pages, it seems more likely" that the title is "a running title" (Herbert 2007, 147).

It is one thing to critique an editor's choices but quite another to provide alternatives. The Digital Temple does, but the solution is far from satisfactory. Here are "Easter Wings," "Easter Wings [1]," and "Easter Wings [2]" (the latter two being the two stanzas treated as separate poems), with images from #w, #b, and #p respectively (Figures 9–11).

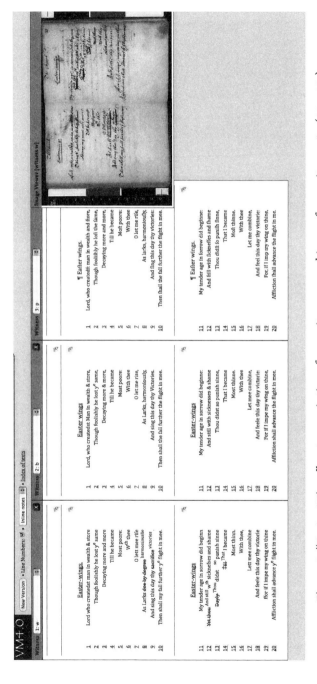

Figure 9. "Easter Wings" as transcriptions from witnesses and image from witness #w (27v–28r)

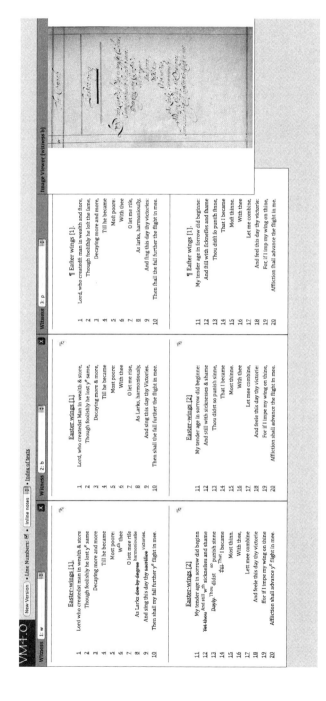

Figure 10. "Easter Wings [1]" and "[2]" as transcriptions from witnesses and image from #b (26v)

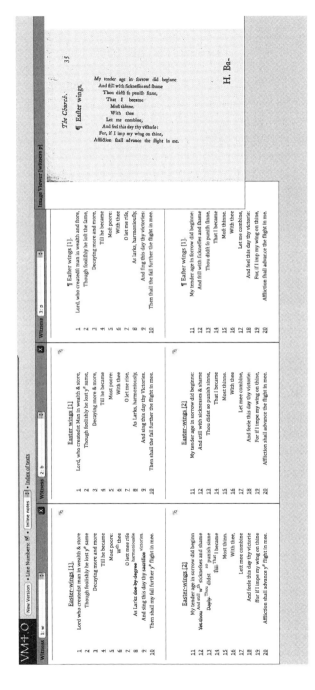

Figure 11. "Easter Wings [1]" and "[2]" as transcriptions from witnesses and image from #p

There are at least two problems with this. The otherwise diplomatic transcription fails to capture the vertical orientation of the first edition (#p), nor does the absolute right-margin alignment do justice to the actual layout of both #p and #b (but not #w). These are technical limitations that could be overcome through more sophisticated tweaking of the XML and eXtensible Stylesheet Language (XSL) engine on which currently runs this already customized iteration of the Versioning Machine. But these limitations are mitigated by access to the images. After all, the chief purpose of a transcription in a digital edition that includes the source images is more functional than aesthetic: to enable efficient data search and retrieval. Of course, visual features of an artefact are data too and could be captured by the encoding and thereby made susceptible to software-enabled querying, which is all the more reason to regard transcription as the capture of a text's linguistic contents, a "view" of the artefact parallel to that of its purely visual properties.

In addition to these presentational considerations, "Easter Wings" is problematic from a low-level encoding point of view, reminding us that encoding decisions are every bit as critical as other editorial matters. The underlying encoding structure of "Easter Wings," displayed as a single poem in Figure 9, actually includes *two* poem divisions (<div/>), each with its own unique identifier. The reason for this is that conformant TEI-P5 allows only one <head/> tag per <div/>, so the following is wrong:

```
<div type="poem" xml:id="easterwings">
        <head>Easter Wings</head>
        <!-- Lines 1-10. -->
        <head>Easter Wings</head>
        <!-- Lines 11-20. -->
    </div>
```

In all three witnesses—#w, #b, and #p—the second heading looks identical to the first. There is neither a chirographic distinction in #w or #b, where both headings are underlined, nor a typographic distinction in #p, where both headings are preceded by a pilcrow (¶). It would seem that the only way to allow the two headings to be represented as the same kind of phenomenon within conformant TEI-P5 is to treat the stanzas as separate poems, each with its own unique identifier:

```
<div type="poem" xml:id="easterwings1">
        <head>Easter Wings <supplied>[1]</supplied></head>
        <!-- Lines 1-10. -->
</div>

<div type="poem" xml:id="easterwings2">
        <head>Easter Wings <supplied>[2]</supplied></head>
        <!-- Lines 1-10. -->
</div>
```

However, it would be possible to mitigate this non-conformance by simply nesting the second <div/> within the first and, by virtue of doing so, making that second <div/> different in kind from the first (because structurally contained by rather than parallel to it):

```
<div type="poem" xml:id="easterwings">
        <head/>
        <!-- Lines 1-10. -->
<div type="poemPart" xml:id="easterwings2" corresp="#easterwings">
                <head/>
                <!-- Lines 11-20. -->
        </div>
</div>
```

Nested within rather than following the first <div/>, the second <div/> explicitly declares its structural subordination (not a term of value) even while allowing both iterations of the poem's title (marked by <head/>) to be more or less the same sort of thing ("more or less" because the second belongs to its parent, the nested <div/>). The simultaneous difference and similarity are also captured through the second <div/>'s attribute values "poemPart," "easterwings2," and "#easterwings." Which is to say, "This section is part of a poem; but because it has its own unique identifier, it is a poem unto itself—even as it points (in a deliberately ambiguous way) to another uniquely identified poem." This is now perfectly valid and conformant TEI-P5 XML. And yet introducing this nested <div/> has important semantic implications. Why a <div/> for this stanza and not for all stanzas? To be consistent, should not the encoding for all poems observe this hierarchy (i.e., of stanza divisions within poem divisions)? This would be entirely redundant, for stanza division is handled in TEI-P5 by the <lg/> (line-group) element. The effort to accommodate the two <head/>s within a single poem seems to be a kind of encoding gymnastics. It is error free from a TEI-XML perspective; but is it correct?

Is the solution simply to create two parallel (non-nested) poem <div/>s and sunder finally that stubborn verso-recto opening? Or perhaps we could abolish the ambiguity in the other direction (in agreement with Wilcox and Hutchinson, after all) by calling that second heading a running title, a formework feature that is part of another hierarchy altogether:

<fw type="header">Easter Wings</fw>

The "header" attribute, according to TEI-P5, pertains to "a running title at the top of the page." What then to do with that "other" running title, "The Church," that appears in all three artefacts (Figures 9–11)? Moreover, <fw/> is designated a "milestone-style" element in TEI-P5, which means that its content is deemed to fall outside of the structural hierarchy consisting, in this case, of text, section, poem, line group (stanza), and line. While it is not difficult to see the running title "The Church" as falling into this category, one is reluctant to designate the second iteration of the title "Easter Wings" a formal feature outside the flow of text that is the poem (or series of poems).

Other encoding scenarios are possible, and conformance to the TEI protocol is recommended but not obligatory. (One may custom design the schema against which a TEI-XML file is validated, adding and subtracting elements and attributes according to need, and doing so, moreover, with tools provided by the TEI Consortium.) It would appear, however, that TEI-P5 semantics resists, on several fronts, a persistent feature of this work's editorial history, namely, the tendency to regard the two ten-line stanzas as components of a single poem. So perhaps the nested structure allowing two identical <head/>s is the superior solution after all, for not only is it TEI-conformant; it also captures something of the ambiguity—and editors' ambivalence?—surrounding the problem of whether "Easter Wings" is one or two poems.

The goal of The Digital Temple is to provide ways of exploring Herbert's verse not possible through more conventional print-based means. Enabling access to materials currently available only in black-and-white facsimiles (without transcription) or to those able to visit the repositories housing them, a digital Herbert might also be used by teachers of early-modern literature and culture to introduce students to the converging worlds of manuscript and print so they might explore more fully the process of literary production. A few examples illustrate the possibilities for incorporating into the reading experience the phenomena of revision and variation among the sources.

One attractive example is the first four lines of stanza 62 in "The Church Porch" (see Figure 1):

> Leave not thine owne deere-cuntry-cleanlines
> ffor this ffrench sluttery wch so currant goes:
> As if none could bee brave but who profess
> ffirst to bee slovens, & forsake their nose.

In #w this stanza appears to be marked for revision by a supra-stanzaic X, and indeed the first four lines are revised in #b and #p. In proximity to "sluttery," the word "country" (with its bawdy overtone as exploited in Hamlet's pun on *cunt*, 3.2.111) may have struck Herbert as too sexually suggestive, even though the common meaning of "sluttery" was "untidiness" or "filthiness." The passage nevertheless is a rare moment of excess in Herbert, and the revised version is not only far tamer but arguably inferior. Look at the awkward meter and rhythm in the revision, line 370: "Beforehand & anticipate their last houre" is a far cry from #w's "ffirst to bee slovens, & forsake their nose," the latter with its perfect pentameter, the forward propulsion of its opening dactyl (or trochee, if you prefer), and the variously placed alliterative s's (final, initial, medial, and final) that string through the line a hissing contempt for foreign dress, manners, and hygiene. One cannot help but wonder whether the X reveals Herbert censoring and restraining himself, regretting having indulged his English xenophobic wit, however light-hearted. Whereas elsewhere in the Williams manuscript passages and phrases periodically are deleted (crossed out) and then revised either there or in the later Bodleian manuscript, Herbert here perhaps hesitated, the X indicating distaste for an earlier indiscretion but (momentary) lack of a commitment to deleting it.

Not only content but also formal features of Herbert's verse are subject to significant variation among the witnesses, which may have been introduced by the Cambridge printers or by someone other than the author. Consider, for example, "Evensong," appearing only in the Bodleian manuscript and first print edition. In the Bodleian manuscript (#b) the poem is arranged into four eight-line stanzas (Figure 12), whereas in the print edition (#p) there are eight four-line stanzas (Figure 13).

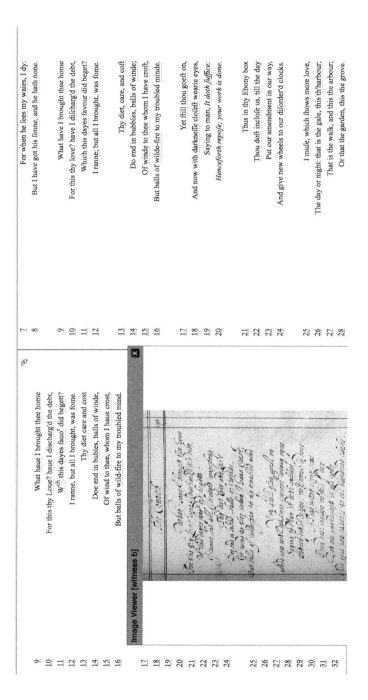

Figure 12. "Evensong" from #b as image (43r) and transcription, and from #p as transcription

Euen-song

1 Blest be the God of Loue,
2 Who gaue mee eies, & light, & powre this day,
3 Both to be busy, and to play.
4 But much more blest be God aboue,
5 Who gaue mee sight alone,
6 W^ch to himselfe he did deny:
7 For when he sees my waies, I dy:
8 But I haue gott his sonne, & he hath none.

9 What haue I brought thee home
10 For this thy Loue? haue I discharg'd the debt,
11 W^ch this dayes fauo^r did beget?
12 I ranne, but all I brought, was fome.
13 Thy diet care and cost
14 Doe end in bubles, balls of winde,
15 Of wind to thee, whom I haue crost,
16 But balls of wild-fire to my troubled mind.

Even-fong.

Bleft be the God of love,
1 Who gave me eyes, and light, and power this day,
2 Both to be bufie, and to play.
3 But much more bleft be God above,

4 Who gave me fight alone,
5 Which to himfelfe he did denie:
6 For when he fees my waies, I dy:
7 But I have got his fonne, and he hath none.
8

9 What have I brought thee home
10 For this thy love? have I difcharg'd the debt,
11 Which this dayes favour did beget?
12 I ranne; but all I brought, was fome.

13 Thy diet, care, and coft
14 Do end in bubbles, balls of winde;

The Church. 55

¶ Sinne.

O That I could a sinne once fee!
We paint the devil foul, yet he
Hath fome good in him, all agree.
Sinne is flat oppofite to th' Almighty, feeing
It wants the good of vertue, and of being.

But God more care of us hath had:
If apparitions make us fad,
By fight of finne we fhould grow mad.
Yet as in fleep we fee foul death, and live:
So devils are our finnes in perfpective.

¶ Even-fong.

BLeft be the God of love,
Who gave me eyes, and light, and power this day,
Both to be bufie, and to play.
But much more bleft be God above,

Who gave me fight alone,
Which to himfelf he did denie:
For when he fees my wifhes, I dy:
But I have got his fonne, and he hath none.

What have I brought thee home
For this thy love? have I difcharg'd the debt,
Which this dayes favour did beget?
I ranne;but all I brought, was fome.

Thy diet, care, and coft
Do end in bubbles, balls of winde;
Of winde to thee whom I have croft,
But balls of wilde-fire to my troubled minde.

C 4
Yet .

Figure 13. "Evensong" from #b as transcription and from #p as transcription and image (p. 55)

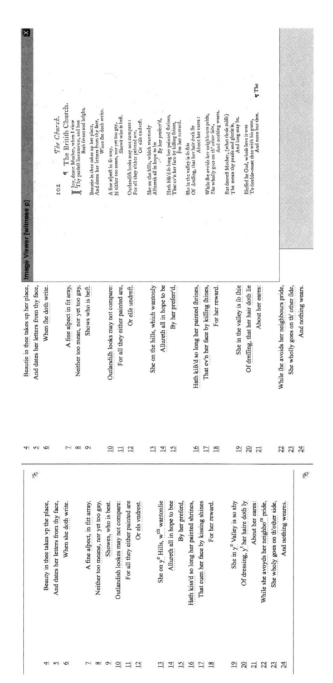

Figure 14. "The British Church" from #b as transcription and from #p as transcription and image (p. 102)

Why the printers (if they were responsible) chose the shorter stanzas is uncertain. It is possible that the rhyme scheme, a four-line pattern rhyming ABBA, determined the stanzaic unit. Or perhaps their copy was an unknown manuscript that arranged the poem into four-line stanzas. Lacking conclusive evidence, however, it is reasonable to assume that Herbert would have preferred witness #b's eight-line stanza, for the smallest repeatable metrical pattern here consists of eight lines, not four: trimeter, pentameter, tetrameter, tetrameter, trimeter, tetrameter, tetrameter, pentameter (or 3, 5, 4, 4, 3, 4, 4, 5). This pattern is repeated three times for a total of thirty-two lines. That longer eight-line stanza, reinforced visually in witness #b, is a subtle feature of the poem's larger music. Given Herbert's significant contribution to English verse forms, it is important to highlight this visual complement to aural effect where it is warranted. Wilcox again prefers the first edition's arrangement, despite solid evidence for a reading that foregrounds Herbert's technical mastery.

"The British Church" is similarly problematic, only here the issue is rhyme rather than meter. The Bodleian manuscript's six-line stanza captures the larger unit, AABCCB, whereas the first edition's three-line unit does not (Figure 14).

Notice that consideration of meter alone supports a three-line stanza. But emphasizing rhyme in this poem and meter in the other is in no way inconsistent, for in both cases the larger stanza captures visually an important aspect of the poem's aural dimension. Favouring the first edition, Wilcox neglects this crucial aspect of Herbert's verse. The Digital Temple overcomes the eclectic print edition's infelicities by displaying the differences and discussing their significance in the apparatus—without unduly (as opposed to necessarily, as in a print context) mediating readers' access to the materials.

A digital parallel text edition of Herbert's verse enhances the reading experience in ways not possible through a conventional print edition. Immediate juxtaposition of the several witnesses encourages the reader to explore Herbert's revisions as well as the additional scribal and printers' contributions to the collection of poems we call *The Temple*. A single TEI-XML file contains all of the information necessary on which to mount a multiple-view display interface. Users of The Digital Temple will be able to examine individual poems in parallel display, to access one of the three witnesses in its entirety, and in both cases to summon individual page images from which the transcriptions were made.

Another (and, some might say, the most significant) feature of digital texts is their susceptibility to data mining and analysis. Indeed, the display advantages I've described will not be fully realized until computer screen representations become more finely detailed than they are now. Meanwhile, digital texts are likely to be used largely as reference tools providing fast and convenient access to information or, more promisingly, to explore an author's idiolect: semantic patterns most discernible through the application of text-analysis software and methods. Given Herbert's reputation as a master of technique and formal innovator, another promising goal of the project is to incorporate tools for analysis of rhythm and meter. These software-enabled research goals depend, however, on the creation of a robust source from which to extract the data.

To illustrate the advantages of a machine-readable text-base I turn now to a couple of basic but crucial encoding issues. The Digital Temple's transcriptions include both diplomatic and modern spellings of all words and abbreviations. The primary reason for including both is to enable thorough and efficient querying. To take a couple of simple examples: if one were to query only the diplomatic transcript for the string *servant*, the search would fail to retrieve instances where it retains archaic orthographic and typographic conventions, as in *seruant* and *ſeruant*. If, however, such a word in the diplomatic transcript were linked to a normalized spelling, the search software could easily be programmed to find all variant instances. Here are several examples using TEI-P5's <choice/> structure (which allows the display software to "choose" to show either the diplomatic or modernized version):

```
<choice>
        <orig>&#x17f;eruant</orig>
        <reg>servant</reg>
</choice>

<choice>
        <orig>creaited&#xFB05;</orig>
        <reg>createdst</reg>
</choice>

<choice>
        <orig>thyne</orig>
        <reg>thine</reg>
</choice>
```

The same is true for abbreviations and elisions:

```
<choice>
        <abbr>impail'd</abbr>
        <expan>impaled</expan>
</choice>

<choice>
        <abbr>yo<hi rend="superscript">r</hi></abbr>
         <expan>your</expan>
</choice>

<choice>
        <abbr>th'</abbr><expan>the</expan>
</choice><choice>
                <orig>inclo&#x17f;er</orig>
                <reg>encloser</reg>
        </choice>
[i.e., "th'incloſer]
```

The query strings *servant*, *create*, *thine*, *impale*, *your*, and *enclose*, all with standardized modern spellings, would fail to retrieve their diplomatically transcribed counterparts—ſ*eruant* (with long-s), *creaited&#xFB05*; (with long-s+t ligature), *thyne*, *impail'd*, *yoʳ*, and *incloſer*—were it not for the accompanying <reg/> and <expan/> tags. Or at least that was my thinking eight years ago when I began the project. Since that time, the onus for facilitating efficient search-and-retrieval has shifted away from the editors of digital texts and toward the creators of search engines. Literature Online and the MarkLogic Server at University of Virginia Press's Digital Imprint are two examples of interfaces capable of dealing effectively with orthographic variety and inconsistency. Nevertheless, I have chosen to retain robust querying capability in the encoding for two reasons. The first is scepticism about search engines' claims to be able exhaustively to deal with diplomatic transcriptions of texts from an era for which there was nothing like a modern dictionary or standardized orthography. The second is the desire to ensure portability to any platform and to offer the user processing flexibility.

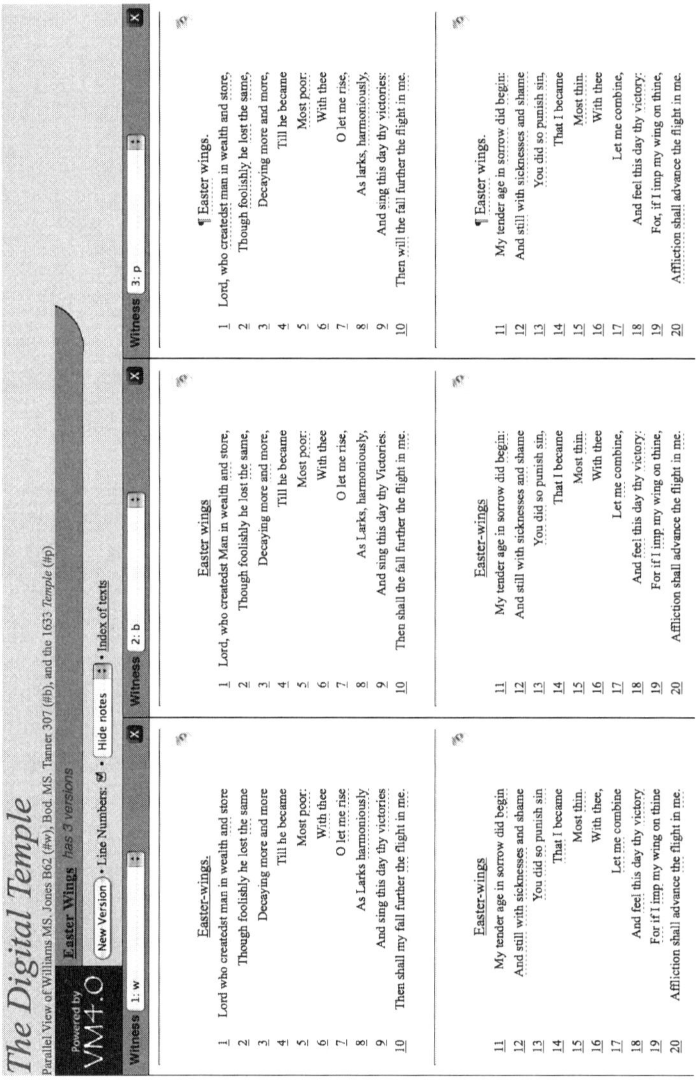

The Digital Temple

Parallel View of Williams MS. Jones B62 (#w), Bod. MS. Tanner 307 (#b), and the 1633 *Temple* (#p)

Powered by VM4.0

Easter Wings *has 3 versions* | New Version · Line Numbers: ✓ · Hide notes | · Index of texts

Witness 1: w

Easter-wings.

1 Lord who createdst man in wealth and store
2 Though foolishly he lost the same
3 Decaying more and more
4 Till he became
5 Most poor:
6 With thee
7 O let me rise
8 As Larks, harmoniously
9 And sing this day thy victories
10 Then shall my fall further the flight in me.

11 My tender age in sorrow did begin
12 And still with sicknesses and shame
13 You did so punish sin
14 That I became
15 Most thin.
16 With thee,
17 Let me combine
18 And feel this day thy victory
19 For if I imp my wing on thine
20 Affliction shall advance the flight in me.

Witness 2: b

Easter wings

1 Lord, who createdst Man in wealth and store,
2 Though foolishly he lost the same,
3 Decaying more and more,
4 Till he became
5 Most poor:
6 With thee
7 O let me rise,
8 As Larks, harmoniously,
9 And sing this day thy Victories.
10 Then shall the fall further the flight in me.

11 My tender age in sorrow did begin:
12 And still with sicknesses and shame
13 You did so punish sin,
14 That I became
15 Most thin.
16 With thee
17 Let me combine,
18 And feel this day thy victory:
19 For if I imp my wing on thine,
20 Affliction shall advance the flight in me.

Witness 3: p

¶ Easter wings.

1 Lord, who createdst man in wealth and store,
2 Though foolishly he lost the same,
3 Decaying more and more,
4 Till he became
5 Most poor:
6 With thee
7 O let me rise,
8 As larks, harmoniously,
9 And sing this day thy victories:
10 Then will the fall further the flight in me.

¶ Easter wings.

11 My tender age in sorrow did begin:
12 And still with sicknesses and shame
13 You did so punish sin,
14 That I became
15 Most thin.
16 With thee
17 Let me combine,
18 And feel this day thy victory:
19 For, if I imp my wing on thine,
20 Affliction shall advance the flight in me.

Figure 15. "Easter Wings" with normalized spellings and expanded abbreviations

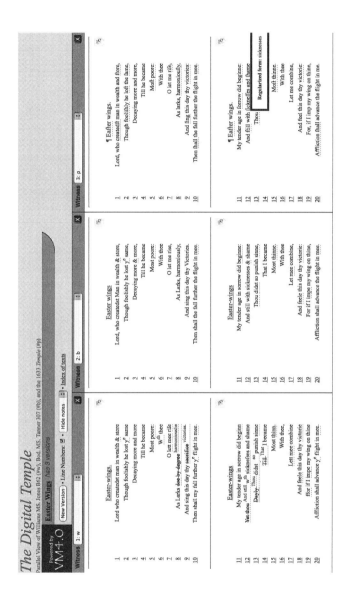

Figure 16. "Easter Wings" diplomatic transcriptions with tool-tip (lower right panel)

Another reason for including such tagging is to provide in the display interface the option of viewing fully modernized texts, mainly for students. A stylesheet designed to do this with "Easter Wings," for example, generates the following result (Figure 15).

An alternative is to provide a tool-tip mechanism by which users can access modern or expanded versions of words individually (Figure 16).

The text box below "ſickneſſes," triggered simply by placing the cursor on the word, reveals the alternate "sicknesses" that is included in the encoding (parallel to the original whose non-Unicode ſi and ſſ ligatures are captured using the <g/> tag from the TEI-P5 *gaiji* module):

```
<choice>
        <orig><g ref="#silig">ſi</g>ckne<g ref="#sslig">ſſ</g>es</orig>
        <reg>sicknesses</reg>
</choice>
```

This second option, from a pedagogical point of view, is perhaps superior to the first. It allows students otherwise alienated by strange orthography recourse to something more familiar even while not avoiding the original, as would be the case with the single-view modernized transcription (Figure 15).

While the orig/reg and abbr/expan pairs serve well my desire to include a modern text (whether fully displayed or just below the display surface and accessed using a tool-tip device), they are not so effective with respect to computer-assisted querying. Inflected verbs archaically spelled, for example, each receive distinct treatment:

```
<choice>
        <orig>creaitedst</orig>
        <reg>createdst</reg>
</choice>

<choice>
        <orig>created&#xFB05;</orig>
        <reg>createdst</reg>
</choice>

<choice>
```

```
      <orig>creait'&#xFB05;</orig>
      <reg>creat'st</reg>
      <expan>createst</expan>
  </choice>
```

Though a good search engine querying 'create' might return all of these instances, the encoding as such does not guarantee this. A solution, offered by the TEI-P5 *analysis* module, is to include the <w/> (word) element with the "lemma" attribute pointing to the English language dictionary headword under which it would be found:

```
  <w type="verb" lemma="create" >
      <choice>
              <orig>creaitedst</orig>
              <reg>createdst</reg>
      </choice>
  </w>
```

This method is more consistent, resolving all words to their appropriate lemmas, verbs to their infinitive forms, and nouns to the singular nominative. The P5-conformant "type" attribute, whose value here is the word's part-of-speech function, contributes to this greater analytical rigor. Abbreviations can be handled in a similar manner, as in the following rendering of the nominative plural *sums* which, in the original, includes a combining tilde over the u implying an additional nasal consonant *m*:

```
  <w type="noun" lemma="sum">
      <choice>
              <orig>su&#x303;mes</orig>
              <reg>sums</reg>
      </choice>
  </w>
```

Real lemmatization, of course, would mean tagging all words in the file that are themselves not dictionary headwords but whose orthography otherwise conforms to the modern standard (as with inflected verbs such as *sinned* and *speaketh*). Indeed, a thorough treatment would include all modern-spelled headwords such as *sinning* (a verbal noun), *sinning* (an adjective), and *sinning* (a present participle), for these are three distinct words (though the OED often lists adjective/present-participle pairs as single entries).

The following poem (offered extempore and with sincere apology)

> Hapless sinning,
> Sinning hipster:
> George the hipp'd aesthete is (haply) sinning.

might be encoded as:

> <l>Hapless <w type="noun(vbl)" lemma="sinning">sinning</w> ,</l>
> <l><w type="adj" lemma="sinning">Sinning</w> hipster:</l>
> <l>George the hipp'd aesthete is (haply) <w type="ppl" lemma="sinning">sinning</w>. </l>

The <w/> element with a "type" attribute, then, introduces a level of detail that enables much finer querying. The question, as with all encoding decisions, is whether such functionality is worth the effort to include it.

What began as an effort to produce an electronic edition of George Herbert's English verse has become more broadly an effort to devise a model for handling early-modern texts in the emerging world of digital humanities. Such projects, though imperfect, point toward the future of scholarly editing. Indeed, by foregrounding difference through parallel display of witnesses, The Digital Temple raises theoretical questions about what it means to be a digital scholarly editor. One might argue that such a method is an abdication of the editor's most important role: to establish the eclectic text as a single ideal, representative text that never existed prior to its being distilled from witnesses. If so, I stand guilty as charged. My purpose is not to establish the text that is Herbert's *Temple*; it is not, in the words of Martha Nell Smith, "to dictate what can be seen," but rather, "to open up ways of seeing" and thereby to "create a climate of possibility for interpretation" (Smith 2004, 315–16). It is perhaps what Randall McLeod might call an exercise in un-editing. And yet, as is likely evident by now, digital editing does not escape being but another form of mediation. Even something as innocuous as lemmatization is a kind of editorial intervention, for it implicitly says that this aspect of the text (as opposed, say, to its prosodic or biographical or theological features) is what matters. Just as the "master text," to cite the editors of the Norton Shakespeare, is but a "dream," so perhaps is the postmodern notion of a master-less text that relieves the editor of scholarly and ideological responsibility (Greenblatt 2008, 67).

WORKS CITED

Barthes, Roland. 1977. *Image, Music, Text.* Fontana communications series. London: Fontana.

Greenblatt, Stephen, ed. 2008. *The Norton Shakespeare.* International Student Edition. New York: W. W. Norton.

Herbert, George. 1876. *The Temple: Sacred Poems and Private Ejaculations.* London: Elliot Stock.

_____ 1941. *The Works.* Ed. F. E. Hutchinson. Oxford: Clarendon Press.

_____ 1984. *The Bodleian Manuscript of George Herbert's Poems: A Facsimile of Tanner 307 [completed in 1633].* Delmar, NY: Scholars' Facsimiles & Reprints.

_____ 2007. *The English Poems of George Herbert.* Ed. Helen Wilcox. Cambridge: Cambridge University Press.

McGann, Jerome J. 1991. *The Textual Condition.* Princeton, NJ: Princeton University Press.

McLeod, Randall. 1993. Fiat Flux. In *Crisis in Editing: Texts of the English Renaissance,* 61–172. New York: AMS Press.

_____ 1998. Enter Reader. In *The Editorial Gaze: Mediating Texts in Literature and the Arts,* ed. Paul Eggert and Margaret Sankey, 3–50. New York: Garland.

Smith, Martha Nell. 2004. Electronic Scholarly Editing. In *A Companion to Digital Humanities,* ed. Ray Siemens, Susan Schriebman, and John Unsworth, 306–22. Blackwell Companions to Literature and Culture 26. Oxford: Blackwell.

A First-Principles Reinvention of Software Tools for Creative Writing and Text Analysis in the Twenty-First Century

Jeff Smith

University of Saskatchewan

jeff.smith@usask.ca

One thing software developers learn young is that, sometimes, another incremental feature release is just not going to cut it. Witness the sea changes from Microsoft DOS to Windows, or from Apple Macintosh OS 9 to OS X. These were not the same old packages of features and bug fixes that previous versions had been, but instead a complete reconception of the very principles and assumptions underlying the software upon which a new code base was built to give form to those updated ideals. Like any other human-made system, software tools are based on a set of foundational assumptions, principles, or beliefs, and once started, they tend to grow from those humble beginnings by incremental modification. Eventually, though, the times change sufficiently to antiquate those foundations, and when that day comes, more incremental change is not going to make things better. That time has come for writing tools.

I do not just mean that we need to take word processors back to the drawing board and redesign their code to get rid of bloat. I mean we have to throw them out completely, along with our entire notion of what the fundamental relationship between writing and software should be. We need to start again. We know a lot more now about the creative process than we did when these tools were born, and we got it wrong. I begin this exploration by outlining four dimensions of creativity that seem to conflict with the current state of the writing/software marriage. Then I present my model of how the writing process works and from that I proceed to construct a blueprint for what writing tools might look like in the future, with examples. Finally, I conclude with some observations about where the challenges lie in achieving this revolution and how we might go about helping it along.

© 2010 Iter Inc. and the Arizona Board of Regents for Arizona State University.

All rights reserved

ISBN 978–0–86698–021–0 (online)   ISBN 978–0–86698–449–2 (print)

New Technologies in Medieval and Renaissance Studies 2 (2010) 63–80

Four Dimensions of Our Misconception

Computer scientists typically view the creative process as ephemeral, hard to pin down and quantify. Since they also tend to believe that a process must be well understood in order to express it effectively in code, discussions about creativity software tend to make them uneasy. Historically, they have dealt with artistic media tools by defining the processes narrowly enough to constrain them into a form that is knowable, predictable, and, therefore, computable. This is a large part of why word processors have rectangular paper extents, top-to-bottom text flow, serial pages, and black text on white backgrounds. Over time, of course, some of these constraints have been relaxed, embracing coloured fonts, for example, and permitting some languages to flow text in different directions, but the underlying assumptions have not changed much. Word processors are literally that: tools for processing words. This has made them a natural fit for the business writing world, because that form of writing tends to be very direct and purposive. A business communication, such as a memo or letter, is guided by efficiency: it should be as unambiguous as possible, concise, and quick to produce.

By contrast, the origins of the content in creative writing are far murkier. Business writers do not spend six months doing deep background research on the milieu of their purchase orders. They do not struggle with understanding the motivation of their antagonist while drafting a job description for the receptionist, and they certainly do not need to track all the references to the theme of loneliness while filling out a customer satisfaction survey on behalf of a supplier. Creative writers do exactly these kinds of things, and the ability to process words has only tangential bearing on those formative activities, because the words are not yet clear in the writer's mind. If creative writers are to be facilitated in those earlier stage ruminations, they will need a new tool. They will need a story processor.

From the perspective of the computer scientist, however, this sounds like a tool steeped in exactly the kinds of imprecision that they removed from the equation in the first place in order to make it solvable. That means changing some fundamental assumptions, and that is why building a story processor is going to require a complete rewrite. Fortunately for our purposes, much has been learned in the past fifteen years about what creativity is, how it functions, and how it can be facilitated. Those intangibles are a little more distinct today, giving us more to work with than our predecessors had. We now know that creativity is starry-eyed, dances in circles, starves in a straitjacket, and suffocates in a vacuum. These are, of course, my own characterizations, and I've phrased them in a way that will underscore how imprecise and un-quantifiable these notions might seem. Now I'd like to explain what I mean by each of those statements and to see if we can tease a bit of quantifiability out of them.

Creativity is starry-eyed

I have a mantra in my research that I have found helpful in guiding my approach to the artistic process: "Creativity is not an act of will; it is an act of awareness." By this I mean that even when an artist thinks she is engaged in an intentionally creative act, I find it helpful to divide her activity into two separate components. The intentional part of the act is about creating ideas or representations which she constantly reviews with her artistic sensibility. This inner awareness then recognizes something artistic about the work and directs further activity. To me, this awareness-oriented view of creativity explains why artists can be inspired by just about anything, whether it is an intentionally constructed artefact or a chance-encountered pattern perceived in their everyday lives.

Further, this helps me to understand the value of experimenting, of keeping a sketchbook or journal, of retaining previous drafts and failed projects. In addition to simply archiving work already done that might later be reused, these histories also retain idea structures and fragments that might later provide new inspiration. Creativity thrives on being inundated with many different ideas and perspectives on an artistic problem; hence it is "starry-eyed," which also connotes a sense of obliviousness. Mihaly Csikszentmihalyi described flow—a state of engagement in which the artist is completely absorbed by her work and her media, to the exclusion of all other awarenesses, including that of time—and tells us that it is crucial to the creative process (Csikszentmihalyi 1990).

From these notions, I extract a few observations that should inform our thinking about story processing tools. If abandoned drafts and fragments of text have potential value, either for inspiring new ideas or in representing multiple perspectives on the work in progress, then they should not be relegated to remotely hidden backup files or allowed to be overwritten when one draft is saved over another. And if artists working at their peak of efficiency are oblivious to the passage of time, maybe we should not be interrupting them with mundane concerns like having to save their files or create backups. Current tools present writers with an unsolvable dilemma:

stay productive and risk losing your work, or protect your work by interrupting yourself when you are at your best. I think we can do better.

Creativity dances in circles

Creativity is not a straightforward, linear process. It rarely proceeds directly from inspiration, to implementation, to completion in one pass. Typically, the work proceeds in iterations, beginning with either inspiration or implementation and proceeding through some degree of development before a new understanding is achieved, which sends the process back to an earlier stage to try again in this new light (Alamargot and Chanquoy 2001). Each such iteration of this process presumably brings the artist closer to the final goal as she spirals in toward the bullseye. Similarly, it has been my observation that as the spiral tightens, the focus of the artist's attention shifts. In the early stages of creativity (ESC) the focus tends to be on large-scale structures within the work, whereas later stages (LSC) focus more on manipulations of the atomic elements of the medium (Smith, Mould, and Daley 2009), such as pixels, words, or notes. In LSC, those larger scale structures tend to have already solidified and no longer require manipulation.

As a consequence of this shifting spiral of artistic concern, a great many tools that are crucial to one phase of a project may be inconsequential at another. Few novelists are liable to worry overly much about spelling when they have not yet discovered their protagonist's motivation. An essayist likely cares nothing about pagination when he is still wrestling with the flow of his argument. A monolithic menu structure that presents all possible tools to the user at all times introduces navigational complexity that might usefully be avoided. The spiralling dance of creative exploration also suggests that splitting the ESC and LSC toolsets into two separate applications is likely a bad idea, so it does not seem advisable that our story processor be constructed as a precursor application. To properly embrace the nature of the writer's creative journey, it will have to handle the entire process.

Creativity starves in a straitjacket

This is the dimension in which computer science and art might be most diametrically opposed. For a programmer, uncertainty is an evil. The better she is able to predict the nature of the information she will be manipulating, the more she is able to avoid doing stupid things with it. This has given rise to a concept computer scientists call strong typing, and is the reason why a calculator program will not accept text or music as input. If the program code can be sure that it will never be asked to multiply the word "cranberry" by the key of C Major then the programmer can make some safe assumptions about the data she will be asked to work with, and can better shape the code to deal effectively with it. However, playing fast and loose with the meaning of information, treating entities of one kind as though they belonged in the realm of another kind, is a hallmark of creative exploration, and I believe that allowing artists to flout the boundaries of convention is an essential part of facilitating their creative journey. Hence I promote a *loosely typed* design philosophy, but in the domain of writing tools, this has to be interpreted more broadly than it is usually intended.

I do not expect writers to want to transform MP3 files into text or create sentence structures from tax data, even though this is the sort of openness that loose typing usually implies. In this case, I am referring specifically to the classifying of story types and structures. There are a number of tools in the market that attempt to facilitate creative writing by creating very limited definitions of what stories are, or how they are structured. Tools such as Dramatica or NewNovelist purport to help writers overcome barriers by providing restricted definitions of what a story is and what parts it has. These formulaic approaches to story I construe as being strongly typed, and I hold that a story processor must be agnostic on such definitions. In addition to typing, there is another way in which existing tools are overly constrained, to the detriment of the earlier creative stages. It lies in the seemingly benign notion of tidiness. Almost every creative media tool I have seen goes to great effort to always present the content in as neat and tidy a fashion as possible. Messiness has been eliminated at the cost of throwing the baby out with the bathwater.

During the early 1990s, I worked for a company that made three-dimensional design and visualization tools for the automotive market. Car designers would use our software to sketch ideas for new cars, and in a matter of days be able to go from first concept to glossy photo of what the car would look like on the showroom floor, complete with overhead lights reflecting off the bumper and smiling sales people standing behind it. It took several years for the insidious part to become evident. The concept-to-showroom time for a typical car, in those days, was about five years, during which hundreds of paper sketches were made, dozens of clay models sculpted and two or three prototypes manufactured by a small army of contributors. The problem with fast-tracking to the visualization of a completed car was that the high fidelity rendering was conveying an unintended and entirely inappropriate message, telling designers that their designs were more mature than they actually were. Subconsciously, they equated the polish of the rendering with maturity of concept. So they stopped refining their work.

I call this the *completion cueing* problem, and now that I have been sensitized to it, I see it in almost all creative media tools. With word processors, the very first draft of a document's outline is as legible, neat, and orderly as the final output. Christina Haas tells us that English students consistently revise their work less and produce poorer results when writing on computers than when writing by hand (Haas 1989). While I cannot claim that this is all attributable to completion cueing, I believe that it is a large part of it. To avoid this trap, story processing tools need to be smart enough to guesstimate the maturity of the work, or allow the writer to indicate the maturity level, so that the software display can provide cues in the visual presentation to help remind the writer how much remains to be done.

Creativity suffocates in a vacuum

A common theme among cognitive psychologists and creativity researchers is that art cannot happen in isolation (Boden 1990; Gabora 2002; Shneiderman 2002). Art builds upon that which has gone before, and it can only be judged against that cultural corpus. In music, for example, a new piano concerto is meaningless if we do not already have some notion of what a piano concerto is, what the rules and traditions are for that form, and what other works in the genre have already accomplished. Furthermore, it can only be judged effectively by someone who is intimately familiar with all those parameters. Asking a woodcarver to judge the concerto would be unlikely to yield more than a superficial assessment. In addition to historical contribution, creativity also thrives on contemporary feedback. This is not to suggest the notion of building art-by-committee, but rather, presenting material in a way that permits rich and contextually meaningful commentary to be exchanged by contemporary contributors.

Some work is already being done on collaborative writing tools, but in my view all have missed the point. Collaborative writing is not about collaborative wordsmithing. In order to collaborate, writers must first be able to exchange ideas, concepts, and attitudes. The writing comes later. Consider the case of two writers who want to collaborate on a story. In one scenario, suppose that they can exchange only unblemished, typewritten drafts. In a second scenario, suppose they are allowed to add sticky notes, highlighting, and marginal annotations to the draft, and in a third, let us allow them to add outlines, backstory sketches, and character studies to the shared and annotated material. In which of these scenarios is the most meaningful collaboration happening? There should be no debate. Clearly, when they are allowed to exchange information to convey their deeper reasoning and to explain how that depth of thought is manifested in their art, writers are then able to align their work to a much greater degree and build on one another's thinking, rather than to be constantly struggling and misunderstanding one another, as they would likely do in the first scenario.

But this richer idea exchange doesn't only bring value to contemporary collaboration. Imagine how much more value there would be for a writer in studying *Hamlet* if she had access to all of Shakespeare's intellectual scaffolding around the work and did not have to rely solely on the text itself to infer such structures. Or what if, in addition to Shakespeare's scaffolding, she also had access to the scaffolding contributed by six of history's leading *Hamlet* scholars. If having access to review and manipulate all of these scaffolds would be useful, perhaps there is one more contributor whose scaffolding would be a valuable contribution to a writer's workspace as well: her own. Any tool that could provide this meta-level information contributed by others would naturally also be able to encode and manipulate the author's own underlying thoughts about her work, connecting those thoughts to the actual passages of text where they are evident.

This is the essence of what I think a story processor should be all about: not just manipulating words, but also manipulating the ideas, the themes, and the concepts that the author brings to bear in shaping those words in the first place. Now that I have described what we know about creativity and how it might apply to creative writing, I will look at what we know about story, about what a writer is trying to produce, and about how she goes about doing it.

A Model of the Writer's Creative Process and Outputs

It is all well and good to declare that we are going to design an annotative story processor, and that doing so will usher in a new era of creative achievement in the literary arts, but for that promise to bear fruit we have to get a much better picture of what a story is, so that we can decide how to process it. I do not mean that we need to create a robust definition of story in any conclusive, irreducible manner, for that would just be inviting another one of those straitjackets I mentioned earlier. What I mean is that we need to create a definition of story, and an understanding of the writing process, that illuminates the various parts and dimensions that will have to be encoded and manipulated in the proposed tool. In that light, I find it useful to characterize the creative writing process as a simultaneous development of three key, interdependent outputs: *testaments*, which are arrangements and renderings of selected *narrative shards* that convey features of the underlying *story model.*

There have been many attempts to define a story model, but the one that comes closest to capturing my meaning is the ficton postulated by Robert Heinlein (1980). A ficton can be described as the world in which a story takes place. This is not just the name of a city or a milieu, but all the details, facts, histories, characters, backstories, settings, and so forth that define the story, its limitations, and its infrastructure. Even in the case where a story takes place in the real world, it has its own distinct ficton by virtue of the fact that, to some degree, the characters, events, or other details are invented. During the course of writing, one of the things I characterize the writer as doing is building this ficton and collecting the list of factoids (the truths that hold good in this invented world, say that the planet has two moons) that describe that world. I call these fictional factoids *fictoids.*

In addition to conceiving this world, I see the writer as also, simultaneously, exploring ways to convey those fictoid details in passages of narrative text. There are many ways to tell a given story and many ways to draw out the conflict, illuminate the characters, and convey the themes. Some elements may take an entire chapter; others might be captured by a single word or by a recurrent idea. In that a story can be broken down into these fragments, which can in turn often be broken down again, I refer to them as story shards, and collectively, they form a kaleidoscope of possible combinations that can be grouped and presented in myriad ways. In the visual arts, we might refer to shards as sketches, and indeed, there are similarities between the two ideas, not the least of which is that the artist often explores different approaches to a single visual element, and similarly, the writer can often explore different shards to illuminate the fictoids of the model that she is trying to express. This highlights a problem with existing writing tools, in that prior drafts are typically treated as defunct, and relegated to some hard-to-reach location in the archival file system, if they are saved at all. I think a creative writing tool should embrace such shards, and maintain them within the workspace in an entirely accessible form, throughout the life of the project. They are not rejects but alternatives.

The third production activity within the writing process is of course the selecting and sequencing of the story shards into various views, which I call testaments, although not all testaments are necessarily intended as potential outputs. Drafts of the story are only one particular type of testament. There are other authorial views possible as well, of value to the writer only. For example, one testament might be a point-form outline of a particular character's emotional arc; another might be a graph of the dramatic tension in a particular sequence of events; and a third might be a list of all the dialogue spoken by character A to character B. These are all ways of looking at the ficton and the narrative kaleidoscope that can be of assistance to the writer, and many such testaments might be produced over the course of her work.

The question that needs to be answered is what form these three output documents should take. It seems that the narrative kaleidoscope is reasonably well defined as some collection of story shards. These can be chapters, scenes, paragraphs, or any other cohesive segment of text that is meaningful to the writer, and there is no reason for regularity or consistency, either. One shard can be a sentence and another can be a chapter, depending on the situation. Similarly, the testaments seem well enough understood, instantiating as various forms of multimedia documents. Some are simply ordered collections of shards, and others might be the output of some automated analysis of such a collection, and while the specific contents of those testaments, and the algorithms that produce them, may not be completely known at this point, we do understand how to represent such things in computers. What remains unclear at this point is the nature of the ficton model. That output is not yet well described. How do we represent abstract ideas in software? How do we make them accessible, selectable, sortable, retrievable, and how do we link them together? How do we connect them to the shards that express them, and how do we illustrate those linkages, where appropriate, in testament views?

Let us look at how writers currently develop such information. By and large, most of them create a number of tangential working documents: backstories, outlines, journal entries, old drafts, short stories, sketches, calendars, and so on. They might even collect multimedia catalogues of images, recordings, and films that inform some aspect of their thinking toward the work in progress. To some degree, these working documents are annotated with marginal notes, sticky notes, or a concordance, that attempt to connect the source materials with his thoughts, plans or even with passages from his output text. These working documents are rarely well organized or annotated, and even then, they are not particularly accessible for our scrutiny. It turns out, however, that there is another group of people who have exactly the same forms of material used to produce a representation that describes a particular person's model of the infrastructure of a subject text. Those people are literary scholars.

The scholar's critical understanding of a text begins with reading. Then there is some thinking, followed by an awful lot more reading, and maybe a bit more thinking, before the whole thing resets and the reading starts again. And through it all, notes and external linkages accumulate like a gently falling snow of ideas. A particular line of text illustrates a particular marginal thought about isolation. The use of a certain word reinforces certain theories about the author's psychological stability. Each such annotation contains some marginal description or explanation, and may also refer to some fragment or fragments of text, either in the subject material itself, or in some other external document. These annotations and marginal linkages to other passages and documents are almost identical to the ones described for the writers themselves. And this makes perfect sense, because the author must be considered the first critical analyst to study any particular work, and while their processes are in a sense reversed, the model each group builds contains essentially the same kinds of information.

My research in conjunction with Yin Liu has developed a tool called Glyphicus (Liu and Smith 2008) to allow humanists to explore text and construct annotative models in exactly this kind of free-form manner. So if the scholar can build a model of his understanding of a text this way, then perhaps it would be possible for an author to build one using similar tools. And this model is ideally suited to encoding fictoids. A fictoid is just a statement that expresses a fact within the world of the ficton, or an idea in the mind of the writer. Example ideas include: "Norman Bates fixates on his dead mother," "There is a green light on Daisy Buchanan's dock," "Pi Patel was set adrift with a hungry tiger," "Loneliness is always self-imposed," and "That which does not kill us only makes us angrier." They can be a single word or as lengthy as a manifesto. What matters is that they convey some specific thought or concept of interest to the writer. Once encoded, the power comes when the writer links these fictoids to the shards, and can view those linkages contextually within the testaments. When all three constructs are thus interconnected, the writer is in possession of a full-blown story exploration and development tool, a story processor. Now let me show some examples of what that might look like.

Penelope: Integrated Story-Processing

While there is no actual story processor application yet, my research currently exists as a number of isolated software experiments, collectively referred to as the Penelope project. The following images are either outputs from these various experimental software tools, run against real data taken from my own novel in progress, or they are artists' conceptions of what those outputs will look like when they have been completed. Figure 1 depicts an early stage sketch of the story's plot outline.

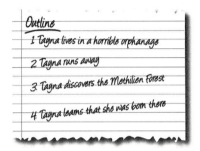

Figure 1. Completion cueing in story outline views, early and late stages

Note the extreme informality of the font and text alignment, which conveys the notion that this is a very preliminary structure in need of further refinement. Contrast this with the same outline presented on the right as it would appear in a typical word processor. Note the much more authoritative impression given by the second version, that this is the outline, and is not to be challenged or changed.

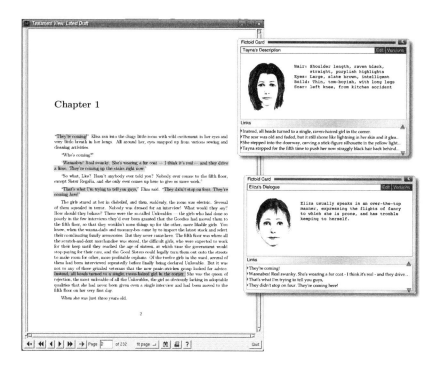

Figure 2. A text entry interface with some annotation enabled

Figure 2 shows the system in text-entry mode, where some annotations have been explicitly turned on by the user. Notice that a fictoid card regarding the physical description of the protagonist is shown and that it contains links to all locations in the story where references are made to her appearance. These associated passages are depicted in the text with colour-coded highlighting, and the list of them in the fictoid card allows the writer to quickly navigate between such passages to maintain consistency if any changes are made to her description. The second card highlights all the dialogue spoken by one of the supporting characters. In addition to having direct links to text passages, fictoid cards can also reference links indirectly, by referring to other cards. In this way, complex structures can be built up quickly. For example, cards for Tayna's description, her dialogue, and her wardrobe can all be summarized in a grouping card called Tayna's attributes, but grouping is not forced to be hierarchical, so there can also be a parent card for all "good-guy" dialogue, or a fashion card for all clothing references. This feature implements a very powerful way to express multiple, parallel structures within a project, in a way that traditional outlining tools simply cannot match.

Also note the character visualizations included in these cards. They were created with a tool that allows users to sketch faces by selecting from a catalogue of feature shapes and is just one of many visualization tools planned for Penelope. Other planning and visualization tools under consideration include a map-making tool, day planners for each character, and an extensive media album to allow the author to manage collections of images and sounds relating to the project. The contents of any of these tools can then be included into fictoid cards, just as the character visualizations have been in this example.

Sentence Word Density by Chapter

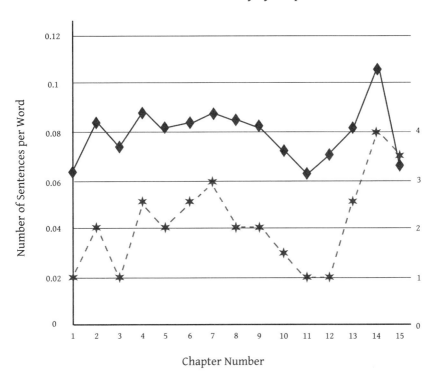

Figure 3. A dramatic tension graph

In my writing style, tense moments are characterized by shorter, choppier sentences. Figure 3 depicts a graph of sentence brevity over the course of the novel, which I used in an attempt to visualize the changing pace of action. The solid line represents this automated tension calculation. Compare that to the dotted line which represents my subjective evaluation of tension, coded on a 5-point scale from "serene" to "climactic." Not only do the two correspond in shape well, but this demonstrates the flexibility of the system to support different types of evaluation tools, as well as its value as an experimental platform into which different analysis tools can be plugged and examined, either by humanities scholars or computer researchers.

Figure 4 is an example of what I am calling a *voice coherence* diagram. David Hoover demonstrated their utility in his analysis of writing styles (Hoover 2007). The graph depicts the results of a stylometric analysis of vocabulary used in dialogue uttered by different characters. By this method, he was able to depict consistency and inconsistency of voice in the works of several novelists, and use it to examine beliefs about how well some novelists were able to impart distinct voices to their characters. I have used it as a touchstone in comparing the voices of several characters during the development of my novel.

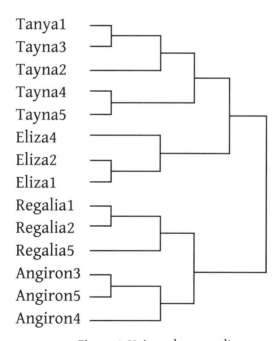

Figure 4. Voice coherence diagram

The entries linked most closely by the branches of the diagram represent the dialogue sets that are most similar in voice. Each entry represents all the dialogue spoken by a given character in a given chapter, although it should be noted that not all characters appear in each chapter. This diagram suggests that each character has a consistent voice, and that Tayna and Eliza, who are children and friends, are more similar to one another than they are to the two adult characters.

Figure 5 is the most important output from the Penelope project to date, in the sense that it is responsible for inciting a major change in the novel it depicts. This simple diagram is what computer scientists call a swim-lane diagram, but I have repurposed it in Penelope into what I call a *geographic flow* diagram. Each column depicts a particular setting in the ficton, organized horizontally by their geographical distance from the orphanage in which the story begins. The vertical axis is chronological time with earlier events at the top. Each oval is an event from the outline that is known to have been expressed in the output testament and involves one of the six main characters. The graph clearly shows the journey of this party of characters as they move further and further from the orphanage during the story's progress. An exception is one sequence at the bottom left, which clearly shows that the protagonist has stepped out of the story to pursue a completely tangential agenda. This diagram demonstrated a crucial fact that I had not realized until I saw it in the graph: I was writing two stories. In response to this evidence, I spent several days contemplating what it meant, and in the end, realized that I was writing a trilogy, and not a single novel, as I had thought. This is hardly conclusive evidence of anything other than my own shortcomings as a storyteller, but I find it a compelling validation of the kinds of contribution that I think story processors will be able to make to the creative writing process.

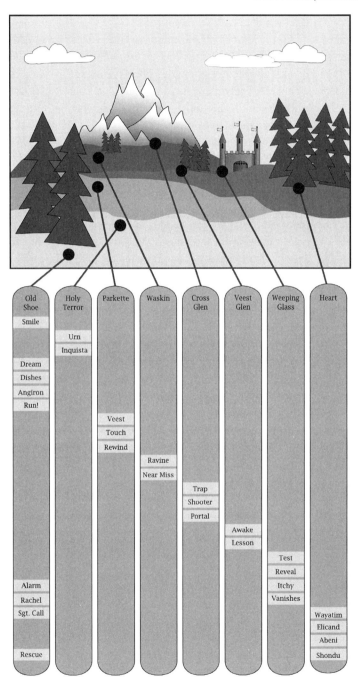

Figure 5. Geographic flow diagram

Looking to the Horizon

None of the features I have discussed represents a challenge to software engineering. All are easily implementable. The challenges lie in packaging these features and making them usable by writers who neither have nor want expertise with computers. I believe those challenges are solvable. The benefits of story processing are not confined to creative fiction. Any form of writing that needs to collect and manage a list of contributing thoughts and ideas will benefit from the separation of modelling and rendering represented by this approach, which is to say that most forms of writing should benefit. Nor do the potential benefits lie only with writers. What has become evident in relation to structure-based creativity tools is that they are usable by more than just the principal artists for whom they were developed. In the case of story processors, if a novelist can use one to develop a mental model of her world and her thematic and conceptual intentions for it, then it can just as easily be used by a literary scholar to build up a similar sort of model about a work under scrutiny. It is not difficult to conceive going from supporting the work of literary scholars to supporting the work of literature educators. Just as the author can create structural models of her work and then derive visualizations of it, literature and creative writing teachers should also be able to use the same tools to demonstrate their points more intimately, by placing the annotations and visualizations inside a representation of the text.

Will this become the foundation for much richer and more explorable scholarly editions in the future? It certainly seems plausible. Especially when we recognize that such a tool is capable of encoding and presenting the apparatus of hundreds of different scholars, not just one or two, and then allowing students to inspect the text in any number of ways, on their own. In the end, this may be the most powerful way to characterize structural story processors: not as a writing tool *per se*, but as a way to marry deeply contextualized, structured information within a text, and to make that information available to any interested party, be they author, critic or student.

WORKS CITED

Alamargot, Denis, and Lucile Chanquoy. 2001. *Through the Models of Writing*. Studies in writing v. 9. Dordrecht: Kluwer Academic.

Boden, Margaret A. 1990. *The Creative Mind: Myths & Mechanisms*. London: Weidenfeld and Nicolson.

Csikszentmihalyi, Mihaly. 1990. *Flow: The Psychology of Optimal Experience.* New York: Harper & Row.

Gabora, Liane. 2002. Cognitive Mechanisms Underlying the Creative Process. In *Proceedings of the Fourth Conference on Creativity and Cognition*, 126–33. Loughborough, UK: Association for Computing Machinery. http://portal.acm.org/citation.cfm?id=581730.

Haas, Christina. 1989. Does the Medium Make a Difference?: Two Studies of Writing with Pen and Paper and with Computers. *Journal of Human-Computer Interaction* 4, no. 2: 149–69.

Heinlein, Robert A. 1980. *The Number of the Beast.* London: New English Library.

Hoover, David. 2007. Corpus Stylistics, Stylometry, and the Styles of Henry James. *Style* 41, no. 2: 160–89.

Liu, Yin, and Jeff Smith. 2008. A Relational Database Model for Text Encoding. *Computing in the Humanities Working Papers* A.43: http://www.chass.utoronto.ca/epc/chwp/CHC2007/Liu_Smith/Liu_Smith.htm.

Shneiderman, Ben. 2002. Creativity Support Tools. *Communications of the Association for Computing Machinery* 45, no. 10 (October): 116–20.

Smith, Jeff, David Mould, and Mark Daley. 2009. Constructures: Supporting Human Ingenuity in Software. *Digital Creativity* 20, no. 1 & 2: 79–94.

Mechanick Exercises: The Question of Technical Competence in Digital Scholarly Editing

Alan Galey
University of Toronto
alan.galey@utoronto.ca

Technical competence and the unknown

> There are known knowns; there are things we know that we
> know. There are known unknowns; that is to say, there are things
> we *now* know we don't know. But there are also unknown un-
> knowns; there are things we *do not* know we don't know.

Donald Rumsfeld, U.S. Defense Department Briefing, 12 February
2002

To borrow the former U.S. Defense Secretary's infamous epistemology, how
might we characterize the various types of unknowns in digital scholarly
editing, and what do editors need to know about using the Web as a delivery platform? Ever a cause for anxiety and wistfulness among overextended
scholars, this kind of question takes on a particular urgency as born-digital
scholarly editions become viable. (By *born digital* I mean not simply editions
that begin life as computer files—nearly all scholarly writing must be born
digital in this sense by now—but rather editions designed for use primarily
in digital environments rather than print.) The traditional humanities curriculum can equip new scholars with knowledge of bibliography (enumerative, analytical, historical, descriptive, and textual [Greetham 1994, 5–8]),
palaeography and codicology, history of the book trades, stemmatics, languages, literary criticism, editorial theory, biography, intellectual history,
reception history, theatre history, archival research methods, and other core
competencies; but what does digital editing add to this already formidable
list? A recent job advertisement for a "Postdoctoral Fellow in Early Modern
Textual Studies and Digital Humanities" invites applicants with competence
in "TEI P5; XML, XSLT, XSL and XHTML encoding; XQuery; eXist XML databases; JavaScript; Ruby on Rails; PHP; CSS; and web-based SQL database
projects using PostgresSQL and mySQL" (ETCL 2008).

ISBN 978–0–86698–021–0 (online)   ISBN 978–0–86698–449–2 (print)
New Technologies in Medieval and Renaissance Studies 2 (2010) 81–101

Such piling-up of knowledge domains on an editor's list of things to learn can seem as daunting as the labours of Hercules, the greatest mythic to-do list of antiquity. Erasmus even compared it to the thankless labours of textual scholarship in his *Adages*: "I should like to know who would not be frightened off ... from engaging in such work, unless he be a real Hercules in mind, able to do and suffer anything for the sake of serving others" (Erasmus 1964, 194; Jardine 1993, 41–45). Erasmus lived in a time of scholar-printers such as John Froben and Aldus Manutius, and their legacy of encyclopaedic skill sets is still detectable in Joseph Moxon's account of the printer's art from 1683–84 (our earliest surviving manual of the trade):

> A *Correcter* should (besides the *English* Tongue) be well skilled in Languages, especially in those that are used to be Printed with us, *viz.* the *Latin, Greek, Hebrew, Syriack, Caldæ, French, Spanish, Italian, High Dutch, Saxon, Low Dutch, Welch,* &c. neither ought my innumerating only these be a stint to his skill in the number of them. (Moxon 1683, 2:260, Mm4v)

Erasmus's question remained a good one in Moxon's time, and even five centuries later. Continuing the trope of the copious list, Jerome McGann responds to digital competence-inflation in the persona of a besieged humanities scholar: "What are you saying? Learn UNIX, hypermedia design, one or more programming languages, or textual markup and its discontents? Learn bibliography and the sociology of texts, ancient and modern textual theory, history of the book?" (McGann 2005, 107). McGann's answer, and the one reflected in the state of the field today, is a clear yes: these are exactly what textual scholars and other humanists must learn if they are to have a voice in the digital reconstitution of the human record.

Yet we lack a name for the type of individual who embodies this synthesis within scholarly editing. The term *corpus editor*, as defined by Gregory Crane, David Bamman, and Alison Jones, describes something close, in that he or she "occupies a middle ground between the algorithm-heavy, knowledge-light approaches of computer science and the wholly manual practices of traditional editing" (Crane, Bamman, and Jones 2007, 52), but their definition still depends upon Fordist notions of specialization. Many computer scientists have always been knowledge-heavy—the best ones, in my experience, make a virtue of curiosity that puts humanists to shame—and many traditional editors have always combined "manual practices" with theoretical inquiry. Frederick Brooks, in his landmark book on the organization of labour and knowledge in software engineering, had to reach outside his own discipline for the term *architect* as a metaphor for the individual entrusted with the conceptual integrity of a project (Brooks 1995, 41–50 & passim).

It was the need to move beyond this two-cultures divide which prompted Northrop Frye, in an unlikely but resonant keynote address to the 1989 conference of the Association for Computing in the Humanities, to remind us that

> three of the most seminal mechanical inventions ever devised, the alphabet, the printing press, and the book, have been in humanist hands for centuries. The prestige of humanists in the past came largely from the fact that they lived in a far more efficient technological world than most of their contemporaries. It is true that today they are sometimes confused about the new possibilities opening up in front of them, though hardly more so than the rest of the human race. (Frye 1989, 8)

Although scholarly editors have been looking to digital technologists for answers to questions about the relation of labour to knowledge, it is worth heeding Frye's reminder that humanists have themselves been technologists and information architects all along.

If the emerging field of digital textual studies lacks a clear answer to my initial question—what does a digital scholarly editor need to know?—it is because any answer depends upon complex relationships between labour, epistemology, and technology, which extend beyond any primarily technical discussion. The following chapter applies the Rumsfeldian taxonomy to scholarly editing and suggests ways digital editors can address questions of technical competence based on the close historical parallels between the digital humanities and textual studies as fields. For the purposes of this discussion, I take *digital editor* to mean anyone undertaking a scholarly edition or similar project designed for delivery over the Web (at this time the main delivery system for digital editions), and *technical competence* to mean the minimum knowledge required for progress in the absence of specialist contractors and research assistants.

Known knowns: Humanities computing and textual scholarship

In the inaugural volume of *Literary and Linguistic Computing* Susan Hockey reports on a workshop held at Vassar College in 1986 that addressed the same question of what humanists need to know about computing (Hockey 1986, 228). She remarks that the place of programming in the curriculum generated much discussion but little consensus apart from agreement that the now-outdated languages "PASCAL, BASIC, and SNOBOL were all thought suitable" for humanists to learn at the amateur level (Hockey 1986, 228). However, the rationales posited by workshop members at the time have endured: that programming inculcates "mental discipline" just as Latin language training has done for centuries; that programming reveals computers' capabilities and limitations alike; and that programming stretches the mind to inspire new ways of thinking about problems (Hockey 1986, 228). More recently, Geoffrey Rockwell echoes the same desire for high-level integration: "The important thing is the integration of skills preparation with intellectual preparation. We shouldn't hide skills and technique—they are what makes [sic] digital humanities different from other programs. Instead, we should think of our programs as an art" (Rockwell 2003, 243).

The integration Hockey and Rockwell describe has long been an ideal difficult to achieve in practice. Peter Shillingsburg similarly attempts to integrate the skill sets of editing and computing, though his book's most recent edition was published before the emergence of the Web as the dominant delivery system (Shillingsburg 1996). Typesetting and other document-centric ways of conceptualizing digital editions are inadequate to the mixed ontologies of Web 2.0, where it is becoming increasingly difficult to tell the difference between a page and a program. Attempts to articulate stable known knowns for digital editing illustrate the value of understanding programming's benefits in abstract terms, as an intellectual exercise independent of any particular language or tool.

The editors of a recent Modern Language Association (MLA) collection, *Electronic Textual Editing*, note the problem that "there are currently few manuals, summer courses, or self-guided tutorials that would help even trained textual editors transfer their skills from print to electronic works" (Burnard, O'Keeffe, and Unsworth 2006, 16). (An exception is University of Victoria's Digital Humanities Summer Institute, which combines the best aspects of a skills workshop, international conference, and summer camp.) However, Burnard and his co-authors write from amid the abbreviations that represent scholarly editing in its most institutionalized form: the MLA's Committee on Scholarly Editions (CSE), formerly the Centre for Editions of American Authors (CEAA), and the Text Encoding Initiative (TEI). David Greetham calls this "an *ex cathedra* statement from the policing organization of our discipline(s)" (Greetham 2007, 133). As the publishers of guidelines for scholarly work, the MLA, CSE, and TEI represent textual scholarship's archival tradition: the part of the discipline that shares many librarians', archivists', and information technologists' reverence for professional standards, best practices, and, most of all, the institutionalizing of a professional desire for "reproducing and uniting the best standards so far developed" (Burnard, O'Keeffe, and Unsworth 2006, 16).

Yet editorial theory and practice over the past quarter-century have come to embody a deep scepticism of institutionalized orthodoxies. Textual scholars today have been trained amid the debates sparked by intensely contested editions such as the Hans Walter Gabler *Ulysses*, the George Kane and E. Talbot Donaldson *Piers Plowman*, the Edinburgh Editions of Walter Scott's *Waverley* novels, the 1986 Oxford *William Shakespeare: The Complete Works* (including the two-text *King Lear*, and a three-text *Lear* in its reincarnation as the Norton Shakespeare), the three-text Arden 3 *Hamlet*, and the 2007 Oxford *Thomas Middleton: The Collected Works*. To these projects we can add more general topics of debate, especially focussed in Shakespeare studies, such as unediting, the (allegedly) bad quartos, multiple-text editions, performance, canonicity, the gendering of texts, the intentions of Shakespeare and his company with regard to publishing playbooks, and the very idea of literature as a distinct category of texts. Should the skills training that comes from "manuals, summer courses, [and] self-guided tutorials" communicate the questions at stake in these debates or simply compartmentalize them?

Few of textual scholarship's known knowns have gone uncontested, especially toward the end of the twentieth century, and there has been little consensus-based progress toward so-called best practices. Instead, dissensus has given us something better: a critical tradition to parallel the archival tradition, advancing knowledge through contestation, debate, and the inclusion of voices from outside the specialist field of scholarly editing, especially from postcolonial studies, book history, performance studies, gender and sexuality studies, film and media studies, and critical theory. To distil editing into a set of institutionally sanctioned practices is to neglect this critical tradition, and to underestimate the challenges it raises. Understanding the often-unacknowledged friction between the critical and archival traditions must be the first thing a digital scholarly editor needs to know, since it will determine how one relates to everything else. This conclusion hardly dispels the unease voiced by Erasmus and McGann, nor does it yet tell us what a digital scholarly editor needs to know. What, then, are the undiscovered regions of the knowledge domain of digital scholarly editing, and how might we identify them on the map of what we do and do not know?

Known unknowns: Foundational technical skills for digital editors

This section describes four technical subjects that are normally the domain of Web programmers, but which digital scholarly editors would do well to understand. I mostly omit discussion of specific software packages because editing is not a task for any one piece of software in the way that a single word processor serves most scholars for writing. I echo William Turkel and Alan MacEachern's premise in their website *The Programming Historian* (required reading for digital editors) favouring a polyglot approach to technologies and languages. No single technology can do everything, despite proprietary software often being marketed commercially as a capital-S Solution (such as Adobe Flash). Encoding, text analysis, and interface design are intellectual endeavours not reducible to abbreviations—text encoding, for example, is about much more than learning any single markup language—but there is nonetheless a need for stable, extensible technologies that enable a range of practice, from the simple to the complex. Some favour the development of a tool or suite of tools, but I am sceptical that these could be anything other than a scholar-built counterpart to Dreamweaver, a tool so generalized that one must bypass its own interface (using the code view pane) to do much specialized or original work. The following list therefore names four areas of knowledge of technical fundamentals that will likely remain pertinent despite the coming and going of software and tools.

1) The history of Web browsers. Browsers, like word processors, are ubiquitous and, therefore, often unnoticed. In the 1990s it was not uncommon to hear the words Netscape or Explorer used to describe any browser regardless of whether it was actually Netscape's Navigator software or Microsoft's rival Internet Explorer. A major recent development in browsers is the maturation of the Web as a platform for delivering applications, not just documents as in the original conception for the Web (Berners-Lee 1990). Scholarly editing is conceptually document-oriented (suited to text encoding) rather than algorithmic (suited to data structures and object-oriented design). Yet browsers are spaces where documents, data structures, and algorithms merge into hybrid forms with complex ontologies. The browser's helpful View Source function gives easy access to a document's source code in HyperText Markup Language (HTML) or eXtensible Markup Language (XML), but increasing complexity in Web architectures means that there is often more to a website than is visible in the source code. Browsers also have a history of conflict with one another and with the very principle of standardized design. Browsers from different makers are not the same, and a single browser may not always function identically on different operating systems.

Ideally one should be able to design Web-based materials according to the independent recommendations of the World Wide Web Consortium (W3C) and have that design function identically on different browsers, as opposed to writing individual workarounds for a specific browser. That ideal was far from reality during the period known as the browser wars, waged largely between Netscape and Internet Explorer since the mid-1990s. We are closer to that ideal now with the Mozilla Firefox browser, which is reasonably standards-compliant and platform-consistent, and to a lesser extent with Safari and recent versions of Internet Explorer, though there are many browsers beyond these major ones, and almost all cling to proprietary implementations of certain features. Wikipedia's entries on Web browsers and their history are useful entry points to this topic (and are reliable at the time of writing), but digital editors should also read a detailed history of this most important of tools (Haigh 2008, 125–47). Digital editors should also become familiar with the online documentation for the major browsers and their design communities, the Mozilla Developer Center and the Microsoft Developer Network.

2) *Text encoding and markup.* Markup of written texts precedes digital computing by centuries, from word-separation by spacing to modern punctuation (Parkes 1992). Although encoding and markup are sometimes conflated under the term *tagging*, it is necessary to understand the distinction between text encoding formats such as ASCII and Unicode and markup languages such as XML. There is also value in understanding markup in more abstract terms than the adding of tags to texts, but that topic is beyond the scope of this discussion (McGann 2004). In particular, one should be aware of how Unicode translates symbols that stand for letters or punctuation visible on the screen into machine-readable codes and back again (Wittern 2007). This knowledge is important for all editors since the careless migration of digital texts between operating systems and applications can introduce errors even though no one has made a typographical error. The Anglocentric history of computing means that keyboards and software handle accented letters awkwardly, so editors working in languages other than English, especially those using non-Latin alphabets, will need to know Unicode well. Even editors working solely in English may need to account for ligatures, swash letters, and other typographical and scribal phenomena.

Systems for marking up texts with tags have a long and varied history, from typesetting software to Standard Generalized Markup Language (SGML) to its Web-oriented derivative, but it is fair to say that XML has superseded them for the present. Along with XML we have several related technologies for key tasks: eXtensible Stylesheet Language Transformations (XSLT), for transforming XML into new forms; XPath, for accessing specific sets of entities within XML documents; and XQuery, for running more complex queries than XPath normally handles. These technologies are usually combined with one another; for example, an XSLT stylesheet is itself an XML file, and uses XPath to select parts of the target document to transform. Perhaps the most fundamental value of XML is its capacity to enforce internal consistency and external conformance by means of a schema or Document Type Definition (DTD), a formal abstraction of the rules that the document is supposed to follow.

A project-wide schema or DTD is a tremendously helpful error-control mechanism, and writing it can be an exercise in formalizing one's assumptions about one's material. The TEI guidelines represent a large-scale, multidisciplinary, and collaborative effort to extend this thinking to the full range of materials that humanists might represent using markup. TEI is more than just a tagset; it is also a mechanism for validating files tagged according to its vocabulary, a protocol for customizing its own tagset, a community for sharing tools and resources, and, most valuably, a locus of debate about humanities materials that makes a virtue of the constraints of markup. In other words, the TEI guidelines should be regarded not simply as a solution to a problem, but as a vocabulary to enrich our questions.

The TEI's *Gentle Introduction to XML* is a good place to start, though humanists will need to look further for introductions to XSLT, XPath, and other related technologies (see the TEI Consortium's website for links to resources). Now that the three major browsers contain XML parsers, one can do a great deal even with the simplest combination of tools: a text editor and Web browser. However, it is helpful to have a single XML editing program that allows one to validate files against schemas and DTDs, run XPath queries, execute XSL transformations, and perform other tasks in one place. Currently the proprietary XML editor *oXygen* provides this functionality and includes the TEI schema.

3) Regular expressions. The simplest and most robust tool for searching and manipulating strings of texts is the standardized grammar known as regular expressions. Basic parts of this grammar will be familiar to anyone who has used a wildcard character in a simple search, as when using *Plo*man* to find matches with *Ploughman* or *Plowman*, and *Le?r* to find matches with *Lear* or *Leir*. Since the grammar is standardized, its rules apply more or less consistently across different programming languages and environments, from JavaScript to Perl to PHP (a recursive abbreviation for "PHP: Hypertext Preprocessor"). Understanding regular expressions has intellectual value beyond practicality; it also disciplines the mind to think about patterns within written language, as Hockey describes, and thus could serve as the basis for user-driven searches of digital editions (Egan 2005).

4) Ajax. Scholars planning digital editions often lack a framework to hold these and other technologies together. With the advent of Firefox as the first popular, standards-compliant, cross-platform Web browser, there has been renewed interest in Web applications that meet third-party standards and build on the free and open-source software ethos. One framework has come to be known by the acronym *Ajax*, or Asynchronous JavaScript and XML, and is a composite of five elements:

> 1. standards-based presentation using eXtensible HTML (XHTML) and Cascading Style Sheets (CSS);
> 2. dynamic display and interaction using the Document Object Model [DOM];
> 3. data interchange and manipulation using XML and [...] XSLT;
> 4. asynchronous data retrieval using the XMLHttpRequest object;
> 5. and JavaScript binding everything together.
> (Garrett)

Some implementations of Ajax add two more components: an XML database such as eXist or Tamino, and a server-side language such as PHP or Java to handle interaction between the database and the client-side JavaScript. Further layers may come into play at the server side, usually requiring advanced expertise and access.

In the Ajax architecture, the interface and the underlying functionality that manipulates the data are closely integrated, written in the same language (JavaScript) and located in the same files. Matthew Kirschenbaum suggests why this kind of integration is important: "from a developer's perspective, the interface is often not only conceptually distinct, but also *computationally* distinct" in many older architectures, and "it wasn't until the comparatively recent advent of languages like Visual Basic that it even became practical to program both a user interface and an application's underlying functionality with the same code" (Kirschenbaum 2004, 524–25). This combining of interface and functionality replicates the humanistic design principle that presentational forms are inseparable from analytical functions because a text's meaning is constituted in part by its material form.

Three general points may be added. Firstly, the most important skill, underwriting all others, is the ability to learn new skills quickly and independently. Yet autodidacticism must be balanced with the second point, that learning how to write code does not necessarily mean one has learned to write good code that is concise, legible, efficient, and elegant. Programming is no less an art than rhetoric, and learning the vocabulary of any one language is only the beginning; more advanced topics include data types, data structures, search and sort algorithms, and object-oriented design. Finally, anyone embarking on a digital edition that requires server resources beyond static web page hosting, such as XML databases and server-side scripting in a language like PHP, will soon encounter the always complex interface between the technological and the institutional. Although it is not difficult to set up a local server on one's own computer—using a package such as MAMP (Mac, Apache, MySQL, PHP) for the Apple Macintosh, or its Microsoft Windows counterpart XAMPP (X-platform, Apache, MySQL, PHP, Perl)—doing the same on a university Web server may require considerable skill in navigating the politics and pragmatics of institutional research support.

Unknown unknowns: Interface and divisions of knowledge

Rumsfeld identified the category of the "unknown unknown" as the most dangerous of all, and in digital editing that category has often manifested itself in matters of interface. Many scholarly editing projects begun in the 1990s did not anticipate how difficult and resource-intensive interface design would be (Kirschenbaum 2004, 524–25), nor how many opportunities for new research it presented. Bethany Nowviskie, for example, reflects on the project history of the *Rossetti Archive*:

> Why did we neglect interface until it was almost too late? ... [P]art of the reason ... was ... an unsavory combination of condescension toward and blind faith in programmers. Our own clarity on the subject has increased, I think, precisely in step with our education in technical issues, programming and stylesheet languages—all the things that academics are too likely to leave to others. (Nowviskie 2000)

The lesson here is that project organization and "education in technical issues" must be closely integrated from the outset, not left to "others," lest unknown unknowns manifest themselves without warning.

Projects today still encounter a lack of tools for visualizing the digital edition and making latent intellectual structures meaningful on the screen. This gap receives little attention because of the wealth of resources researchers now enjoy in related areas like text encoding and text analysis, which have evolved along with their own working languages of choice. A neophyte computing humanist sitting down to learn the fundamentals of text analysis or text encoding soon learns what tools he or she needs on the workbench in order to make something happen and to produce the early results, however modest, that are essential to the success of the autodidactic learning process. This is known as the *hello world!* stage, in which the traditional first task upon learning a new programming language is to make those words appear on the screen. For text analysis and text encoding there are also resources ready to help, like those offered by the TEI and the Text Analysis Portal for Research (TAPoR), but there is no corresponding centralized resource for interface design in the humanities.

One could formulate the problem like an examination question for the present generation of digital humanists:

XML is to markup as Perl is to text analysis

as _____ is to interface design.

One should think carefully before filling in any one acronym or tool. The widespread assumption throughout the late 1990s that hypertext would solve all technical and theoretical problems has proven chimerical. For many theorists and non-specialist commentators, hypertext was an empty vessel into which they poured their hopes without bothering to understand digital texts at the level of code—they simply did not know how much they did not know. The pattern persists, and whereas the technologies mentioned above represent known unknowns, this blank represents the unknown unknown continuing to obtrude into contemporary digital humanities' orderly world of tools.

No single tool or technology can provide the things we have not yet learned to expect from a digital edition, yet consumerist reliance on commercial applications may lead non-specialists to think of interface development as simply a matter of tags, stylesheets, and hyperlinks. The prevailing thinking in software marketing, especially since the late 1990s, crystallizes in the word *solution* as a noun meaning software that solves a problem as soon as it comes out of the box. What You See Is What You Get (WYSIWYG, pronounced whizzywig) Web-design software encapsulates complexity, simplifying design to the point where Web authoring becomes a species of word processing—hence the idea of a web page, symptomatic of the constraints imposed by document-oriented computing. What you see is what you get, but you get only what you can see. Even Ajax may not be the right answer to the blank in the above homology, since the question may contain a category error. Perhaps we need not so much an acronym as an art, to echo Rockwell.

Among digital editing projects one finds two characteristic responses to the existence of unknown unknowns. One is the DIY ethos in which individual scholars stay on top of the copious desiderata of programming languages and databases. Turkel and MacEachern describe the best rationale for this ethos in *The Programming Historian*: "If you don't program, your research process will always be at the mercy of those who do" (Turkel and MacEachern 2007, ch. 2 sec. 2), which is also the message of the present chapter. However admirable such an approach might be in terms of individual autonomy and work ethic, it is difficult for many scholars to sustain in terms of time and career development. (A helpful document in that regard is an MLA report titled "Guidelines for Evaluating Work with Digital Media in the Modern Languages.") A more debilitating side-effect of prioritizing technical work can be what Anthony Kenny calls "distortion of research" (Kenny 1992, 9), a neglect of the important non-digital aspects of humanities scholarship, especially the critical debates ongoing in one's area of study. As Kenny warns, "There is a danger that projects may be undertaken not because they are likely to lead to academically interesting results, but simply because they are susceptible to computerization" (Kenny 1992, 9).

The other common response to unknown unknowns is the collaborative ethos in which one delegates labour—and with it, knowledge—to team members or contractors, with the lead editor providing skills in project management and funding procurement instead of first-hand technical competence. Shillingsburg argues:

> Scholarly editors are first and foremost textual critics. They are also bibliographers and they know how to conduct literary and historical research. But they are usually not also librarians, typesetters, printers, publishers, book designers, programmers, web-masters, or systems analysts. … [Thus] textual scholarship requires the services of Internet technologists. (Shillingsburg 2006, 94–96).

Shillingsburg's conclusion, however appealing, perpetuates the black-boxing inherent in the WYSIWYG approach, in which the user can work without ever having to see the underlying code. Similarly, a shared technology services model like Project Bamboo's, tempting to over-taxed textual scholars, carries the risk that cross-disciplinary influence will flow in only one direction, from the supposedly technology-oriented disciplines like computer science, information studies, and cognitive science to the text-oriented humanities, but not back again. Although encapsulation is essential to computing generally, people are not software, and we should be cautious about applying principles of software design to project organization, interdisciplinarity, and human relationships.

There is a growing division between projects where the humanists regard the technologists as providing services, and those where it is difficult to tell the humanists and the technologists apart. (I now actively avoid the former kind of project.) The division deepens with the belief, popular with digital humanists and funding agencies, that collaboration is self-evidently good. Yet collaborating specialists may dig ever deeper into their disciplinary niches, drawing rigid borders between what they need to know and what they do not. By contrast, it can be liberating and enlightening for a non-technical humanist to start a digital project by painstakingly learning to write her own DTD or schema, treating it as an intellectual exercise in the modelling of materials and not rote implementation of rules dictated by past practice. Ideally, one emerges with a better understanding of one's materials and one's digital tools and of the relationship between them, which in the humanities may be anything but straightforward. The most viable collaborations are intellectual ones, based on the meeting of different minds where all parties emerge changed; the least viable are those that attempt only to balance out skills deficiencies. At worst, the latter approach can render apprenticing scholars (postdoctoral fellows, research assistants) more valuable as continuing subordinates than as future colleagues bound for careers beyond the project.

Thus one may become too technically competent or competent for the wrong reasons. A gifted programmer working on scholarly editions risks exploitative collaborations or conceiving of research materials and questions exclusively in terms of computation. To prevent this, literary and textual scholars must overcome two conceptual constraints. The first is the idea of infrastructure as the guarantor of excellent research. (I use the word *excellent* here mindful of Bill Readings's cautions about its stealth function in academic politics [Readings 1996, 21–43]). Although infrastructure of the kind that Shillingsburg describes is worthwhile and necessary (Shillingsburg 2006, 80–125), the broader institutional discourse still tends to use infrastructure to denote equipment, tools, and shared services rather than knowledge and the capacity to hire knowledgeable people. The second constraint is the assumption of an unbridgeable gap between those working with code and those working with texts and ideas, such that a humanities scholar and a programmer cannot be the same person. To draw a distinction between programming and abstract, poetic thinking is to misunderstand both. Yet in many electronic editing projects the labour divides precisely along these lines: editing stops where interface design begins, with another specialist entering the picture, often as a research assistant rather than an equal collaborator. The division of labour between programming and humanistic inquiry is often necessary, but the division of knowledge is impoverishing.

Conclusion: The missing term

I have argued above that digital editors need to possess technical skills themselves, not just in their research assistants and collaborators, and that the distinction between skills and knowledge is artificial. Does, then, a digital scholarly editor need to be a programmer too or merely able to hire one? If one is committed to the critical tradition of scholarly editing, not just the heaping-up of digitized texts and tools, the answer must be that the project leader should be a programmer, even if she does not do most of the programming. True technical competence cannot be bought. A more heartening rationale for humanists learning programming is described by Stephen Ramsay in a conversation with Turkel and the hosts of the *Digital Campus* podcast, Dan Cohen, Mills Kelly, and Tom Scheinfeldt, in an episode on humanities programming. Ramsay describes the empowerment he felt by learning how to control his digital environment at the level of code—how to "build it, hack it, break the warranty" (Cohen, Mills, and Scheinfeldt 2008, 30.00). For him and his students, upon crossing the programming threshold "the digital world … suddenly seems … less deterministic than it might have been before." Kirschenbaum makes a similar case to a mainstream audience in a recent *Chronicle of Higher Education*: "Computers should not be black boxes but rather understood as engines for creating powerful and persuasive models of the world around us. … I believe that, increasingly, an appreciation of how complex ideas can be imagined and expressed as a set of formal procedures—rules, models, algorithms—in the virtual space of a computer will be an essential element of a humanities education" (Kirschenbaum 2009, B10).

Behind Ramsay's and Kirschenbaum's rationales we may detect the liberal arts tradition of the enlightened, autonomous individual, technically equipped to make informed judgments of a kind that Alan Liu expresses more pointedly: "My highest ambition for cultural criticism and the creative arts is that they can in tandem become 'ethical hackers' of knowledge work—a problematic role in the information world but one whose general cultural paradigm needs to be explored" (Liu 2004, 7–8). With all these convincing rationales available, what remains to prevent humanists from becoming programmers? All the technological conditions have been in place long before now: computers are cheap; the tools are free (from browsers and text editors to XML databases like eXist, and local server environments like MAMP); online tutorials and knowledge bases are free and ubiquitous; online communities for new programmers are thriving and ready to help (and free); the open-source ethos has resulted in many reusable Web programming components being made available for free; and the Web as a distribution platform is mostly free (though servers and their support do cost money). Where, then, are all the programming humanists?

An explanation for their absence may be found in the fourth, unstated category of Rumsfeld's taxonomy, as Slavoj Žižek explains:

> What [Rumsfeld] forgot to add was the crucial fourth term: "unknown knowns," things we do not know that we know—which is precisely ... the disavowed beliefs and suppositions we are not even aware of adhering to ourselves. ... The situation is like that of the blind spot in our visual field: we do not see the gap, the picture appears continuous. (Žižek 2008, 457)

A disdain for the mechanical constitutes the most potentially troublesome blind spot for digital scholarly editing, and the unknown known it conceals is the idea that computers are venues for labour and not for thinking. This is a distinction as old as the liberal arts that gave rise to the modern university system. By invoking the liberal arts tradition in his defence of learning code, quoted above, Rockwell implicitly contextualizes programming and similar skills within the humanities' known knowns (as Hockey does by invoking Latin). It is worth remembering, though, that the liberal arts tradition draws its rationale from the often-unstated Aristotelian distinction between the liberal arts and the servile arts (Adler 1937, 430–44; Burke 2000, 84). If the liberal arts are traditionally defined as those needed by a free citizen of the state, then the servile (or useful) arts are those needed by the servants of the citizens, like the rude mechanicals of *A Midsummer Night's Dream*.

Yet that dichotomy is transforming into something else even as the difference between digital humanities and other humanities disappears. Liu describes this related ideological formation:

> Wherever the academy looks in the new millennium, it sees
> the prospect of a world given over to one knowledge—a single,
> dominant mode of knowledge associated with the information
> economy and apparently destined to make all other knowledges,
> especially all historical knowledges, obsolete. Knowledge work
> harnessed to information technology will now be the sum of all
> worthwhile knowledge—except, of course, for the knowledge of
> all the alternative historical modes of knowledge that undergird,
> overlap with, or—like a shadow world, a shadow web—challenge
> the conditions of possibility of the millennial new Enlighten-
> ment. (Liu 2004, 7)

With Liu's argument in mind, it is worth recalling that the object of Greetham's
critique of the MLA's *Electronic Textual Editing* collection was not what knowledge the book offers its readers, but how the book assumes that knowledge
should function in the world. If the archival tradition and its conservative
worldview embody the kind of illusory continuity that Žižek describes—an
ideology, in other words—then we need a critical tradition that operates in
the gaps of the digital humanities as an Enlightenment project, making the
discontinuities visible.

Such a critical tradition might regard programming as a link to historical
modes of knowledge work that resist what Liu calls the "one knowledge" of
the information economy. Early modernists in particular should be sensitive
to the fluidity between the liberal and servile arts, since the dichotomy began to lose its coherence in the period leading up to Moxon's time in the late
seventeenth century (Prest 1987, 13). Indeed, as Jonathan Sawday describes
in a chapter on early modern "reasoning engines," Francis Bacon and other
seventeenth-century thinkers attempted to rescue the idea of the mechanical from its past associations with socially inferior labour, though at the cost
of a certain instrumentalism (Sawday 2007, 210–16). The same ambivalent
transformation may happen in our time as digital editing, along with digital
knowledge work in the humanities generally, comprise not the "tradesman's
entrance" to the academy, as Willard McCarty calls it, but rather "a computing that is *of* as well as *in* the humanities: a continual process of coming
to know by manipulating representations" (McCarty 2004, 265). The digital
humanities at their best represent not only a synthesis of disciplines, but also
a synthesis of different types of labour and knowledge.

Ours is not the first generation of textual scholars to reckon with the problem of mechanical knowledge. Book history, an interdisciplinary cousin and

historical contemporary of the digital humanities, has reckoned with applied technical knowledge in its own conception of its known unknowns. As the New Bibliographers' chronicler F.P. Wilson contends,

> often ... the bibliographer reaches conclusions that are demonstrable and irreversible. The reason is that he is dealing with an Abel Jeffes or a James Roberts not in his relations with other human beings, whether of the government, or the Stationers' Company, or the playhouse, but in his relations with a mechanical process (Wilson 1970, 34).

Bibliography and book history have been negotiating between the different epistemologies of the mechanical, linguistic, and aesthetic for decades. D. F. McKenzie, for example, did not just lead the reintegration of bibliography with book history and literary interpretation, but also established and operated the Wai-te-ata Press at Victoria University of Wellington, New Zealand, using an 1813 Stanhope hand-press that he operated himself and used to teach his students (McKitterick). This figure of the scholar at the press, attempting to guarantee what Brooks called "conceptual integrity" in software design (Brooks 1995, 256), returns us to Moxon's *Mechanick Exercises*:

> *it is necessary that a* Compositor *be a good English Schollar at least; and that he know the present traditional* Spelling *of all English Words, and that he have so much Sence and Reason, as to* Point *his Sentences properly: when to begin a Word with a* Capital Letter, *when (to render the Sence of the Author more intelligent to the Reader) to* Set *some Words or Sentences in* Italick *or* English Letters, &c. (Moxon 1683, 2:198, Ee1v)

What Moxon is writing about, and what he demonstrates here in print, is the fundamental link between the details of text and the ubiquity of markup: the latent architecture of information that gets manifested and modified through the productive constraints of a mechanical process. The difference between Moxon's technology and the ones I have described above is one of scale but not of nature. What digital textual scholars need to know, then, may be learned by reckoning with our unknown knowns concerning knowledge work, and by rediscovering what we already know about our own mechanic exercises.

Note

This essay reflects conversations with many people, and I particularly wish to thank Gabriel Egan, Matthew Bouchard, Martin Mueller, Harvey Quamen, Stephen Ramsay, Seamus Ross, students in my 2008–9 graduate seminars, and audiences at gatherings organized by the Society for Digital Humanities, the HCI-Book group, and the Folger Shakespeare Library. Any errors are my own.

WORKS CITED

Adler, Mortimer Jerome. 1937. *Art and Prudence: A Study in Practical Philosophy.* New York: Longmans.

Berners-Lee, Tim. 1990. Information Management: A Proposal. http://www. w3.org/History/1989/proposal.html.

Brooks, Frederick P. 1995. *The Mythical Man-Month: Essays on Software Engineering.* 2nd ed. Reading, MA: Addison Wesley.

Burke, Peter. 2000. *A Social History of Knowledge: From Gutenberg to Diderot.* Cambridge: Polity.

Burnard, Lou, Katherine O'Brien O'Keeffe, and John Unsworth. 2006. Introduction. In *Electronic Textual Editing*, 11–21. New York: Modern Language Association of America.

Cohen, Dan, Kelly Mills, and Tom Scheinfeldt. 2008. Digital Campus Episode 25: Get With the Program. April 21. http://digitalcampus.tv/2008/04/21/episode-25-get-with-the-program/.

Crane, Gregory, David Bamman, and Alison Jones. 2007. ePhilology: When the Books Talk to Their Readers. In *A Companion to Digital Literary Studies*, ed. Susan Schriebmann and Ray Siemens, 29–64. Malden, MA: Blackwell.

Egan, Gabriel. 2005. "Impalpable Hits: Indeterminacy in the Searching of Tagged Shakespearian Texts." A conference paper delivered on 17 March at the 33rd annual meeting of the Shakespeare Association of America in Bermuda, 17–19 March. http://gabrielegan.com/publications/Egan2005a.htm.

Erasmus, Desiderius. 1964. *The "Adages" of Erasmus. A Study with Translations.* Trans. Margaret Mann. Cambridge: Cambridge University Press.

ETCL. 2008. Postdoctoral Fellowship in Early Modern Textual Studies and Digital Humanities (2009–11) at the Electronic Textual Cultures Laboratory (ETCL) at the University of Victoria. *Humanist.* September 11.

Frye, Northrop. 1989. Literary and Mechanical Models. In *Research in Humanities Computing,* ed. Ian Lancashire (Selected Papers from the 1989 Association for Computers and the Humanities-Association for Literary and Linguistic Computing (ACH-ALLC) Conference): 3–12. Vol. 1. Oxford: Clarendon Press.

Garrett, Jesse James. Adaptive Path: Ajax, A New Approach to Web Applications. http://www.adaptivepath.com/ideas/essays/archives/000385.php.

Greetham, D. C. 1994. *Textual Scholarship: An Introduction.* New York: Garland.

_____ 2007. Review of *Electronic Textual Editing,* ed. Lou Burnard, Katherine O'Brien O'Keeffe, and John Unsworth. *Textual Cultures* 2, no. 2: 133–36.

Haigh, Thomas. 2008. Protocols for Profit: Web and E-mail Technologies as Product and Infrastructure. In *The Internet and American Business,* ed. William Aspray and Paul Ceruzzi, 105–58. Cambridge, MA: Massachusetts Institute of Technology Press.

Hockey, Susan. 1986. Workshop on Teaching Computers and the Humanities Courses. *Literary and Linguistic Computing* 1, no. 4: 228–29.

Jardine, Lisa. 1993. *Erasmus, Man of Letters: The Construction of Charisma in Print.* Princeton, NJ: Princeton University Press.

Kenny, Anthony. 1992. *Computers and the Humanities.* London: British Library.

Kirschenbaum, Matthew G. 2004. "So the Colors Cover the Wires": Interface, Aesthetics, and Usability. In *A Companion to Digital Humanities,* ed. Susan Schreibman, Ray Siemens, and John Unsworth, 523–42. Blackwell Companions to Literature and Culture. Oxford: Blackwell.

_____ 2009. Hello Worlds: Why Humanities Students Should Learn to Program. *Chronicle of Higher Education* 55, no. 20 (January 23): B10–B12.

Liu, Alan. 2004. *The Laws of Cool: Knowledge Work and the Culture of Information.* Chicago: University of Chicago Press.

McCarty, Willard. 2004. Modeling: A Study in Words and Meanings. In *A Companion to Digital Humanities*, ed. Susan Schreibman, Ray Siemens, and John Unsworth, 254–70. Blackwell Companions to Literature and Culture. Oxford: Blackwell.

McGann, Jerome J. 2004. Marking Texts of Many Dimensions. In *A Companion to Digital Humanities*, ed. Susan Schriebmann, Ray Siemens, and John Unsworth, 198–217. Blackwell Companions to Literature and Culture. Oxford: Blackwell.

_____ 2005. Information Technology and the Troubled Humanities. *TEXT Technology* 14, no. 2: 105–21.

McKitterick, David. Oxford Dictionary of National Biography article: McKenzie, Donald Francis (1931–99). http://www.oxforddnb.com/view/article/72097.

Moxon, Joseph. 1683. *Mechanick Exercises, or, The Doctrine of Handy Works.* Vol. 2. London: Joseph Moxon.

Nowviskie, Bethany. 2000. 'Interfacing the Rossetti Archive'. Conference paper presented at the October 2000 conference of the Humanities and Technology Association. http://www2.iath.virginia.edu/bpn2f/1866/dgrinterface.html.

Parkes, M. B. 1992. *Pause and Effect: An Introduction to the History of Punctuation in the West.* Aldershot: Scolar.

Prest, Wilfrid. 1987. Introduction: The Professions and Society in Early Modern England. In *The Professions in Early Modern England*, ed. Wilfrid Prest, 1-24. New York: Croom Helm.

Readings, Bill. 1996. *The University in Ruins.* Cambridge MA: Harvard University Press.

Rockwell, Geoffrey. 2003. Graduate Education in Humanities Computing. *Computers and the Humanities* 37, no. 3: 243–44.

Sawday, Jonathan. 2007. *Engines of the Imagination: Renaissance Culture and the Rise of the Machine.* London: Routledge.

Shillingsburg, Peter L. 1996. *Scholarly Editing in the Computer Age.* 3rd ed. Ann Arbor: University of Michigan Press.

_____ 2006. *From Gutenberg to Google.* Cambridge: Cambridge University Press.

Turkel, William J, and Alan MacEachern. 2007. *The Programming Historian.* NiCHE: Network in Canadian History and Environment.

Wilson, F P. 1970. *Shakespeare and the New Bibliography.* Ed. Helen Gardner. Oxford: Clarendon Press.

Wittern, Christian. 2007. Character Encoding. In *A Companion to Digital Literary Studies*, ed. Susan Schreibman and Ray Siemens, 564-576. Malden MA: Blackwell.

Žižek, Slavoj. 2008. *In Defense of Lost Causes.* London: Verso.

A HISTORICAL INTERMEZZO:
IS TEI THE RIGHT WAY?

SGML, Interpretation, and the Two Muses

Ian Lancashire

University of Toronto
ian.lancashire@utoronto.ca

Standard Generalized Markup Language (SGML) is an International Standards Organization (ISO) standard syntax for designing encoding languages
such as HyperText Markup Language (HTML) and the languages promoted
by the Text Encoding Initiative (TEI). By enabling people to write many such
encoding languages, SGML is to (artificial) encoding languages what Noam
Chomsky's hypothetical universal grammar is to human natural languages
like English and Chinese. Both SGML and universal grammar are generative:
they enable language-making but are not languages themselves. The analogy,
of course, falters if pressed too far. Arguably, universal grammar is based in
the human genome, which reduces people to gene-survival bodies, but SGML
and TEI are human-built and may or may not have anything to do with our
survival. As well, although natural language could only have followed from
language-enabling genes, other encoding languages like COCOA (a scheme
first devised for use with the software called WordCOunt and COncordance
on the Atlas Computer in the 1960s) predate SGML tagsets and do not obey its
rules. Also unlike universal grammar, which establishes parameters for the
making of natural languages without specifying any content for them, SGML
has a little implied linguistic content—the entities that ISO has devised for
characters in world languages—although it is "designed to mimic the regular
expression notation of automata theory" and to supply a "formal analytical
world of coherent constructs" (Sperberg-McQueen and Burnard 1994, 556–
57), not a real world. It would be more of a mistake to say that SGML is itself
an artificial language than that it is a universal grammar for making one.

If SGML can be used to generate encoding languages, comparably to how
universal grammar generates natural languages, then arguably no one
SGML-conformant markup scheme is innately better than any other. SGML
encoding systems serve different communities, as human languages do. Just
as one culture ought not impose its natural language on another, so the
SGML tagset of one community should not be imposed on the SGML tagsets
of other cultures or communities. For example, HTML, an SGML-conformant
encoding language, dominates world text encoding as the natural language

ISBN 978–0–86698–021–0 (online)   ISBN 978–0–86698–449–2 (print)
New Technologies in Medieval and Renaissance Studies 2 (2010) 105–119

of English does international science and business. HTML serves an international culture by supplying codes for online typesetting on the World Wide Web. The TEI encoding guidelines in whatever flavour, however extended for what specific purpose, serve the different cultural purposes of a smaller community within the knowledge industries. Anyone reading the latest TEI guidelines, known as P3, will immediately see that HTML neither meets all the encoding needs TEI aims to supply nor is rendered obsolete by it. TEI guidelines

> particularly do not address the encoding of physical description of textual witnesses: the materials of the carrier, the medium of the inscribing implement, the layout of the inscription upon the material, the organisation of the carrier materials themselves (as quiring, collation, etc.), authorial instructions or scribal markup, etc. (Sperberg-McQueen and Burnard 1994, 557)

In contrast, HTML gives us designer tags for layout. Chauvinist attacks on one SGML tagset by advocates of another can be settled, either by measuring the relative success of each one in meeting the needs of a common culture, or by showing that the two encoding languages serve different autonomous cultures equally well.

When TEI P3 came out in 1994 with an SGML Document Type Definition (DTD), it specified a sizable tagset. TEI began in the humanities and the first principle that representatives of professional societies, universities, and text archives agreed at a preliminary meeting at Vassar College on November 12–13, 1987, was the creation of a standard format for data interchange (not creation) in humanities research (Ide and Sperberg-McQueen 1987). But P3 opens by stating that it is "addressed to anyone who works with any text in any form" (Sperberg-McQueen and Burnard 1994, 1). It occurred to ISO committees that others would want to create standard tagsets because SGML does not "codify the semantics of processing" and because "the idea of common semantics has some appeal" (Sperberg-McQueen and Burnard 1994, 129). The name for such a common rule-set for text processing is "a document architecture." TEI claims its goal is to specify a general-purpose document architecture, not just for the humanities and for text-based scholarship, but for anyone. This is an astonishing claim, for within it seems to be the assumption that SGML was devised only for TEI, or for the maker of any universal document architecture. It would be as absurd to say that HTML has exhausted the possibilities of SGML. Although TEI P3 may provide a method for encoding many more textual encoding problems than HTML recognizes, there is little likelihood that P3 or its successors will be a standard encoding DTD, even one that permits extensions to many other approaches to text. If a group as small as the humanities consists of so many small academic cultures with different specific purposes, consider the complexities awaiting SGML in users all over the world.

There is one reason to be sceptical about the possibility of a uniform SGML document architecture. All SGML tagsets reflect the specific purposes of their creators, according to the prime maker of the syntax. Charles F. Goldfarb says that SGML "mandates how one declares a set of elements, attributes and entities for a *specific purpose* and then uses these declared constructs to mark up content" (Goldfarb 1990, x, my italics). Any purposeful action—here giving names to words and passages to texts, and to their relationships—is taken by a living being whose purpose is underscored by an understanding of a situation. In this context, that understanding includes both an interpretation of text and a theory of text within which interpretation makes sense. Goldfarb's description of anticipated applications for SGML implies that ISO was moved to design SGML at first for the use of professionals who needed online, (then) technical-writing tools for the exchange and storage of electronic documents. SGML thus enables authors, editors, offices, and publishers to devise tagsets for their own electronic texts. It seems that the ISO did not undertake SGML in the belief that any one tagset produced with it would be suitable for all purposes or all texts of a given type.

If the ISO had believed so, it might have produced at least one tagset itself, but implicit within SGML is the assumption that a tagset reflects one author's or one culture's specific purposes. The perspective of the encoder determines the semantics of the encoding language. Nowhere do Goldfarb or the ISO indicate that they did not specify a markup scheme from a lack of knowledge of textual objects and structures. Instead, they said that they were "allowing the intuitive understanding apparatus of the native speaker to infiltrate strategically SGML's formal analytical world of coherent constructs" (Sperberg-McQueen and Burnard 1994, 556–57). For any text there are at least two important perspectives: the author's and the reader's. When TEI P3 claims that it is "addressed to anyone who works with any text in any form," it expresses a purpose of universal applicability that is fundamentally at odds with what we know about the differing capabilities of author and reader in representing text structures. TEI also is not acting in the spirit of SGML standard.

Encoding a text with a markup language requires three kinds of interpretation by the encoder: (1) judging that a tag can be truthfully applied to a word or passage; (2) assenting to the encoding terminology as both meaningful and properly describing text; and (3) believing that the syntax of the encoding language (the ways in which tags are characterized in terms of one another) allows for the description of relationships among tagged words or passages in text. The first kind of judgment can be exercised freely within SGML and TEI P3. Encoding is the intellectual responsibility of the encoder in this respect. Different persons will encode differently, given the same tools; and the spectrum of variation from one interpreter to another will probably be wide. TEI P3 alludes to this level of interpretation in encoding "as any means of making explicit an interpretation of a text" and "of making explicit what is conjectural or implicit, a process of directing the user as to how the content of the text should be interpreted" (Sperberg-McQueen and Burnard 1994, 13).

Any author can interpret and so authoritatively encode his or her own text. Yet if an electronic text is SGML-encoded by someone other than its author, then the question arises: does the interpretation of text by the encoder match the author's interpretation? If that cannot be recovered, or if it is judged irrelevant, then does it match a generic reading or interpretation, or lacking that, one reader's perspective at one time? Because so much research encoding in the humanities today is done by editors of the texts of dead authors, the TEI guidelines mainly concern the tagging of texts by someone other than their author. In non-electronic contexts (such as critical editions), readers will recognize the impact that the editor's interpretation has on the editing of the text, but electronic texts in online libraries are published with the SGML tags largely hidden. The humanities are very sensitive to how editorial accretions distort texts. Even within small areas, individuals are notoriously sceptical and resist harmonization, unlike colleagues in the sciences, who tend to accept not only the same empirical method and test for new knowledge but also to operate within a common set of assumptions or beliefs, which Thomas S. Kuhn calls a paradigm. Because retrieval gains its power from, and is constrained by, the tags available in the source, then if those tags are applied in an eccentric way and import anachronistic, impressionistic, or unpopular "intuitions" about it, a scientifically rigorous implementation of elements will not ensure effective retrieval in a worldwide network.

My concern here is with the second and third types of judgment. They are predetermined by the encoding standard syntax (SGML) and by the semantics that TEI provides for that syntax. Most text encoders are not computer scientists and cannot be expected to have the necessary technical skills to modify the TEI DTD by changing the names of elements or by respecifying their relationships. Occasionally TEI P3 recognizes that it expresses only one of many possible ways of representing texts. For example, the editors state that "There is no single DTD which encompasses any kind of absolute truth about a text" (Sperberg-McQueen and Burnard 1994, 19) and that the element "<seg>" can extend "the semantics of the TEI markup scheme in a theory-neutral manner" (Sperberg-McQueen and Burnard 1994, 424). The second remark implies that TEI P3 is not theory-neutral.

The specific theoretical perspective that helped shaped P3 are given in Sperberg-McQueen's article that provides nine axioms, the first of which states: "A markup language reflects a theory of texts in general" (Sperberg-McQueen 1991, 35). This axiom does not say that *marking up a text* reflects a theory of texts: that is, Sperberg-McQueen is not referring to the kind of interpretation an encoder makes in applying tags to specific places in one text. He means the theoretical assumptions in the second and third types of interpretation. If read with the first sentence on page 1 of P3, that it is "addressed to anyone who works with any text in any form" (Sperberg-McQueen and Burnard 1994, 1), TEI says to electronic-text encoders: "Give up your own theories of text and accept ours, because with ours you can describe rigorously anything that can characterize any text." It may be doubted whether any extension or modification of the TEI Document Type Definition will be enough to adjust it to a different theory of text. Finally, no text encoder can reach into SGML itself and alter its syntax.

The second level of interpretation can be seen in the sample tags common to Goldfarb's manual on SGML and TEI P3. This judgment identifies and names textual objects, attributes characteristics to them, classifies them and their attributes, and specifies their relationships. Both Goldfarb and TEI use the element names "<front>," "<body>," and "<back>" to label the three broadest textual divisions, as if texts were people or animals. These names are metaphoric when applied to text. They implicitly compare a text to a creature viewed from the front, from inside, and from the back. The terms "<front>" and "<back>" suggest outward appearances—a perspective adopted by someone standing outside the text—because "<body>" can only name the entire thing. In other words, we encounter the text only after we pass the "<front>" tag, and we leave it as soon as we pass the "<back>" tag. This seemingly innocuous naming convention conceals an error in interpretation. In it, the start and the end of a text—typically the title page and the index—are described as surfaces rather than substance. Whether true or not in this century is doubtful, but the TEI intuition does have a basis in the practice of publishers who normally supply the title page and end matter for a book. In Middle English, however, the front is the opening line of the text, is part of the body.

In early modern English, the title page often summarizes the content of the book and gives advice on how to use it, information typical of the author: again, the front belongs to the body. For Shakespeare's period, the tags "<opening>," "<middle>," and "<closing>" might make more sense than the TEI structured elements, although these names also conceal a debatable metaphor: two doors, windows, flaps, gates, or other boundary entrance and exit. One of Gary Larson's amusing *The Far Side* cartoons shows a featureless desert and a couple in a car passing a sign telling them that they are entering "the Middle." The joke depends on our appreciating the absence of any recognizable boundary between the middle and what surrounds it. Texts are rather like this. An epic that starts narratively in medias res, in the middle, as Milton's *Paradise Lost* does, is nonconformant if we mean by divisions the action narrated by the poem. Encountering Barnardo's words, "Who's there?" in *Hamlet* 1.1.1, is the reader entering the body or the middle, well before knowing anything about the prince or his dilemma? Might Shakespeare and his audience not consider act one scene one to be the front or the opening? The lesson here is that any element-names for the three broadest divisions in a text may be out-of-place and misleading, depending on which text we are encoding.

Any code that gives an intelligible name to content—a name drawn from a natural language and there endowed with meaning—carries baggage with it. Let me give two other examples, chosen at random from TEI P3. The element class name *agent* "defines a group of elements which contain names of individuals or corporate bodies" (Sperberg-McQueen and Burnard 1994, 767), yet the word *agent* normally does more than indicate one or more persons: the term ascribes action to a person, a body, or (yes) a substance. If *agent* means some human entity, then how is it different from the TEI element class name *name*, defined as "elements with proper nouns as content" (Sperberg-McQueen and Burnard 1994, 799)? Or, the element class name *interpret* "defines attributes common to all interpretative elements": yet if encoding is "any means of making explicit an interpretation of text" (Sperberg-McQueen and Burnard 1994, 793, 13), then all elements are interpretative and the grounds for an *interpret* tag are unclear.

A class name having the support of a large committee does not make it less of an interpretation. It will be objected that the sciences invest heavily in naming conventions so as to make interpretation precise and reliable, and that TEI rescues the world of text encoding from ambiguity, obfuscation, and unnecessary misunderstanding by giving encoders a common terminology with which to register their disagreements. Scientific names, however, denote discrete phenomena identified. The facts that we observe in texts—characters and spaces—are of little general interest because they belong to a technology of language storage, not to language itself. Neither the sciences nor the humanities have embraced a lexicon for textual elements of content because neither accepts one theory on what text is. Textual features cannot be observed in the same way that stars, geological structures, ants, fundamental particles, and neurons can. TEI need not have used anthropomorphized names for its main textual division tags. Strings selected at random from noise would have done, but if those string-names rigorously denoted unambiguous phenomena in texts the likelihood is that they would not serve their purpose.

Any SGML tagset claiming to provide a lexicon of tags for textual content belongs with literary and linguistic theory and will have to defend its interpretation in that academic context. This is what Northrop Frye had in mind at the first ACH/ALLC conference in 1989 when he said:

> Critical schools, like philosophical ones, are better thought of as programming models. The importance of the computer is in bringing them down to manageable scope, so that their essential assumptions can be worked through in a reasonable time before they modulate into or merge with something else. (Frye 1989, 7)

TEI P3 has not defended its theoretical coding of texts against alternate text grammars devised by other theorists, although because non-computational literary theories do not stay still, as Frye says, the task of making rivals is not easy. The use of SGML, then, requires interpretation. Although it does not recommend any tagset, there is still no circumstance in which SGML content-based encoding can be done without interpretation. Tag names, whether for elements or for their attributes, are not devised to be meaningless. They encode a theory on what texts are like. Charles Henry, who closed the humanist debate, made this clear: "To appropriate Barbara Herrnstein Smith's term, an encoding system always has the tendency to privilege an epistemological bias" (Henry 1996).

The adoption of SGML by ISO made available to TEI a paradigm within which a self-consistent terminology could be applied to all fields of textual computing and in which puzzles could be solved and new applications developed. Thus it is not the deficiencies of TEI themselves—including the inability to encode brevigraphs, ligatures, and the order of composition in early books typeset by formes—that causes most alarm, but the limitation of SGML as an epistemological paradigm. That SGML tags require interpretation need be no serious problem for its practitioners. On the contrary, researchers in the humanities defend competing theories all the time and would no doubt find a theory-based encoding method useful in realizing electronically representative texts according to the tenets of their theories. Yet the perplexing trouble with SGML, in my opinion, is that its syntax imposes limits to a researcher's interpretation of texts. SGML has assumptions that fit it better for artificial (symbolic, logical) languages than for natural languages.

SGML is based on a positivist epistemology. Tag elements and structures are routinely expressed as delimited, well-formed, knowable objects in unambiguous relationships. Axioms 4-5 in Sperberg-McQueen's theoretical essay, "Texts are linguistic objects" and "Texts occur in/are realized by physical objects" (Sperberg-McQueen 1991, 37, 40), are consistent with the assumptions of the makers of SGML. Both axioms and SGML itself—as a method of describing text—fly in the face of a scepticism found, for instance, in the literary theory of Roman Ingarden and Wolfgang Iser, who accept generally the phenomenological philosophy of Edmund Husserl, Martin Heidegger, and others. All deny that objects can be understood independently of the subjects who apprehend them (Makaryk 1993, 139–44, 562–63, 633–36). If one accepts the premise, then the positivist theory in SGML may work, although perhaps only because it is a tautology. It is the indeterminacy of "textual objects"—the things we perceive in texts—that frustrates attempts to describe them in a regular expression automaton.

SGML elements, in my opinion, are opportunities only for tagging what is known, determinate, non-fuzzy objects and relations, not for handling objects that are indeterminate because their attributes as attributes are in doubt. As well, any SGML element gives a name and attributes to a delimited section of text. Everything to be tagged must be delimited or segmented. Anything we cannot clearly delimit cannot be named. Yet clusters of textual objects, types of fuzzy sets, have indeterminate numbers of members, cover spans that can vary widely from one place in a text to another, and frequently may overlap (depending on how they are defined). Associative clusters of images, for example, are a frequent characteristic of literary writing. We can impose linkages among them, of course, and set arbitrary limits to the size of any cluster, but such measures respond more to the mind of a researcher desperate to set order to a flux than to the reality of text as a product of the human mind, either as author or as reader.

Multiple overlapping structures reveal the tip of the problem. SGML limits us to encoding two non-overlapping structures in one text file, and to recognizing only one structure at a time. Goldfarb recommended that such multiple structures in poetry be managed, not by the Concur function in SGML, but by hypertext links (Goldfarb 1990, 304), yet these non-linear, non-hierarchical relationships are not very clearly explained in his book. The prevailing structural relation among textual objects, tagged as SGML elements, is hierarchical or non-hierarchical. This leads Goldfarb to say that "the document is simply the element that is at the top of the hierarchy for a given processing run" (Goldfarb 1990, 11n5). To some degree, associative relations—such as govern the networklike organization of concepts—prove to be within the capabilities of SGML when TEI developed linking elements such as "<ptr>" (pointer), "<link>," and "<linkGrp>" to represent associations between one place in a text and another, and common linkages among a group, that is, what TEI calls a web (Sperberg-McQueen and Burnard 1994, Chapter 14). Yet it remains unclear how a flat, lattice-like structure, one characterized by fuzzy boundaries and spreading activation, can be adequately represented in SGML. Establishing firm links among parts of a text, as the anchor tag does in HTML, sets in place as rigorous and unambiguous a structure as any hierarchy. Imprecisions and uncertainties, where they exist, are expressed in TEI with weights and percentages as clear, quantifiable attributes of the elements to which they apply.

Yet anyone encoding texts today faces two muses. One is the disorganized, hard-to-predict, invisible, and messy thought and language process from which utterances come. What this muse professes, the second muse selects from, edits, and formats. Colin Martindale's phrase "the clockwork muse" well names the second muse, who like a strict housekeeper lives to curb and channel the inventions that the first muse gives its unruly child or occupant (Martindale 1990). The first muse is the author. The second muse is the reader-editor or publisher for whom texts represent a landscape to be tamed, described, and mapped for use. Texts can be certainly interpreted sensibly as having grammatical and syntactic units, as being delimited by punctuation and paragraphing, and as being modelled on discourse modes that have readily named and delimited elements with attributes. Like an intellectual nanny, HTML encourages writers to use headings, paragraphs, lists, tables, and other explicit markers of text division and to make distinctions in encoding text elements to avoid confusing tags, such as italics. HTML recognizes the associative nature of thinking, how the first muse operates, and determinedly tames it with the anchor tag. Hypertextual links in HTML and TEI are unambiguous. They have a source and target that the writer must predetermine and explicitly encode. Networks of anchor tags thus become convenient ways of structuring tables of contents, notes, and cross-references. SGML privileges the second muse because its epistemology cannot cope with the first muse, which is responsible for many distinctively human characteristics of text.

Can people think linguistically and speak in nested structures, hierarchically, as Ian Watson's science-fiction novel *The Embedding* suggests (Watson 1973)? Does natural language operate like well-structured computer code, without GOTO and other ill-formed statements? Under some circumstances the answer is a qualified yes. After all, what can authors and readers not decide to do if they declare it to be so? For research purposes, however, an encoding language should be devised that can mirror the structures by which the human mind (the subject in phenomenological criticism) generates the encoded texts, for these structures—imposed by the first muse—may never be recognized by the second muse for explicit identification. The first muse's structures are fuzzy networks, embodying many-to-many relationships in ill-defined segments: these account for the association of concepts and experiences in the text, not as found in sequences of words (sentences) but in the conceptual hypertexts that give purpose to the text's creation in the first place.

There are differences between the assumptions about text structures inherent in SGML and those found in the brain's processing of natural language. Let me cite two. First, SGML defines an element as having or not having fixed attributes. The human brain stores the attributes or features differently, in a distributed way. Elements, the entities that we experience and discuss, are stored as more or less strongly associated networks of the features by which we know them. Feature networks are the primary nodes in the mind's structure. Elements are actualized implicit networks of those features and require effort by long-term memory to set up initially. (That is, something we remember is not stored separately in memory as a node with attributes, but literally as a web connecting attributes or features.) These may well continue to exist in memory after memory of the thing has gone, because the loss of the network does not affect the attribute nodes. Such networks—such memories of a thing—change from one person to another, and within the same person from one day to the next, because they reflect the individual's experiences and the dynamics of the individual's mind. TEI P3 develops a structure that "identifies and groups together individual features, each of which associates a name with one or more values," and includes in this structure two elements for alternating (ambiguous and uncertain) features and feature values (Sperberg-McQueen and Burnard 1994, 475, 498–99).

The methods recommended by TEI to represent knowledge about these feature structures look to be flexible enough to encode an artificially created model, one assembled by a researcher who fully understands and sets the relations of features and their values. However, the feature structure in the human mind, whether author or reader—such as the long-term memory of something—is dynamic and changes from one minute to another according to the impact of sensory experiences and thinking. The boundaries, features, and feature values of a "feature structure" (that is, a network) are as indeterminate in texts as they are in the mind because texts are created and experienced in time. Second, SGML recognizes two-dimensional verbal structures (that is what a hierarchy is), but the brain encodes knowledge in networks that have at least four dimensions, because time is a factor, just like length, width, and depth. A text is written by an author, and read by a reader, over a period of time. The feature structures of a text change during that period. This dynamic makes for an instability and a systemic ambiguity that cannot be known in advance for the purpose of editorial encoding.

The more we edit it in artificial memory (on paper, in computer memory), the more we purge text of fuzziness and endow it with the traits of an artificial language, one suitable for conveying information. SGML is one of the devices our second muse developed to make us behave in company. To the degree that the humanities publishes research, it must publish it clearly; and so SGML-based encoding makes sense as a communication tool. However, many fields of research in the humanities aim to understand the workings of the first muse, either in the writings of well-known authors or in the general populace. One research method with a long tradition—going back to Biblical exegesis—adds tags (or glosses) to a text and then retrieves them in specialized lists (or concordances). These tags sometimes highlight non-literal entities in a text, ones perceived by prior analysis and then refined during the retrieval or indexing process. Lacking an author (muse or God) who will explain what he meant so that it can be tagged, early researchers of the meaning of sacred texts developed ways of making the text itself reveal this content. Exegetes recognized four modes of meaning: eschatological, moral, anagogical, and literal. They attributed the non-literal modes to the mind of

God, who they believed authored the text, and in tracing the activation of all modes they were acting, in their own minds, in the image of their mysterious God. The first muse resembles such a God as they imaged within themselves.

I have for some while imagined that computer analysis can elicit the traces of an author's memory in the text. The process of having a program elicit tags from the text itself may be called dynamic or virtual encoding. The tagset is suggested by the text itself, not by the researcher. For example, software like Oxford Concordance Program, Wordcruncher, and TACT can easily produce a keyword-in-context concordance of a text in which contexts, often with citations such as book, stanza, and line, are listed under keywords in alphabetical order. This output can be read as tagging each context with a keyword. If the context is ten words wide, then each word in it will be "tagged" by itself and nine other words. Here, of course, the keywords take the same form as they possess in the context. The encoding does not lead to especially surprising results. If the keywords are lemmatized, or if they represent a combination of two keywords (both of which must be present in the context), however, the tag becomes non-trivial. Such concording automatically identifies certain kinds of non-linear groups in a text. These groups include repeating collocational clusters, which change in frequency through an author's career, and over the course of a long work, and in that way can be described as multidimensional networks. They sometimes look as if they could be related to long-term memory. By postponing the definition of a tagset to indexing and information-retrieval processes, software gives users freedom to explore the text and the relationships among its parts.

TACT uses extended-COCOA (which takes its name from the tag format of the predecessor of Oxford Concordance Program), Wordcruncher, and start-of-line encoding methods popular with researchers for the past thirty years. The TACT ".MKS" or markup file used by the indexing program Makebase does not ask the user to specify relationships among tags. This omission does not mean that the user cannot establish such relationships later. In fact the definition process is deliberately postponed until the retrieval and the analysis. Decisions about what is and is not a relationship among tags are made by the user in making inquiries to programs like Usebase and Collgen, not by the editor in creating the text. This method is conventional in the humanities. The editor of a work seldom, through the editing and its apparatus, imposes one interpretation on the text, her own or his own. Scholarly editions—printed as well as electronic—do not bind a text to a single interpretation. For this reason, the heavy interpretative tagging fostered by some SGML tagsets impedes critical inquiry on texts. Usebase enables users, interactively, to declare a working hierarchy in three ways, by formulating queries, by devising templates for reference citations, and making distribution graphs. Because TACT moves interpretative tagging from the edited text to the database, that is, because the system uses virtual tagging, this method maintains the same distinction between an edited text and the process of interpretation of it as is traditional in humanities scholarship.

A dynamic encoder enables users to experiment with tags without changing the source text. Multiple encodings are easily managed by revising the ".MKS" file in TACT or the control file in another program. An ".MKS" file or an Oxford Concordance Program command file in this respect functions like an SGML Document Type Definition, but they do more than a DTD aspires to. Command files required by concordancers define the alphabet, collating sequence, diacritics, comment delimiters, and word separators, as well as the tags and their delimiters. Users can interpret the writing system of the text as suits them. For example, someone interested in the sequencing of text segments could replace letters with punctuation marks in the Makebase alphabet or just identify letters as diacritics. If a text comes heavily encoded with grammatical or metrical tags delimited by angle brackets, a researcher could delete reference to COCOA delimiters and instead make reverse angle-bracket pairs ">" and "<" into displayable comment delimiters so that source text became ignorable comments and tags became the sole text. This simple switch allows the researcher to retrieve and analyze the information-rich encoding while still seeing, in the context retrieved from searches, the text to which it applied.

One goal of the SGML community is to do away with conflicting encoding schemes, especially ones that rely on individual pieces of software. By making SGML its standard for both communication and textual research, however, researchers can overlook the limitations of its syntax for specific purposes and thus of all generic SGML-based software. SGML is a valuable product serving the needs of industry, governments, and now education for rapid electronic communication. One advantage of conformance to the SGML standard in publishing research is homogenous worldwide retrieval not just on one text but on a universe of documents. The HTML tagset already serves part of this need. If all texts are encoded in HTML, one search request—transmitted from any computer—and one browser can operate on many millions of documents. Presumably the TEI DTD can function in a similar way if the world academic communities agree to use its tagset, which even now meets many needs of their intellectual culture. Other needs, however, remain unmet. The inability of TEI (and SGML itself) to describe texts in ways discussed by non-positivist theories of knowledge is a greater problem than most, because it affects the paradigm that TEI has accepted. TEI should reengineer SGML to overcome the limitations in it. Application software is also needed that will make SGML encoding both easier for scholars to manage as well as more faithful to the intellectual structures artificially stored in texts. It is a waste of human resources to devise a tool that enslaves the user. Computers should make electronic texts human-readable; people should not have to rewrite their texts to make them machine-readable. Textual structures should not be defined in terms of SGML because those texts are impoverished in the process. Writers and readers are more gifted than automata.

August 2, 1997

Note

A version of this paper was given first in a session on text encoding and textual theory in December 1996 at the Modern Language Association 112th Convention in Washington, D.C. That paper in turn grew out of my controversial remark, "SGML by its very nature imposes interpretations" (Lancashire 1995). My thanks to the editor, both blind peer-review readers, and Murray McGillivray for their interest in this twelve-year-old summary of a decade's participation in TEI. I further develop some ideas in this essay in a forthcoming book.

WORKS CITED

Frye, Northrop. 1989. Literary and Mechanical Models. In *Research in Humanities Computing*, ed. Ian Lancashire (Selected Papers from the 1989 Association for Computers and the Humanities-Association for Literary and Linguistic Computing (ACH-ALLC) Conference):3–12. Vol. 1. Oxford: Clarendon Press.

Goldfarb, Charles F. 1990. *The SGML Handbook*. Ed. Yuri Rubinsky. Oxford: Clarendon Press.

Henry, Charles ("Chuck"). 1996. Re: 9.430 Inappropriateness. *Humanist*. January 5. http://www.digitalhumanities.org/humanist/Archives/Virginia/v09/0407.html.

Ide, Nancy, and C. M. Sperberg-McQueen. 1987. The Preparation of Text Encoding Guidelines. Poughkeepsie, NY, November 13.

Lancashire, Ian. 1995. Re: 9.327 encoding accented characters. *Humanist.* November 29. http://www.digitalhumanities.org/humanist/Archives/ Virginia/v09/0307.html.

_____ Forthcoming. *Forgetful Muses: Reading the Author in the Text.* Toronto: University of Toronto Press.

Makaryk, Irena Rima, ed. 1993. *Encyclopedia of Contemporary Literary Theory: Approaches, Scholars, Terms.* Toronto: University of Toronto Press.

Martindale, Colin. 1990. *The Clockwork Muse: The Predictability of Artistic Change.* New York: Basic Books.

Sperberg-McQueen, C. M. 1991. Text in the Electronic Age: Textual Study and Text Encoding, with Examples from Medieval Texts. *Literary and Linguistic Computing* 6, no. 1: 34–46.

Sperberg-McQueen, C. M., and Lou Burnard, eds. 1994. *Guidelines for Electronic Text Encoding and Interchange, P3.* Chicago: Text Encoding Initiative.

Watson, Ian. 1973. *The Embedding.* London: Gollancz.

Ian Lancashire's Two Muses: A Belated Reply

Murray McGillivray

University of Calgary

mmcgilli@ucalgary.ca

Ian Lancashire's essay "SGML, Interpretation, and the Two Muses" contains much that seems fixed in its own time, now distant from us because of the rapid progress of technologies. It speaks from an apparently ancient environment for humanities computing (now more often digital humanities) in which now-extinct technologies (or nearly extinct, or thoroughly transformed through generations of evolution) such as COCOA tagging (Hockey 2000, 27–30), WordCruncher, the Oxford Concordance Program, TACT, and TEI P3 ruled the primeval forest. The article is framed as an assault on P3, which was at the time the recent high-profile introduction of a then richly funded international group, the Text Encoding Initiative (TEI), a group that had been attempting to solve a problem that itself appears even more remote and ancient now, namely how to conduct textual computing in a way that would be independent of operating systems and software so as to facilitate moving texts from system to system and avoid loss of work and data both when systems and software became obsolete and when transferring files from one system to another. It is now more than hard, in our age of ubiquitous computing, seamless file transfer, multilingual capabilities, and Google, to believe that such a problem ever existed, even though it was a real one and considered particularly thorny at the time the TEI began.

I have taken up Gabriel Egan's challenge and written in belated reply to Ian Lancashire's article not because the specific challenge to TEI P3 needs an answer. The question is simply moot, since no one nowadays uses P3, or considers COCOA tags or TACT concordancing a viable alternative—or perhaps knows about them, except us old-timers— although TACT lives on in the Text Analysis Portal for Research (TAPoR) initiative and COCOA in R. J. C. Watt's Concordance software. Rather, Lancashire's paper seems to me to raise issues and take positions that transcend their practical (their contemporary software and encoding standard) setting and that merit discussion even many years later.

ISBN 978–0–86698–021–0 (online)   ISBN 978–0–86698–449–2 (print)
New Technologies in Medieval and Renaissance Studies 2 (2010) 121–136

To list them as they arise in the paper, these issues and positions are as follows:

1) "Encoding a text with a markup language requires three kinds of interpretation by the encoder: (1) judging that a tag can be truthfully applied to a word or passage; (2) assenting to the encoding terminology as both meaningful and properly describing text; and (3) believing that the syntax of the encoding language (the ways in which tags are characterized in terms of one another) allows for the description of relationships among tagged words or passages in text."

2) "Any code that gives an intelligible name to content—a name drawn from a natural language and there endowed with meaning—carries baggage with it."

3) "The facts that we observe in texts—characters and spaces—are of little general interest because they belong to a technology of language storage, not to language itself."

4) "SGML is based on a positivist epistemology. Tag elements and structures are routinely expressed as delimited, well-formed, knowable objects in unambiguous relationships.

5) "Everything to be tagged must be delimited or segmented. Anything we cannot clearly delimit cannot be named. Yet clusters of textual objects, types of fuzzy sets, have indeterminate numbers of members, cover spans that can vary widely from one place in a text to another, and frequently may overlap (depending on how they are defined). Associative clusters of images, for example, are a frequent characteristic of literary writing."

6) "Multiple overlapping structures reveal the tip of the problem. SGML limits us to encoding two non-overlapping structures in one text file, and to recognizing only one structure at a time. [Charles] Goldfarb recommended that such multiple structures in poetry be managed ... by hypertext links ... Yet it remains unclear how a flat, lattice-like structure, one characterized by fuzzy boundaries and spreading activation, can be adequately represented in SGML. Establishing firm links among parts of a text, as the anchor tag does in HTML, sets in place as rigorous and unambiguous a structure as any hierarchy."

7) "[A]nyone encoding texts today faces two muses. One is the disorganized, hard-to-predict, invisible, and messy thought and language process from which utterances come. What this muse professes, the second muse selects from, edits, and formats. Colin Martindale's phrase 'the mechanical muse' well names the second muse, who like a strict housekeeper lives to curb and channel the inventions that the first muse gives its unruly child or occupant. The first muse is the author. The second muse is the reader-editor or publisher for whom texts represent a landscape to be tamed, described, and mapped for use."

8) "For research purposes, ... an encoding language should be devised that can mirror the structures by which the human mind (the subject in phenomenological criticism) generates the encoded texts, for these structures—imposed by the first muse—may never be recognized by the second muse for explicit identification."

9) "The process of having a program elicit tags from the text itself may be called dynamic or virtual encoding. The tagset is suggested by the text itself, not by the researcher... . By postponing the definition of a tagset to indexing and information-retrieval processes, software gives users freedom to explore the text and the relationships among its parts."

The broad claims underlying these individual assertions are really two in number: that (authorial) language in (one presumes primarily) literary texts is "fuzzy" or "lattice-like" or "characterized by fuzzy boundaries and spreading activation," and that it is therefore not a match to the definite structures and positivist assumptions of SGML and other encoding languages. I will return to these broad claims at the end of this essay, but to reach them will examine the individual steps in Lancashire's argument as mentioned above.

It is worth noting in starting out, however, that Lancashire's argument brings the matter of text encoding into an arena it rather rarely fully enters, one in which the questions addressed to the enterprise are ontological, epistemological, and above all ethical. It would be an interesting historical task, but one with lesser contemporary relevance, to take up Lancashire's argument on its native territory and deal with the question of whether SGML is an appropriate vehicle for the use of humanists in describing textual objects—although probably such a discussion could be carried on in terms that addressed both SGML and its current successor XML—but I would propose that what is most interesting about what he has to say lies, in fact, in these realms of the ethics, ontology, and epistemology of textual encoding in the general case.

> *1) Encoding a text with a markup language requires three kinds of interpretation by the encoder: (1) judging that a tag can be truthfully applied to a word or passage; (2) assenting to the encoding terminology as both meaningful and properly describing text; and (3) believing that the syntax of the encoding language (the ways in which tags are characterized in terms of one another) allows for the description of relationships among tagged words or passages in text.*

Immediately I am caught up, as I expect many readers will be, on the word "truthfully," which encapsulates one of Lancashire's unstated assumptions, namely that to tag or encode a text is to make an assertion about reality, in this case the reality of the text, one that can be truthful or could be (by implication) not merely false but lying. What is at stake for us here that we react so strongly to the word? A fairly common way of thinking about text encoding is to assume that the application of a tag could be erroneous (the tag is applied incorrectly to a textual object it should not have been applied to through inadvertence or misunderstanding of the encoding scheme) or perverse (the encoder understands what the tag is supposed to be used for but employs it in another way anyway for reasons that make sense to her or him in the particular encoding situation but do not match broader encoding conventions of the encoding community) but could not constitute falsehood because tagging does not have truth-value. This view of the morally neutral character of the encoding enterprise arises because we commonly adopt a functional approach to tagging, employing a system with further processing in view and therefore thinking primarily of what a particular tagging will allow us to do later.

Lancashire's use of "truthfully" instead challenges us to consider encoding as a linguistic activity with propositional content. And indeed propositional content would seem to be a genuine aspect of descriptive encoding particularly (perhaps not so much of merely procedural markup destined, for example, to provoke aspects of print display). Descriptive tagging inevitably draws in aspects of the semantic, as the adjective "descriptive" implies, both the semantics associated with particular tags and the semantics associated with grammar/syntax of the encoding scheme. Examples of both the semantics of tags and the semantics of tag-relations encoded in a scheme are present in the following example from the TEI P5 Guidelines:

```
<p>
 <q>My dear <name type="person">Mr. Bennet</name>,</q> said <rs
type="person">his lady</rs> to him one day,
 <q>have you heard that <name type="place">Netherfield Park</name>
is let at last?</q>
</p>
```

In the example, both "Mr. Bennet" and "Netherfield Park" are properly (truthfully) qualified as "<name>" because they are in fact proper nouns, the semantics associated with that tag, whereas "his lady" is only a "reference string" or "<rs>" because not a proper noun, and the application of the more specific tag to it would constitute not just an abuse of the tagging scheme but a false description.

Likewise, the names and the reference string are part of (occur within) the paragraph ("<p>"), and it would be not merely a tagging blooper but false to assert there to be a paragraph within either name (e.g. "<name>Mr. <p>Bennet</p></name>") or indeed within any conceivable proper name in our current cultural universe (a universe in which a proper name could contain a paragraph or more would need a different syntax with different semantic implication). Lancashire's assertion of the ethical dimension of tagging therefore seems to me to be correct, and I understand his tripartite division of the interpretation applied by the encoder to refer to 1) the accuracy of description (truthfulness) involved any particular act of applying descriptive tags, 2) the relevancy of the semantics (capability of description) of a particular tagset to the text being tagged and 3) the appropriateness of the semantics defined by the tagging grammar/syntax to the encoding situation.

2) Any code that gives an intelligible name to content—a name drawn from a natural language and there endowed with meaning—carries baggage with it.

This is undoubtedly true, and users would presumably react with scorn to a tagset that tried to apply the tag "<sonnet>" to a prose paragraph, "<title>" to punctuation marks, and so on. But surely the fact of being drawn from natural language is not the point here, since tags that are not "drawn from natural language" (perhaps "<11001011>") or only drawn at second-hand from natural language, such as "<rs>" above, will also carry baggage, and the baggage will be precisely the semantics of the tag within the encoding system.

3) The facts that we observe in texts—characters and spaces—are of little general interest because they belong to a technology of language storage, not to language itself.

"The facts that we observe in texts," or the ontology of textual objects, could not possibly be constrained to "characters and spaces," because there is no essential difference between the (linguistic or semiotic) interpretive gesture by which we identify a noun, a sentence, an instance of alliteration or rhyme, a paragraph, a verse line, and so on, and the (linguistic or semiotic) interpretive gesture by which we identify characters and spaces. The distinction Lancashire attempts to draw between "a technology of language storage," a reference presumably to printed texts and also those stored in electronic devices or displayed on screens, and "language itself" (presumably spoken language and increasingly, as his essay goes on, language in the brain) is a logocentric one of the kind effectively critiqued by Jacques Derrida who shows that our culture consistently represses the physicality of spoken language and of "the spirit" or Logos precisely by rejecting the category of the written—which is nevertheless the basic condition of all language, including spoken language—as posterior, dead, fallen (Derrida 1976). And besides the general untenableness of the position that written and electronic texts do not constitute instances of language, it must be pointed out that if it is possible to be untruthful in tagging as in (1) above, it must also be possible to be truthful, which means that assertions about "a word or passage" conveyed by applying tags to them must also have a factual content and compose, when those tags are truthfully applied, part of "the facts we observe in texts."

4) SGML is based on a positivist epistemology. Tag elements and structures are routinely expressed as delimited, well-formed, knowable objects in unambiguous relationships.

Although it is not necessarily clear what Lancashire means by calling an epistemology "positivist" here and elsewhere in the essay, the sequence of sentences here gives the best insight. As the logical positivism of Rudolph Carnap and others in the philosophy of science reduced knowledge to the series of propositions derivable logically from sentences reporting observational facts, so (the claim is) SGML (and presumably all similar encoding schemes that name segments of text, such as XML and COCOA) reduces text to "delimited, well-formed, knowable objects in unambiguous relationships." It would be pointless to deny that some such reductive thinking has in the past been part of the discourse of the text-encoding community, since this is clearly

a good description of the position taken in an article that persuaded many
that adoption of SGML for humanities work would be a good thing, namely
that "Text is best represented as an ordered hierarchy of content object[s]
(OHCO), because that is what text really is" (DeRose et al. 1990).

In fact, however, it is hard to describe this position as positivist because it is
really not claiming that facts about a text can be deduced from observations,
which would be a positivist position, but rather that there is an underlying
structure of the text that is normally invisible though it may be manifested
in different ways, and that that underlying structure constitutes the only
reality of text:

> The essential parts of any document form what we call "content
> objects," and are of many types, such as paragraphs, quotations,
> emphatic phrases, and attributions. Each type of content object
> usually has its own appearance when a document is printed or
> displayed, but that appearance is superficial and transient rather
> than essential—it is the content objects themselves, along with
> their content, which form the essence of a document. (DeRose et
> al. 1990, 3)

It would be much more accurate to call this an essentialist or idealist view
than a positivist one: the assertion is that underlying the bibliographical
semiotics (indented lines, emboldening, font sizes, columns, and so on) of a
document is its essence, characterized by invisible "content objects" which
are invariably in hierarchical relationships, no other kinds of relationships,
and which may be moved to other media or given another "superficial and
transient" appearance without changing the (essential) reality of the text.

This apotheosis of document structure as the essence of "what text really
is" leaves on the floor behind it two discarded victims, the physical book
or manuscript, whose reality is explicitly denied in being described as "superficial and transient," mere "appearance," and the language contained in
that book or manuscript, reduced to "content," and mentioned largely as
an afterthought as in the quotation above, since it is the "content objects"
rather than what they contain that constitute the reality of text in this view.
The essentialist or idealist position of DeRose et al. on the nature of text
held sway with many computing humanists through the 1990s and informed
the basic structure of TEI encoding. Hard-core textual idealism has more
recently been ceding its dominant position within the TEI, and the new pro-
visions in P5 for designating areas within two-dimensional graphic images

such as page images, for example, constitute a particularly dramatic instance of new willingness to consider the material form of text as potentially worth describing in code.

But this does not mean that the TEI standard in its basic conception, or idealist text-encoding more generally, is well-prepared to meet the needs of the current materialist and social approaches to documents that go under the names of book history, material philology, and manuscript studies. These approaches or fields of study, which have deep roots in earlier bibliographical, codicological, and palaeographical study but a new political and social-historical awareness inflected to varying extents by New Historicist accounts of culture, society, and textuality, have recently been powerhouses of the production of new knowledge. They have in common a close attention to the materiality of the printed book or manuscript as object, to the traces of its creation as a product of distinct social circumstances and socially imbricated modes of production, and to the evidence it provides of the history of its use and the interactions with it of readers and owners. It is currently unclear whether TEI can be adapted sufficiently for these purposes. These approaches will demand a language for document-centric descriptive tagging, materialist in conception and elaboration, a language yet to be conceived but which will need to be based on a completely new epistemology and ontology of text encoding, and a new politics.

Although I dispute his terminology and may even have a different analysis of the underlying situation, I agree with Lancashire's basic point here that tagging approaches are neither epistemologically nor politically neutral. Idealist approaches tend to portray the encoded text as independent of its historical place, its conditions of production and reception, and indeed of the physical form in which we find it, which is reduced to a "carrier." They thus participate in and perpetuate a liberal humanist ideology that tends in its broadest form to deny or downplay historical and social circumstance, erase class, gender, and racial differences and tensions, and substitute a vision of essential equality and inalterable human nature for the reality of inequality, oppression, tension, and change.

5) Everything to be tagged must be delimited or segmented. Anything we cannot clearly delimit cannot be named. Yet clusters of textual objects, types of fuzzy sets, have indeterminate numbers of members, cover spans that can vary widely from one place in a text to another, and frequently may overlap (depending on how they are defined). Associative clusters of images, for example, are a frequent characteristic of literary writing.

Although phrased as an aphorism, the statement in the first two sentences appears to apply in the first instance to the imposition onto text of markup consisting of an on-tag and off-tag, as in XML and its precursor SGML, for example in "<rs type="person">his lady</rs>." Lancashire's statement should probably even for those languages be expanded to account for those situations where a "milestone tag" identifies a location only, not a segment or delimited span, and for those situations where multiple locations and/or segments are linked one to the other with tagging: "Everything to be tagged must be precisely locatable. Anything we cannot so locate cannot be tagged."

It is not clear that the aphorism is correct in more general application to all possible markup languages. Certainly inline tagging as routinely applied now in TEI, HTML, and similar implementations or grammars works by delimiting textual features with tags at precisely their beginning and end, but it is relatively easy to conceive of a standoff markup that allows for uncertainty as to where elements start and end, for example by giving a range of byte-offsets within which the start or end might be and therefore a range of possible locations for the start or end tag.

Lancashire does not give an example of "clusters of textual objects, types of fuzzy sets" other than "clusters of images ... [in] literary writing," I suspect that he may be referring, among others, to situations such as the following cluster of images in the first sentence of Milton's sonnet on his blindness:

> When I consider how my light is spent
> Ere half my days in this dark world and wide,
> And that one talent which is death to hide
> Lodg'd with me useless, though my soul more bent
> To serve therewith my Maker, and present
> My true account, lest he returning chide,
> "Doth God exact day-labour, light denied?"
> I fondly ask.
> (John Milton, Sonnet 19)

In the first line when first encountered, "my light is spent," besides being a topical reference to the failure of Milton's eyesight, would seem to raise the image of the burning out of a candle or lamp (OED spend *v*.1, spent *pa. pple. and ppl. adj.*) and thus perhaps allude to the parable of the wise and foolish virgins of Matthew 25, and this image is extended, though also given a new twist, by "dark world and wide" in the second line, where darkness seems to be an image of the evil of the surrounding world, making "light" of the preceding line possibly "virtue," "faith," or "Christian witness." The allusions to the parable of the talents, also in Matthew 25, which begin in the third line, retrospectively create at least two other meanings for "my light is spent," one in which the monetary meaning of "talent" (which also of course carries its modern meaning of skill or capability in the poem) influences "spent" in the direction of "expended, frittered away," and another in which the unprofitable hiding of the talent ("Log'd with me useless") allows the reading of "my light is spent" as "my sighted life has been occupied (unprofitably, without the creation of a major work)." Finally, the "outer darkness" of the biblical passage afflicts the whole complex of light and dark imagery with the prospect of Gehenna.

In other words, the phrase "my light is spent" resonates on the level of imagery in at least four different ways and participates in two distinct literary allusions in the course of four lines of verse. The relations of this phrase to other words and images in these lines are dynamic (that is, they change as new relations are suggested in the course of a reading or over time with study), overlapping, and create a shifting network or web rather than a distinct object. They are also expansive, depending for aspects of meaning on at least one intertext—and no doubt many more, as an Early English Books Online Text Creation Partnership (EEBO-TCP) full-text search for "wide world" and other terms will show—and activating several different possible semantics of the key terms, and in fact more than one grammar for the phrase I have focussed on, as the sentence progresses. I would not claim that even poems as a class are generally this dense and rife with networks of imagery, but discourse analysis can locate analogues to this kind of thing, though most often considerably more diffuse and extended, in political speeches, advertising copy, and popular genres. And although it is possible to think of ways in which it could be tagged, though not necessarily with existing tools, it is not clear that linguistic structures of this complexity will respond well to the demand that they be composed of hierarchically organized discreet components or even that they be identified by tagging.

6) Multiple overlapping structures reveal the tip of the problem. SGML limits us to encoding two non-overlapping structures in one text file, and to recognizing only one structure at a time. [Charles] Goldfarb recommended that such multiple structures in poetry be managed ... by hypertext links ... Yet it remains unclear how a flat, lattice-like structure, one characterized by fuzzy boundaries and spreading activation, can be adequately represented in SGML. Establishing firm links among parts of a text, as the anchor tag does in HTML, sets in place as rigorous and unambiguous a structure as any hierarchy.

Of course, XML is even more restrictive of overlapping structures, since it does not retain the SGML "CONCUR" capability, though that was hardly ever made operational in any way in SGML software. There are probably multiple problems to be addressed, rather than a single problem revealed by the overlapping hierarchy difficulty, since as just noted, whatever we take a "flat, lattice-like structure ... characterized by fuzzy boundaries and spreading activation" to be, it may not best be described by tagging at all, let alone tagging in a rigid hierarchy or even multiple rigid hierarchies of "content objects." There are now various workarounds to the hierarchy problem in TEI, but it remains a tricky one for folks primarily interested in material documents, because the text-structure elements best identified by essentialist markup, such as the paragraph, often overlap with the material facts of book structure, such as the page. They even overlap with linguistic objects. I have permission to share a quite usual instance of this last that I received in my email this week, with the name changed:

> Subject: Your parcel
> From: Helen Black heblack@ucalgary.ca
> Date: Fri. October 2, 2009 3:28 p.m.
> To: Murray McGillivray <mmcgilli@ucalgary.ca>
> Message: went off in the courier this afternoon, HEB

Such an arrangement of textual content is par for the course in email messaging, does occur in more formal textuality (such as William Carlos Williams's poem "This is Just to Say"), and has an equivalent in the tendency of some extended early-book titles to launch into the subject matter of the book, though this is obscured in the Short Title Catalogue. In poetry, it is the rule that sentences overlap verse units. Of course, such overlaps between formal document structure elements and a unified sentence are rarer in prose, but overlaps between discrete segments of discourse or argument and the formal containers, such as paragraphs or chapters into which they are sometimes awkwardly placed is quite routine. Lancashire is quite right to observe that hierarchically ordered text encoding is going to have difficulty with many linguistic structures, including but not limited to those in literary texts.

> 7) [A]nyone encoding texts today faces two muses. One is the disorganized, hard-to-predict, invisible, and messy thought and language process from which utterances come. What this muse professes, the second muse selects from, edits, and formats. Colin Martindale's phrase "the mechanical muse" well names the second muse, who like a strict housekeeper lives to curb and channel the inventions that the first muse gives its unruly child or occupant.

The first muse is the author. The second muse is the reader-editor or publisher for whom texts represent a landscape to be tamed, described, and mapped for use.

8) For research purposes, ... an encoding language should be devised that can mirror the structures by which the human mind (the subject in phenomenological criticism) generates the encoded texts, for these structures—imposed by the first muse—may never be recognized by the second muse for explicit identification.

Despite his citation of reader-response theorists, Lancashire here appears to retail a quite conventional mid-twentieth-century romantic account of the mysterious wild creation of (one presumes) literary texts by inspired authors who do not know quite what they are doing, and their reception by pedestrian readers and editors, whose only role is to try to tame the resultant texts while clearly failing to understand them. In fact, most thinkers about language and textuality would now recognize that much as the brain of an author may often be the crucible of the text, not only does the author (even if unitary and in some rare historical circumstance able to work without the direct collaboration of others, for example, publishers and editors) not exist in a social or linguistic vacuum, but the reader contributes just as much and in some cases more to the creation of meaning in the text.

In fact, the brain of the author is not just theoretically but actually inapproachable even if the author is alive, so if there are two muses the text-encoder must consider, they are on the one hand the physical (paper or electronic) document with its material particularity and elaborated linguistic and semiotic structures, however these may have resulted from the linguistic processes of the author(s) and other participants in the creation of the text, and on the other the reader (including the encoder her- or himself) in whose creative semiotic and linguistic engagement with the document meaning is created. To speak this way is not to deny Lancashire's claim that useful work can be done by partly automated research to reveal aspects of an author's use of language—and maybe an author's brain (Lancashire 1993)— but to acknowledge more fully that it is the document itself and its employment of linguistic and text-semiotic codes that is the object of study and that conscious evaluation of reader responses, and the semantic ambiguities that allow them, may have a continuing role to play.

9) The process of having a program elicit tags from the text itself may be called dynamic or virtual encoding. The tagset is suggested by the text itself, not by the researcher. ... By postponing the definition of a tagset to indexing and information-retrieval processes, software gives users freedom to explore the text and the relationships among its parts.

It is doubtful that the creation of an encoding language or tagset is the best or even a required tool for hearkening to these two muses in computer-aided analysis that explores the meaningfulness of textual objects. As Lancashire himself observes in statement 7 above, encoding as a tool is more classificatory than creative, which makes it a rather unlikely candidate for organizing processes of discovery. It is noteworthy that the example Lancashire himself gives of virtual tagging is of a process most people would not think of as constituting text-encoding at all, namely the iterative employment of concordancing to locate patterns in the use of collocations.

Our current landscape as digital humanists, if that is what we call ourselves, is increasingly constituted by full-text access to millions of pages of documents, whether these are in text files or in page images. Every week more books and periodicals from before the computer age are available, often in both forms in the same resource, with the text-files in a text-base, produced more or less automatically and more or less cleanly by Optical Character Recognition (OCR) processes, acting as indices to the images which are then presented to the reader after full-text searching of the text-base. Something like this methodology underlies older projects such as JSTOR and is the way that all production-volume book digitization projects in the private sector and most of those financed by public institutions run. This is an environment that the text-encoding model of what digital humanities work consists of is less than perfectly equipped to encounter. To manually tag hundreds or thousands of instances of (for example) the paragraph in producing an electronic version of a prose text is beside the point in one way if the user is able to search for instances of the words she or he wants to find without using that information anyway and identify them the old-fashioned way by page number via the page image, and beside the point in another way if the paragraphs are already pretagged, as it were, in the associated images, for example by having their first lines indented. What is more essential is a system that can interpret, or learn to interpret with human input, the coding already present in the typographical codes, layouts, systems of ordination, and so on, of document images and in their paper or parchment precursors.

Such a system might in the course of its operation use an encoding scheme like TEI tagging (but perhaps one adapted to be more oriented to the physical structure of the document than its ideal structure) to record its findings and make them available for pre-indexing to increase search speeds. Such pre-indexing would in turn allow more sophisticated searches of full-text-bases, for example looking for both *Truman* and *Roosevelt* within the same paragraph, or within a title, and could reduce false positives. But rather than searching for the hidden essence of the documents, such a system would ideally depend on information already encoded visually in the material documents themselves, for example by learning to look for a right-hand page with a lot of space at the top and a sequence of words in larger, bolder type on one line as an indication of a chapter (it could also look for the word "chapter" in some books). Such a system would be a facility that digital humanists would use, for example by directing queries to it, and one they can be trusted to improve by critique, but it would hopefully not be a system that digital humanists would create. On the one hand, the programming issues are too wide-ranging and multifarious, and on the other hand the humanities content in the decision-making is too diffuse, for it to be worth their time.

Much more worthwhile for digital humanists, both in terms of the immediate rewards of the actual enterprise and in terms of the appositeness of our knowledge to the task, would be study of the ways in which the kinds of intra-document and extra-document semantic networks I have discussed in connection with the brief Milton excerpt above could be efficiently located as objects of study, the kind of objects Lancashire alludes to. The current tools for searching texts are blunt instruments not just because of the inadequate cleanliness of the data in many image-associated text-bases, but also when scanning a scrupulously prepared text such as a single novel, primarily because they are de facto restricted to searching for strings, whether or not with stemming or lemmatization, whether or not in proximity to one another. The most profitable way forward for document searching of all kinds is going to have to involve smarter search agents, agents that process not only document structure but also and especially detailed grammar and semantics on their way to identifying content.

The programming issues for grammatically and semantically sophisticated searches are to the highest degree non-trivial and certainly involve not only Artificial Intelligence (AI) methodologies but a ramping up of AI to the level of secure identification of grammar and semantic content. But humanists with a computing edge need not be involved in the hard-core programming. There are a wide range of issues, from historical language change to modern dialectology to the processes of allusion and the nature of intertextuality, in which humanists have an interest and to the understanding of which digital humanists might contribute. Human understanding of our various discourse communities and how they operate, including historical discourse communities and including the position of the individual, whether innovative literary artist or not, within her or his discourse community, is in its infancy, and the newly opened field of materials for exploration of these issues is very wide indeed and thanks to various digitization initiatives increasing daily.

With his critique of the ethics, ontology, and epistemology of text encoding, and his concept of virtual tagging, Ian Lancashire points us to a future in which the role of computing in the digital humanities is revived. The generation of researchers whose primary interest for more than twenty years has been in clarifying document structures, having contributed substantial new knowledge in that domain, may well cede its place to researchers more keenly interested in the materiality and social and historical origins of our documentary heritage as it persists to be investigated in individual material objects and in the large libraries of such objects now being opened to digital methods of study. As well, Lancashire's critique of the epistemology, ontology, and politics of tagging points out some kinds of linguistic and semiotic territory for which a text-encoding approach is inadequate, both within the single literary text and across texts. The rise of the macrocosm of image-linked historical text-bases will allow the investigation of that linguistic and semiotic territory by tools smart enough to reveal historical discourse and text-production communities, their ideologies, their verbal obsessions, and the interrelations of individuals and groups within them, tools that could also be pointed with profit at, and that might be partly developed by scholars interested in, the microcosms of individual literary texts. Although I dispute some of its basic positions, this neglected article of Ian Lancashire's deserves a wider readership, which I am very pleased to see given it in this book.

WORKS CITED

DeRose, Steven J., David G. Durand, Elli Mylonas, and Allen H. Renear. 1990. What is Text, Really? *Journal of Computing in Higher Education* 1, no. 2 (Winter): 3–26.

Derrida, Jacques. 1976. *Of Grammatology.* Trans. Gayatri Chakravorty Spivak. Baltimore: Johns Hopkins University Press.

Hockey, Susan M. 2000. *Electronic Texts in the Humanities: Principles and Practice.* Oxford: Oxford University Press.

Lancashire, Ian. 1993. Phrasal Repetends and "The Manciple's Prologue and Tale." In *Computer-Based Chaucer Studies*, 99–122. Centre for Computing in the Humanities (CCH) Working Papers 3. Toronto: Centre for Computing in the Humanities, University of Toronto.

PART TWO
DISSEMINATING ELECTRONIC PUBLICATIONS:
THE POLITICS AND PRAGMATICS OF PUBLICATION

How We Have Been Publishing the Wrong Way, and How We Might Publish a Better Way

Peter Robinson

University of Birmingham

p.m.robinson@bham.ac.uk

A virtue of longevity is that it grants time for a second act. The first act allows pursuit of error: in the second, what is learnt can be parlayed into a better way. Indeed, as our lives have accelerated so that what was once the experience of a lifetime can be packed into a few years, or less, we now have time for third acts, for fourth acts, and maybe even more. I begin this way because in twenty years of making computer tools for scholarly editing I have made two major changes of direction, so that I can now claim to be in the third act of some drama involving computers, scholarly editors, and the academic and wider community. Twice, I have gone some distance down a road better not travelled and come back to try another path. In this paper, I will first say something of the first two roads I tried. This is not just of personal historical interest: many scholars went down those roads with me; there are still scholars who believe that one or other of these roads is the right road, and indeed the second road still dominates in many of those institutions which do the thing called "humanities computing." I will then describe the route I am currently following, and explain why this model is different and (in my view) the way many of us should go. In the terms of the title: almost all the digital publications we have made in the last years, following these first two roads, have been wrongly made. This was excusable: we did what we could, knowing what we did. But we are beginning to glimpse a better way.

One could characterize the first direction I took, roughly from 1989 to 1998, with a single abbreviation: SGML (Standard Generalized Markup Language). There were endless discussions about arcane points of markup, many committees, masses of computer printout, and screens full of pointy brackets, equals signs, and quotation marks. We had lots of printed documentation explaining how one could make texts with all kinds of varieties of Text Encoding Initiative (TEI) markup, many texts interpenetrated with pointy brackets, equals signs, and quotation marks, and hardly any software. A constant refrain of TEI meetings was "that [regardless of what it was] is an implementation matter." This trump card was played at moments when the

ISBN 978-0-86698-021-0 (online)   ISBN 978-0-86698-449-2 (print)

New Technologies in Medieval and Renaissance Studies 2 (2010) 139–155

conversation was verging dangerously upon the practical. The implication was the following: we must not allow what is practical to impose upon the purity of our theory. It also happened to be a very safe gambit, as there was little chance of whatever was being discussed actually being implemented. Useful indicators of the thinking can be recovered from works published at the time (Hockey and Ide 1996; Sutherland 1997; Sperberg-McQueen and Burnard 1994, sections "Textual apparatus" and "Transcription of primary sources"; Robinson 2009b), the last of which was originally written for a conference in 1997 and reflects the community's thinking of the time.

A consequence of this concentration on texts and their markup in a software void was that, unsurprisingly, SGML devotees (and for a while, I was one) came to think that what really mattered was, well, the text and its markup. There was a positivistic fervour about the work of the TEI at this time: a confidence that texts could be absolutely described and validated. One should get the right markup in the text; a task for which one needed mastery of the 1,000 plus dense pages of the TEI guidelines. One could see the first major software tool that I made for editing, Collate, in this light. I devised and wrote most of Collate between 1990 and 1992, in the heyday of SGML. Collate could be used to create SGML files of breathtaking complexity, mapping the word-by-word relations of multiple versions of a single text (the record was, and will now remain for ever, the 1,246 versions of John 18 collated in Birmingham by David Parker and his team) into streams of interlocking markup. Here was a perfected text. What happened to our perfected text after that was not our concern: software would surely appear, some day, to take advantage of all that we had poured into the text, and until then the text could sit in a text archive somewhere.

However, I was also looking for ways to publish collaborative work on the manuscripts of the *Canterbury Tales.* We used the one SGML publishing system accessible to us, and with the capacity to do much of what we wanted, DynaText (firstly a creation of Electronic Book Technologies, then a company possession traded through a succession of owners, and now no more). At first (1996) we were pleased with DynaText. It handled our SGML files, without compromises or difficulties. It did give access to the transcripts and collations and to our editorial discussions. However, we discovered that there were things that DynaText could not do. The display was inflexible, and inherently unattractive, and could not do what seemed a very simple thing: just display a page of transcription of a manuscript. We began to look for alternatives, and found that there were none. There was little SGML software at all. The reason for this was that SGML was so constructed, with all kinds of little byways and exceptions, that it was extremely difficult to write software for SGML.

Many other people too were looking for ways to publish the texts they were making; they felt it was not sufficient just to make beautifully encoded texts and they were frustrated with the tools available. And so, I and others left this first road and started out on another road. One acronym and one word may characterize this second road: the acronym was XML, and the word is Web. For those of us brought up in the hermetic universe of SGML, this was a flood of light. Almost overnight, as the Web invaded every corner and brought XML with it as its favoured lingua franca for all operations of any complexity, XML applications (parsers, publishing systems, editors, tools of every kind) appeared everywhere. XML offered us the tools to make much better publications than could SGML, and the Web offered us a platform from which these publications could reach every user. XML and the Web seemed to offer all that we could possibly need. By 1998 I had come to think that it was not enough to make beautifully encoded texts or to present these in the coarse environment DynaText offered. We wanted to make editions that would reach out to the readers, that would be beautiful things in their own right, as beautiful at least as the best print editions which they might supplant. We wanted them to be endlessly flexible, to provide any reader with all the tools and resources an editor might use, and hence to enrich the reader's experience of the text. Further, these editorial objects would be so desirable, so obviously superior to their print predecessors, that editors would clamour to make them, leaving behind print forever; readers would immerse themselves in them in numbers never known for print editions; institutions and grant agencies would want to support and fund them and their makers.

This was how I was thinking when I started developing what became the Anastasia electronic publishing system in 1998. I wanted something I could use myself to make the kind of editions I had in mind, and to publish them on CD-ROM and on the Internet. I wanted something which (so I supposed) would be so easy to use that scholars with reasonable computer skills, or with access to only limited computer support, would be able to make complex and satisfying electronic scholarly editions. Why not just use a system already made? I could not see then any piece of software which could do what I want, and do it so readily that I could reasonable expect others to use it also. There were various reasons for the failure of existing systems to do what I then wanted. A very early decision was that we should present our editions through standard Web browsers, not through some form of bespoke program interface (as DynaText and other programs of that time, for example Soft-

Quad's Panorama, had used). Browsers were then very crude, and treated identical strings of encoded text in alarmingly different ways. Matters have considerably improved since, with support for Unicode now sophisticated and reliable. In retrospect, this was one of the best decisions I made at that time: our editions have been lifted by the wave of browser improvements over the years. This did mean however that our XML had to be converted to HyperText Markup Language (HTML) for publication. All the XML software publishing software I surveyed then used eXtensible Stylesheet Language Transformations (XSLT) to convert data to HTML.

I found and still find XSLT an extraordinarily difficult programming environment for what we want to do. It works well where there are many XML records with identical and straightforward structure, such as the address books and sales catalogues in the sample documentation. XSLT is for satisfactory for users with this kind of data. But the data in our editions does not fit this pattern: it is, like most scholarly data, unpredictable, idiosyncratic, with no text ever quite like any other text, and no part of a text ever quite like any other part of a text. XML notoriously has difficulties with overlapping hierarchies, so that it forces the encoder to choose whether to make the hierarchy that of the text (volume, chapter, paragraph, sentence) or that of the document (volume, quire, page). XSLT exaggerates the difficulty and makes it easy to process the document according to the primary hierarchy, typically that of the text (so it is simple to output a chapter, or a paragraph) rather than of the document (so it is difficult to output a page). As a primary need of our editions was to show a page of transcription beside an image of a page of a manuscript, this was a critical factor.

A second reason for making our own software was that the typical XML processing system required complex configuration of a server running applications that passed requests from the user through a series of handlers, to extract the XML and transform it to HTML (usually using XSLT; or if not, some form of database handling such as PHP Hypertext Preprocessor to embed HTML) before passing it back to the user. This made CD-ROM distribution problematic: it was hard enough to get these pieces working together on one's own server, with several experts around to help; it was inconceivable that one could expect average computer users to do this. Although CD/DVD-ROM publication might seem obsolete, there are many scholars who want to run an application on their own computer, and we would like them to be able to do this.

A third reason was that, in my view, it was unreasonable to expect individual scholars to run the circuit of Apache, Simple API for XML (Sax), Linux-Apache-MySQL-Perl/PHP/Python (LAMP), Macintosh-Apache-MySQL-Perl/PHP/Python (MAMP), Document Object Model (DOM), XSLT, and various other frightening words in order to make a publication out of their XML. So we designed Anastasia as a single tool to do it all: to process the XML; to offer scripting of the XML conversion; search tools; and a local server capable of sending pages to a browser running on the user's computer. The theory was that if we made it easy enough, many scholars would take this up and electronic editions would sprout.

My first version of Anastasia was released in 2000, and used to publish an edition of the *Hengwrt Chaucer Digital Facsimile* (Stubb 2000). The second version, substantially rewritten by Andrew West, was released in 2001. We achieved one of our aims: in the following years we were able to publish a series of electronic editions, which people found attractive, easy to use, and presenting large and complex bodies of material in an accessible way. Specifically these were: my edition of *The Miller's Tale*, Paul Thomas's edition of *The Nun's Priest's Tale*, the edition of the Parliament Rolls of Medieval England by Chris Given-Wilson and others, Prue Shaw's edition of Dante's *Monarchia*, and the New Testament Transcripts project at the Institute for New Testament Research in Münster. Further, we published these on CD-ROM and the Internet, as we proposed. However, we had limited success creating a tool that other scholars would use. I know of just three substantial uses of Anastasia by other scholars: the Laures Database at Sophia University, Tokyo (a tour-de-force of XML encoding and presentation, far less well known than it deserves), the Eumaios project of Martin Mueller, and the Dafydd ap Gwilym project at Swansea. I believe these projects achieved more, faster, with the Anastasia software than they might otherwise have done, but three projects was fewer than we hoped.

I came to see that Anastasia fell between two constituencies. For the scholars at whom we originally aimed it was too difficult and demanding of software skills. For the technical officers who might have used it to mount XML on their own servers Anastasia did not look like or work like any piece of software to which they were used. For those who were used to databases, it was not a database; for those who were used to XML, it did not use XSLT. Besides, it used Tool Command Language (Tcl), which was decidedly unfashionable.

I have described this at some length because we were almost alone in our decision to make a new tool, usable by many scholars. In the years 1998–2005, technical officers and technical directors at computing installations around the world, in companies, libraries, in the few institutions specializing in supporting humanities computing, determined that the rush of new XML tools could do what they wanted. The tools were complex to configure, install, use, and maintain, but in the institutional computing environment, with paid technical officers operating with stable hardware and software, these demands were easily satisfied. Skilled technical officers could readily run the gamut of Apache, Sax, LAMP, DOM, XSLT, PHP, XML databases of various flavours: that is what they are good at, that is what they are paid to do. Using these new tools, centres such as the Institute for Advanced Technology in the Humanities (IATH) in Virginia, the Humanities Text Initiative at Ann Arbor, Michigan, the King's College London Centre for Computing in the Humanities, and the Maryland Institute for Technology in the Humanities (MITH) were able quickly to produce marvellous bodies of electronic resources. Think of the Rossetti and Blake archives, the Fine Rolls project at King's, the Middle English Compendium at Michigan. The rapid success of these projects had a further effect: funding agencies identified these centres as the clear leaders in their fields and poured money into them, which in turn allowed those centres to gather more resources and make yet more impressive digital publications.

In this period, it seemed we had a perfect consensus. Funders were happy: they were giving large sums of money to well-managed organizations that produced digital publications of distinct sets of material ("The collected papers/works/letters of _____," "The _____ Project/Archive/Digital Edition"), with the funder's name blazoned on the edition. The scholars who led these projects were happy: their careers received the boost of both funding won and publication achieved. The centres which mounted these projects were happy: they got money to employ more people, buy more equipment, move into yet more impressive premises. The scholarly community and public at large were happy, or should have been (though they were rarely asked): they got wonderfully realized digital materials delivered to their computer, for nothing.

Such a paragraph as the last one leads up to a "but . . ." statement. What has this picture of perfect achievement omitted? I am reminded of a comment by Manfred Thaller, in a seminar in Edinburgh in March 2008 on directions in humanities computing. He said, in a discussion about achievements in digital scholarship, that we could build a bridge over the English Channel. It would be the best bridge ever, offering a superlative experience for those who managed to drive over it. But the cost of building that bridge would be so high that there would be no money for building the roads we need to get cars to the bridge. The point of the metaphor is that excellence in one area comes with a price in other areas, and the price may actually be so high as eventually to disable the excellence. If cars cannot get to our super bridge, there will be no reason to maintain it; it will fall into disrepair and finally collapse. All that money would have been far better spent on improving the networks of lesser roads actually used by many people and not on one grand project.

Humanities computing centres (including those with which I have been associated) have built many superb bridges in the last years. Local roads are built by local interests: in the scholarly community, individual scholars. In textual scholarship, the bread-and-butter work of editing is done by one or two scholars, typically working alone over long periods, on the less glamorous corners of our culture, on individual writers, collections or themes of local or sectional interest. This work might first take shape as a doctoral thesis or as a by-product of literary or historical research as a scholar realizes that a work crucial to a particular point of understanding has never been edited, possibly existing only in various problematic and inaccessible forms. In the print age there was a well-accepted process leading to the print publication. The editor creates a print edition, using whatever tools are available: pen and paper, or typescript, up to the last decades, more recently, a word processor. He or she finds a publisher who makes the new edition into a book that goes to libraries and archives, and that is that. The editor's name appears large and clear on the title page, and he or she wins due credit from those who value editing.

One would expect there to be an electronic equivalent to this. Surely, the added value of digital scholarship is so evident, so accepted, that scholars will flock to the new medium. This is particularly true of scholarly editions. The average scholarly article looks much the same in the electronic medium as it does in the print medium: you will read it from the screen rather than from paper or print it (as most people do). But scholarly editions, with their multiple texts and apparatus intricately linked, amount to perfect instances of hypertext, even if we cannot link to images of the original documents. Who would publish a scholarly edition in print, now that the digital medium exists? The answer is almost everyone. With a few exceptions, almost every scholarly edition published in the last decade has been published in print, and in print only. Particularly revealing are editions originally conceived as primarily digital, but which over the years have reconfigured themselves so that they have become primarily print or exclusively print, such as the Cambridge Ben Jonson and the Oxford Jonathan Swift. The situation is even more extraordinary when one compares it to what has happened to scholarly articles, which are usually available in electronic form even ahead of the print form. Yet scholarly editions in digital form can be greatly superior to their print counterparts, where the digital form of an article offers little advantage over print.

Why has this happened? The price of the success of the centre-based model of digital humanities, and the concentration of resources in those centres, is that scholars without access to these centres cannot make digital editions. To make a high-quality digital edition these days, you need expert knowledge of encoding systems, high technical ability, and considerable software and hardware skills to publish the digital edition, as well as expertise in what you are editing. It should be as easy for a scholar to make a digital edition as it is to make a print edition, but a full decade after the appearance of XML and its associated technologies, it is still easier to make a print edition than to make a digital one. The effect is a massive distortion of the scholarly landscape. We have a few high-profile and impressive websites, generally focussed on a single set of resources: a single collection, a single author, a single work. These are built at huge expense by a few scholars working within a few centres. Around that is nothing: a perfect expression of Manfred Thaller's metaphor of the bridge with no roads.

This is even more extraordinary given that the whole direction of computing over the last years has been towards giving more power to the individual user. With the most basic computer, loaded with free or cheap software (usually, just an Internet browser), a cheap Internet connection, and the most basic computing skills, you can make a sophisticated website complete with pictures, music, personalized layout, your own diary, and links. You can write or edit a Wikipedia entry, or a book review, or an article, and they can be read instantly by others or even submitted to a traditional publisher, who in turn could publish your article on the Web. Yet you cannot make, with anything like similar reasonable facility, a scholarly edition incorporating, say, a diplomatic transcript of a single manuscript source, or a critical edition of a text with an apparatus of variants from multiple versions. You could of course put all this into a Microsoft Word or HTML document, and turn it into a print publication or a website. But this would not be regarded as a serious scholarly edition in digital form. It would lack the XML encoding necessary to support what has become the consensus view, over the last fifteen years or so, of what a scholarly digital edition in digital form should be. According to this consensus: the logical relations between the parts of the edition (between the words in the text and the apparatus; between the edition itself and the surrounding editorial matter) and the scholarly knowledge embedded within the edition (that these characters represent a scribal abbreviation, to be read in a particular way; that this reading is an emendation) should be expressed in a formal and highly prescribed encoding, as developed over the last decades by the Text Encoding Initiative. Further, in the last years as digital library systems have developed, the consensus has further demanded that the digital edition should be described with appropriate metadata, so that it and its parts can be stored and retrieved through the digital equivalent of a catalogue.

I do not challenge this consensus; indeed, I could hardly do so, as I have over the last decades been one of the leaders in creating it. The consensus is not wrong: what is wrong is the way it is enacted. If you want to make a scholarly edition in digital form, you will be told: learn about the TEI encodings and about metadata, go to these courses to help you do this, speak to these experts at these centres who will help you on the way. Yet if you want to drive a motorcar, you will not be told that you have to learn the standards which govern the car's electrical systems or its mechanics; you will not need to go to courses on these matters or consult anyone. These have been abstracted now to such a degree that you have only to turn on the engine and it runs. Elsewhere in this collection Alan Galey and Robert Whalen advocate the need for scholars making digital editions to take and run the technical courses in XML and related technologies. I disagree. There will be a continuing need for a few specialists who do understand these matters, just as there is a continuing need for a few people who understand Latin and Ancient Greek. But to insist that all editors who want to make digital editions should understand these things seems to me as short-sighted and narrowly limiting as the requirement of Oxford and Cambridge Universities (maintained until 1960) that incoming undergraduates in all subjects have a basic qualification in Latin or Greek. Relaxation of this rule harmed the teaching of classics at schools (Bulwer 2005) but can hardly be said to have reduced the quality of incoming students or the work of the universities.

It was fundamental that standard encodings and metadata be established and the first users of these encodings had to understand them, in the same way that the first generations of car users needed to know the details of their car's functioning. But once the standards are established, they should disappear into the background. This has not happened in humanities computing. As a result, TEI and metadata encoding, which were at first the great enabling powers of our discipline, have become obstacles. The requirement to learn them suits those who want to teach courses on them; it suits the centres that employ these people, which provide all the tools for making and publishing these editions that the scholar needs, and it suits the funders of these centres. It does not suit everyone else, including the scholars who want to make scholarly editions but do not understand why they need to learn these complex systems and have no access to these centres. Almost all scholars are in the position. A model of scholarship which declares that only a few scholars in a few institutions can make scholarly editions is unsustainable.

I object not only to this model that leaves out the many individual scholars, but also to the editions made according to the prevailing prescription. Although they use the standard TEI encodings and metadata, the editions are made of elaborate structures of interwoven files, hooked together into an interface by many hours of bespoke programming to give access to the many parts of the edition, and to provide searching and other tools. I know this because I have made several such editions. The result is that the various parts of the edition—the transcripts, the images, the editorial annotations and discussions—are accessible only through the interface provided by the edition's creators. For years, we who make these editions have poured countless hours of work into ever-more complex and ingenious interfaces, and these are beautiful objects. They do what we want them to do, and we are pleased; we show them at conferences and we bask in the applause. We even win prizes for them. But we have created monsters. Say you want to see an image of a particular page of a manuscript, or a transcript of a page, or an editorial discussion of a reading in that page. How do you do this for, say, a *Canterbury Tales* manuscript, or a Parliament Roll, or a Blake or Rossetti poem, or for one page of Codex Sinaiticus, or one page of an edition of *The Origin of Species*? There is only one way to do this: you have to go through the interface provided by the edition's makers. Because these editions are (generally) extremely well considered and well made, you do get superb access through the interface. But there is inconvenience in having to learn a different interface for each edition.

Far more serious than inconvenience is the implications this approach has for the data included in these editions, since if the interface fails the data might as well not exist. Computer interfaces are subject to entropy to a degree beyond almost any other manmade object. As soon as your electronic publication goes onto the Web, or a user installs it from a CD-ROM, bits start falling off. This view does not work in this browser on this computer; when Microsoft or Apple upgrade their operating system, some more bits fail; when a standard in some scripting language is properly enforced, a part of your edition which relied on an undocumented feature fails. There are physical hazards too: CD-ROMs and DVD-ROMs decay, servers disappear along with the centres that used to maintain them. You can mutilate a book in many ways, removing the table of contents, indices, whole sections even, and the book may still be useful. But once the interface to a digital edition is gone, all those transcripts, those images, those commentaries, are gone or have reverted to a heap of file names, or items in database tables, or something else entirely from which some hapless programmer might have to conjure sense. In a very few years, all these publications, with all this data so lovingly gathered and published, will become inaccessible.

According to this analysis, the current model for the making and publication of scholarly editions in digital form has two major problems. Firstly, individual scholars without access to specialized computer resources are unable to make them. Secondly, those scholarly digital editions which have been made are constructed on an unsustainable model, with resources sealed within an interface requiring complex and continuing infrastructure to maintain. The conventional answer to these two problems is: more of the same. Give more money to groups like the TEI and various metadata organizations to run more courses, to create more experts. Give more money to the centres which made these editions to update the interfaces, leading to the situation that so much is spent sustaining these interfaces that there is no money left to make anything new. One of the hottest terms in humanities computing these last years has been cyber-infrastructure. It is not unfair to translate this as a plea to give more funding to support existing humanities computing structures, and to create some new ones. We could, of course, continue like this. Each year, we will produce collectively one or two grand new digital resources like the Codex Sinaiticus Project, or our Commedia project. The round of digital humanities courses, conferences and publications may continue unabated; humanities computing centres and digital libraries may continue to recruit clever young men and women who know how to negotiate TEI XML and the many flavours of metadata. My objection is that this model of what I call corporate humanities computing is seen as the only road, and that resources are invested into this approach which might be better used elsewhere.

I am not the only person who is aware that all is not well. Indeed, within corporate humanities computing, there is an increasing awareness of the two problems I have outlined. Several projects are now addressing the making of tools for collaborative editing and successful implementation of these will mean that many more scholars, in specific domains, can contribute to the making of valuable resources. Simultaneously, new approaches to bodies of resource metadata are attempting to model the linkages between the parts of a complex digital object so that the individual parts and their connections with one another are not dependent on *ad hoc* interfaces. For example, there is use of Metadata Encoding and Transmission Standard (METS) to link sets of images with one other, and with related text files, or, more generally, the ambition of Open Archives Initiative Protocol Object Reuse and Exchange (OAI-ORE) to provide a full set of tools by which all relations among resource objects may be represented. It is a concern, however, that much of the work in these new areas is being done by the same people and institutions that created the problem in the first place. The dialect has changed, but the language remains the same.

What should we do about this? Ten years ago, faced with what seemed to me the failure of the first model of humanities computing, I thought the solution would be a very smart and very capable piece of software that would allow every scholar to become a digital editor. Ten years on, after the failure of Anastasia to transform textual scholarship, I do not believe that any one tool, and perhaps not even many tools, could achieve this transformation. At Scholarly Digital Editions (SDE) and the Institute for Textual Scholarship and Electronic Editing (ITSEE) we are in fact making a successor to Anastasia: the SDPublisher system first distributed in April 2009. But the way forward, in my mind, does not lie in tools, or particular software systems. Hence, at the time of writing we are implementing the first steps towards a radically different approach to these problems: my third road. It happens (as it usually does) that our approach arose as a response to a specific set of circumstances. In ITSEE we have the following:

> 1) Several groups of scholars working in different areas who have immense knowledge of the texts they are editing, who have access to basic computer tools but no specialist knowledge (and no inclination at all to learn) of XML, TEI, and their related technologies;
> 2) A need to create transcripts of texts from manuscripts and print editions, to be used as the basic blocks of the editions we make;
> 3) Limited resources for making interfaces;
> 4) Little infrastructural support from the university or elsewhere, and what there is comes from the Institutional Repository;
> 5) A need to give the most convenient access not only to the resources we create, but to those held by our principal partner, the Institute for New Testament Textual Research in Münster, Germany, and beyond to resources held anywhere.

We could not go any of the ways outlined earlier in this article. Our scholars would rebel if we tried to force them to learn TEI encoding. We have no funding for the making of more than the most basic interface. But we have a lot of raw digital resources: some 100,000 images of manuscript pages, taken from microfilm; around 10,000 pages of transcripts of manuscript pages, many of them from pages for which we had images. Our task shaped itself accordingly as finding how we could give access to these materials, in a form convenient to our scholars, and in a way that would allow them to add their own materials.

As we were pondering this, a revolution was occurring across the Web. As well as the elaborately crafted fixed-form top-down websites characteristic of the elaborate digital publications we have discussed earlier in this publication, we began to see something different: sites assembled from many different resources, to the taste of the user. A powerful example was the user interface for Google account holders. When you first log in to Google you are given a blank screen and a set of icons, each representing a tool for accessing a resource: the stock market, weather, news-feeds, sports results, appointments diary, note book, and so on. You choose what you want on your desktop and put it where you want. It occurred to us that we could do the same. Each of our digital objects represents a resource, and all we needed to do was work out a way of letting our user choose the resource she wanted. The key to doing this, we realized, was metadata. If we could figure out a way of labelling each of our many resources precisely, unambiguously, and usefully, then we could make it possible for our users to go directly to it. Other benefits came into view. If we did this right, we would not need to construct elaborate interfaces since we could rely on others to do this for us.

From the metadata, it would be possible to deduce what the resources we were providing were and how they are related to one other, and then to create various sophisticated interfaces levering that information into access routes through the data. This route meant that the resources themselves could be anywhere: all we would have to do would be to point at the resources through the metadata. Still better, we would not have to make all the metadata ourselves. With a little care, we could make it possible for others to create the metadata also. Indeed, we would not need to store the metadata on our own computers. The metadata and the resources could be anywhere; all we would need to do is read the metadata and access the resources. This sounds utopian, perhaps. But within the two major editorial projects with which we are most immediately concerned—the New Testament editions led by Birmingham and Münster scholars and the *Canterbury Tales* project editions led by myself and Barbara Bordalejo—we already have many individual scholars used to collaborating in the way this envisages. Nor can we see any outright technological bar to what we had in mind: there are already federated systems on the Web exchanging information millions of times a day, running searches, querying distributed databases, in ways that seemed directly analogous to what we had in mind. It seemed possible: at least, worth a try.

Here is not the space to describe fully our attempts (at the time of writing, very much in flux) to achieve these goals (Robinson 2007; Robinson 2009a). The reader may see where we have got to at the Virtual Manuscript Room, where she may also find documents spelling out the thinking behind this approach and how we are implementing it. We regard every fragment of a digital edition, even down to a single letter, as a distinct resource. In practice, we break the text into the smallest logical unit above a word (typically, a line of verse; a sentence of prose), we decompose the sources of the text (manuscripts, print editions) into pages, accessed both as digital images and as text transcripts. To every such fragment—a page image or transcript, a text transcript—we attach a metadata statement, precisely describing what that resource is. We say three or four things about every resource. First, we say these two things:

> 1) Its URI, the http:// Web address from which the resource may be retrieved
> 2) Its type. Is this is a digital image? (if so what resolution and how derived?) or a page transcript? (if so, to what standard of transcription?) or a description (as in a TEI <msDesc> element) or a commentary (textual, discursive, analytic)?

Then, we say one or both of the following:

> 3) For resources which are related to a text we identify precisely the text to which the resource relates (say, chapter 1, verse 1 of the Gospel of John, or the first line of the General Prologue of the *Canterbury Tales*)
> 4) For resources which are related to a text source we identify precisely the part of the text source (say, folio 2 verso of quire 18 of Codex Sinaiticus or folio 8 recto of the Hengwrt manuscript of the *Canterbury Tales*)

By grouping these statements we can say such things as "this resource is a digital image of folio 8 recto of the Hengwrt manuscript, and shows the text of lines xxx-yyy of the General Prologue of the Tales" or "this resource is a transcript of the text of lines xxx-yyy of the General Prologue of the Tales, as it appears on folio 8 recto of the Hengwrt manuscript." By packaging these statements into metadata and sending them to the Web, we can then allow suitably configured systems to find (for example) digital images of manuscript pages containing John 1:1, wherever they are on the Web, and to find transcripts of those pages matching those images. It should be evident how one could from this metadata find ways to identify all the manuscripts containing a particular text, the images of the pages actually with that text and the transcripts of those pages, and then give access to the corresponding resources.

It is too early to say whether the system we are developing will be adopted by others, or will remain (at best) a scholarly footnote, a curious experiment on a road to nowhere (rather, I fear, like the Anastasia software). But a few observations are in order. Whether or not others accept our system, the facilities upon which we have focused are needed, and will come to be implemented, in one form or other. You could see the scheme I here outline as an extension of the standard digital library toolset. Digital library systems are superb at storing single digital objects and their associated metadata: the quarto text of *Hamlet*, for example. They are not good at addressing particular fragments of the text (line 1 of scene 1 of *Hamlet* in the quarto) or of the text source (the digital image of the page holding that line), and not good at identifying precisely the characteristics of the resource (if it is a transcript: what type of transcript, done to what standard?). Digital library systems, in time, will come to do these things, and when they do, they will satisfy our needs. If they do so by building on the scheme I describe here, then our effort will have been well worthwhile. Even if all we achieve is to provoke others to do what we are trying to do, it will have been well worthwhile.

I have at least one reason for thinking we are moving in the right direction. In early discussions with the two programmers working on this system I said, half-jocularly, that the less code we had to write the more successful we would be. My idea was that given the ferment of development in the digital library and text encoding worlds in the last decades, the various parts of what we needed would already exist. Further, our aim must be to work "with the grain" and within existing frameworks. Not only would this make our task easier, but also it would considerably improve the chances of acceptance of our work by the communities we address. In the event, we think we can achieve what we want just by the creation of a very few data structures within XML encoding (essentially, some "unified identifier" attributes) and within a Resource Description Framework (RDF) ontology. For the rest, we can rely on standard Web systems, to harvest and search the metadata, and standard Web browsers to carry the results to the reader.

As I review what I have here written, I am astonished how far scholarly editing has travelled in two decades. In place of the highly ordered world of the single scholar making the single publication of the single work—a model which fits perfectly the patterns of credit and authority so familiar in the academy—something is appearing which is a good deal more chaotic, unsettled in its boundaries and uncertain in its end products. In the familiar paradigm, the edition is driven by the vision of a single editor: we need a new edition of work X, and I will make it, I will get the resources I need (copies of manuscripts, money and time) to make it, I will publish it with publisher Y. In the model now emerging, the making of the edition is not driven by the vision of a single editor. Rather, it is driven by the desire of many to understand and to explain. In the environment we are developing in Birmingham and Münster, a monastery can put up images of manuscript pages, a scholar can identify the text on those pages, and other scholars can transcribe, collate, and annotate the same text. This has many implications for editorial practice. In the past, the authority of editions has been derived from the authority of the editor. Collaborative editing cuts across this model, raising questions about the aims of the editions so made, about their reliability, about accrediting those who make the parts, and about the relationship between reader and editor. But these are subjects for other papers, indeed for many other papers.

WORKS CITED

Bulwer, John. 2005. Review of *The Teaching of Classics*, ed. James Morwood. *Scholia Reviews* ns 14: 13.

Hockey, Susan, and Nancy Ide, eds. 1996. *Research in Humanities Computing 4: Selected papers from the Association for Literary and Linguistic Computing-Association for Computing in the Humanities (ALLC-ACH) Conference at Christ Church College Oxford, April 1992*. Oxford: Clarendon Press.

Robinson, Peter. 2007. Current Directions in the Making of Digital Editions: Towards Interactive Editions. *Ecdotica* 4: 176–90.

_____ 2009a. Towards a Scholarly Editing System for the Next Decades. In *Sanskrit Computational Linguistics: Proceedings of the Third International Symposium, Hyderabad India, January 15–17 2009*, ed. Amba Kulkarni and Huet, 346–57. Lecture Notes in Computer Science / Lecture Notes in Artificial Intelligence. New York: Springer.

_____ 2009b. What Text Really is Not, and Why Editors Have to Learn to Swim. *Literary and Linguistic Computing* 24, no. 1 (April 1): 41–52.

Sperberg-McQueen, C. M., and Lou Burnard, eds. 1994. *Guidelines for Electronic Text Encoding and Interchange, P3*. Chicago: Text Encoding Initiative.

Stubb, Estelle, ed. 2000. *The Hengwrt Chaucer Digital Facsimile.* Leicester: Scholarly Digital Editions.

Sutherland, Kathryn, ed. 1997. *Electronic Text: Investigations in Method and Theory.* Oxford: Clarendon Press.

Open Access and Digital Libraries:
A Case Study of the Text Creation Partnership

Shawn Martin

University of Pennsylvania

shawnmar@pobox.upenn.edu

Many people operate under the assumption that Open/Closed Access is a binary proposition. Either the material is available to everyone on the Web or it is closed to a limited number of subscribers. The reality, however, is much more complicated. What is the use of a digital library, no matter how open, if it is unable to sustain and maintain itself over time? What is the point of a well-funded collection that is closed to the people who need it most? There are in fact many models for maintaining both Open and Closed Access digital libraries. Though the conversation often focuses on the furthest ends of the spectrum (greedy publishers extorting money to content, or, conversely, benevolent academics making knowledge freely available to the world via grants), there are in fact many models that are in between these extremes that exhibit characteristics of both Closed and Open Access models. In particular, the Text Creation Partnership (TCP) tries to work with commercial publishers to create a middle road between these extremes. By investigating the many types of Open and Closed Access models, and seeing how models like the TCP fit in this landscape, it is possible to make better determinations on how to build digital libraries in the future. How should the community come together to find a more moderate path, and what will that road look like?

Introduction

"In considering how best to organize the publishing side of scholarly communication, it will also be important to be open to new business models" (Unsworth 2006, 32). Most recently, many new business models being discussed revolve around Open Access, which, according to Peter Suber, means that the resource is "digital, online, free of charge, and free of most copyright and licensing restrictions" (Suber 2007). Recently, the discussion about Open Access has revolved around how open a resource is. On the one hand, most academic grant-funded projects are open and freely available to the world. Yet such projects often tend to be small in scope and dependent on the dedi-

ISBN 978-0-86698-021-0 (online)   ISBN 978-0-86698-449-2 (print)
New Technologies in Medieval and Renaissance Studies 2 (2010) 157–170

cation of one faculty member or research group at a particular university. On the other hand, commercially funded databases like Early English Books Online (EEBO) from ProQuest Information and Learning, among many others, tend to be extremely large in scope and less dependent on the commitment of faculty members. Nevertheless, commercially produced databases also tend to be very expensive and limited only to small numbers of people (those who belong to research institutions able to pay the large subscription fees required). So, ideally the academic community would like to have the best of both worlds, a large comprehensive database of research material that is open and freely available to the world. How is it possible to create such a thing?

The answer can be found in one word: sustainability. Any electronic resource, regardless of whether it is Open Access, cannot survive without monetary and community support. These two things are essential to sustainability, yet they are extremely elusive. The key is to create a business model that captures all of the desirable features and that, rather than falling toward one extreme (Closed Access commercial model) or the other (Open Access academic model), finds a middle ground in which the resource is mostly freely available and is sustainable over time. Many models have attempted this in various ways. Of course, the largest and most well known is Google Books, a massive digitization project that is now in the midst of legal settlements with the Authors' Guild, the Association of American Publishers, and many others about the exact nature of what can and cannot be scanned and given away freely. Additionally, national governments like France have sponsored national digital library programs like Gallica. Finally, there are projects driven by volunteer labour such as Project Gutenburg and its distributed proofreaders.

All of these projects have their strong points. Google especially may fundamentally change the way that scholars and librarians think about digital content creation. Nevertheless, much of the legal work is still in negotiation, and it remains to be seen how Google's digitization will affect electronic collections. Gallica is also intriguing, but not entirely applicable to countries like the United States where government funding of that magnitude seems unlikely. Project Gutenburg is a tremendous asset to the world but, it could be argued, has limited utility for advanced textual scholarship where it is paramount that the text be completely accurate and editions be verifiable. So, there is definitely more work to be done to discuss how projects like Google Books, Gallica, and Project Gutenburg are useful to scholarship, but largely outside the scope of this article. Rather, this paper will focus on the myriad of digitization projects now being undertaken by scholarly projects and libraries at universities primarily in the United States (and to an extent in the UK and Canada) and how to make such projects sustainable over time.

In the United States, as in other countries, there has been much talk recently about how to create such a model. Recently, Ithaka—an organization funded by the Mellon Foundation and dedicated to accelerating the productive uses of information technology for the benefit of higher education—released a report on sustainability and revenue models, which provides some guidance on this issue. It identified two large categories and several subcategories of revenue models (Guthrie, Griffiths, and Maron 2008). Though Ithaka's report is helpful in thinking about revenue models, it does not fully capture all of the arrangements that universities have made for scholarly resources, particularly in the humanities. Currently there seem to be at least eight broad types of model that universities have used for digital libraries in the humanities:

1) *Subscription* The university pays the publisher for access to a resource it has created.

2) *Ownership* The university pays the publisher for rights broader than just access to the resource it has created.

3) *Grants* The university gets a grant to pay for the creation of the resource it wants to use.

4) *Single Institution* The university supports creation of the resource it wants to use with internal funds.

5) *Multi-institution/Consortium* Multiple universities cooperate to build the resource they want to use.

6) *Publisher/Consortium* Universities cooperate with the publisher (usually a university press) to create a resource they want to use.

7) *Multi-institution/Endowment* Universities contribute to a common endowment for access to the resource they want to create and use.

8) *Multi-institution/Subscription* Universities pay the publisher a subscription to a resource they want to use and that eventually becomes Open Access.

By discussing the strengths and weaknesses of each of these models, particularly in the United States, and highlighting one particular model, the Text Creation Partnership (TCP) that employs aspects of all of these techniques, I hope to suggest how the community can arrive at a more complex picture of the ways in which the Open Access environment works.

Generally, arguments tend to discuss such models in a binary way like this:

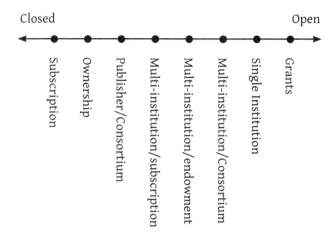

In reality, we need to adopt a more complex graph that would recognize that in addition to a resource being open or closed, it can also be sustainable or unsustainable. Therefore, a resource that is open might not be sustainable and a resource that is closed might be unsustainable. Such a graph might look something like this:

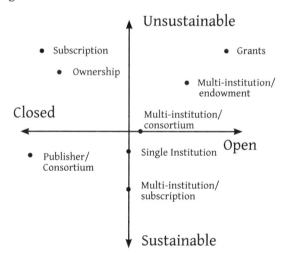

Ideally, any new project should try not to go to any of the extremes, but rather remain in the gray area between them. TCP is just one of the projects that attempts to do this, and, arguably could be a model for future digital library development.

TCP Background

In 1998, ProQuest Information and Learning published the Early English Books Online (EEBO) database containing images of virtually every book printed in England or in English between 1470 and 1700, amounting to roughly 125,000 titles, or in essence the works listed in the Short Title Catalogues I (Pollard and Redgrave) and II (Wing), the Thomason Tracts, and the English Tract Supplement. These were scanned images of their already existing microfilm collection. The publication of EEBO was naturally a major step forward in electronic availability of primary source titles. Nevertheless, at least for the University of Michigan library, it did not present a major step forward in holdings. The university library already held all of these titles in microfilm, and, although the ability to view individual titles from one's home computer, have multiple views of the same book, and so forth, were great access advantages, they did not add greatly to the existing collection.

Librarians at Michigan felt that the true value for this collection lay not in digital facsimiles, but in the possibility of full-text searching. It would allow researchers and students to search individual words or concepts across titles and engage with the sources in ways previously unimaginable. ProQuest saw the advantage of adding full text, but felt that the cost of converting these images into full text would be millions of additional dollars and add so tremendously to the price of the product that libraries would be unable to afford it. Thus the TCP project was born. Rather than taking no for an answer, the University of Michigan felt that it could get support for the creation of full-text versions for at least a subset of the EEBO collection. Under the leadership of Mark Sandler, then collection development officer at the University of Michigan Library, ProQuest agreed to partner with the University Library for the purpose of creating full text for a subset of 25,000 titles in the initial phase, with the understanding that the project might continue depending on the support it got (Sandler 2004).

Another important point to add about the TCP project is that it allowed both commercial publishers and academic libraries to compromise and get something they wanted. For libraries, it is important that these texts become publicly available to the world, not just paying subscribers. So, all of the texts that TCP creates will enter the public domain after a period of five years. During those five years, the commercial publishers have exclusive sales rights and the ability to develop specific tools to search the text that TCP creates. This creates a great opportunity for them to recoup their investment and generate new sales because of increased functionality.

What is unique about the TCP initiative though is not so much the partnership between private and public enterprises; rather, its unique structure and new prototype for cooperation between university libraries, the academic community, and commercial publishing is the most important aspect of the project. The TCP is not a traditional grant-funded project but a partner-funded initiative that seeks library contributions for the creation of full texts. Additionally, a full text that TCP creates is not just another product, but a benefit to the academic community because all the texts enter the public domain. So, in essence, universities are paying for texts which they own and will have the ability to distribute beyond their own campus communities rather than just having ownership of the file for their own local and restricted use, as they would for any other commercial product. This model has been largely successful with (at time of writing) nearly 20,000 texts available. In fact, it has been successful enough to be extended to two other similar commercial databases namely, Evans Early American Imprints, a collection of every work printed in Britain's American colonies and later the United States between 1639 and 1800 (based on the Evans Bibliography) available from Readex Incorporated, and Eighteenth Century Collections Online (ECCO), a database containing over 150,000 titles printed in Britain between 1700 and 1800 available from Thomson-Gale. EEBO-TCP has begun a second round of funding to complete the remaining 25,000 unique titles.

Essentially, how the model works is each partner institution according to its size contributes a set amount of money to the TCP and that contribution is matched by the commercial publisher. All of the money that is collected goes directly to creating texts. So the more money that is collected, the more texts the project is able to create, and the less expensive each text becomes for each contributing partner. In all, this model has allowed TCP to sustain a budget of about $1.4 million per year over approximately seven years, far more than any grant-funded or institutional model would be able to do. Also, these funds allow the project to create texts to a fairly high standard: each text is transcribed twice by two people working independently, then any discrepancies are corrected by a third person, and they are then reviewed by a group of experts from the University of Michigan, Oxford University, the University of Toronto, and the National Library of Wales. Though there are certainly some mistakes that slip through, the important thing is that each text is as accurate as it can be given the constraints that TCP faces.

It is hoped that the EEBO-TCP model can be extended even further to other similar collections. There are a few important caveats to this. Firstly, ECCO actually does already have some full-text searchability. Thomson-Gale used

Optical Character Recognition (OCR) software to generate text files from the images of books in its collection. Necessarily, whenever a printed page or the digital image of it was blurred, or either of them had the printed lines not quite horizontal, or contained unusual (such as non-Latin alphabet) characters, the OCR process produced imperfect results. Thus there is an argument that at least a portion of ECCO needs to be accurately transcribed for scholarly use. Secondly, only around 75,000 out of roughly 125,000 texts in EEBO will be transcribed by TCP. The remaining 50,000 titles are largely reprints or later editions of the same titles. Though some would argue that those titles need to be transcribed as well, in the majority of cases we would simply be reproducing an existing transcript, since in this period most reprints of books simply copied their predecessor edition without introducing significant changes. Since images are already available within EEBO to those scholars who need to see the small differences that were introduced in reprinting, transcriptions of such reprints are not a top priority. In all, these works comprise a seminal corpus of primarily English-language materials, although other languages are also included, and represent a wealth of primary source material for every avenue of scholarly endeavour. The TCP hopes to create a cross-searchable, public domain collection from these (and perhaps other) databases that will form a vast base of material for digital library development for many years to come.

Strengths and Weaknesses of Various Models

Generally all of the above models fit into two larger categories. First there is the commercial model, meaning products usually produced by publishers looking to sell access to the content. Second is the institutional model, meaning projects usually produced by faculty at a particular university and not seeking to raise income. Both of these larger models have subcategories, each with its own advantages and disadvantages. Nevertheless, TCP is a model that really does not fit into either category. Rather, it is a kind of hybrid model of which there are few examples. Though this model is complex, it is also more likely to be the kind of model which is successful in an increasingly complicated electronic environment.

Commercial models have the advantage of being able to produce large amounts of material in a relatively short amount of time. Because of the relatively large amount of money publishers have (compared to universities), the interface and database system usually have better functionality than those produced at universities. Also, commercial products have better marketing and outreach infrastructures behind them. So it is easier to get the word out about new developments. Yet, commercially produced databases also tend to restrict access, and sometimes very heavily. There tends to be less scholarly input in them, because of the amount of time it would take to involve multiple scholars and librarians, and commercial databases do not always improve their systems as technology changes because once a publisher has sold the content to a university and made a sufficient profit, it is in the publisher's interest to move on to new revenue-generating projects.

Examples of such commercial models would include the following:

> *Subscription* This is a model parallel in many ways to what libraries and publishers did in the print world. In essence, the library pays a subscription and the publisher then provides access to the campus community to a particular set of titles. This has the advantage of being a straightforward and familiar arrangement. However, as opposed to the print world, libraries actually do not own any of the content and are in essence renting it from a publisher. Therefore, librarians and the researchers that use them do not have the same abilities to copy, loan, or use electronic materials in the same way that they do with printed books.

> *Ownership* This model is similar to the subscription model. However, it allows libraries broader rights over particular materials. For instance under this kind of arrangement, a library might maintain rights to copy or print materials outside of the library or to make backup copies for the use of scholars and students.

Institutional models are familiar in humanities departments. Scholars are used to getting grants to complete a book or a project which results in an exhibition or special issue of a journal. In the digital world, these models have been migrated into funding online databases of primary resource materials, similar in some ways to commercial products like EEBO. These models have the advantage of being open to the world, have significant input from the scholarly community and are therefore of greater utility for scholars and students. Yet, they also tend to be fairly small and narrowly focussed. So they may be quite useful to scholars in particular areas of study, but not so useful to researchers outside of the field.

Examples of institutional models would be as follows:

> *Grants* This is probably the most common model within the humanities. A funding agency such as the U.S. National Endowment for the Humanities (NEH), the Social Sciences and Humanities Research Council of Canada (SSHRC) and the UK Joint Information Systems Committee (JISC) gives a set amount of money to a faculty member or group of faculty members to create a database of materials for their area. When that money has run out or the faculty member leaves, however, these projects often die or are unable to garner the same amount of interest that they once did.

> *Single Institution* This model is similar to grants in that an institution is giving money to a centre or program that in turn creates digital resource material. It is more stable than a grant because the institution generally makes a commitment to maintain the program over a long period of time. Nonetheless, institutional models still tend to be small and narrowly focussed because institutions do not have the same amount of purchasing power as a large commercial publisher.

These four models tend toward the extremes of the Open/Closed Access spectrum with institutional models on the open side and commercial ones toward the closed. Recently though, both publishers and universities have been experimenting with other kinds of models that attempt to combine aspects of both. Such experimenting allows economies of scale so that universities can create larger resources in a way similar to commercial publishers and permit these resources to remain open. Publishers, realizing the trends toward Open Access, have also collaborated with universities to create publishing models that they hope will allow them to make a profit while at the same time adhering to the demands of their customers.

Examples of these kinds of hybrid models include the following:

> *Multi-institution/Consortium* In this model, institutions come together to produce a large database of material. By pooling their resources, it is hoped that they will be able to rival large commercial publishers and to be able to maintain Open Access. The Open Content Alliance and the Internet Archive demonstrate some ways in which consortia of libraries are coming together to create electronic resources. These projects do have the advantage of creating larger collections but still tend not

to have the functionality of commercial databases because of their relative lack of expertise in interface design and back-end production.

Publisher/Consortium Most often, universities have collaborated with university presses and scholarly societies on projects like the Humanities E-Book project. Again these projects are larger than grant and institutional electronic resources and often will have better interfaces, but are still significantly smaller than large commercial databases.

Multi-institution/Endowment The most well-known example of this type of model is the Stanford Encyclopedia of Philosophy, which brings multiple institutions together to create an endowment which will then allow the encyclopaedia to be maintained in perpetuity. Though this model may work for some seminal resources in the humanities, it is also expensive and probably not sustainable. It would be impossible for the community to come together to support a similar endowment for every electronic resource needed for humanities research.

Multi-institution/Subscription This is the most common type of model for commercial publishers to come together. In this model, commercial publishers will charge a subscription for a certain amount of time and then release their materials into the public domain. Highwire Press at Stanford has tried this model. Though it remains to be seen how successful that particular project is, it has the potential to bring together the best of all possible worlds marrying the large content capabilities of commercial publishers with the academic and Open Access needs of universities.

How does the TCP model fit in with these models? It most closely resembles the *Multi-institution/Subscription* model, but it is much broader than that. TCP tries to negotiate the philosophical differences between commercial publishers and the academic community in order to achieve its goal. In general, the TCP tries to find a middle ground between all of these approaches. One of the more intriguing aspects of the model is that it gets the money to create the product. Rather than grant funding, which often is not sustainable over thousands of texts like this, the TCP has opted to let academic institutions, normally libraries but also departments and grant funds as well, contribute funds to the project, which are then matched by the commercial publishers. That money is used to fund text production, and the more institutions that join, the more text can be created, thus making each text less expensive.

Also, TCP is doing much more than creating another product. The University of Michigan is committed to university ownership, public domain access, and scholarly communication. Universities that are part of the TCP project actually own the texts and will eventually be able to distribute them beyond their own campus community. TCP is committed to working with scholars, librarians, publishers, and members of the community to ensure that the needs of all three are met, whether that means enhancing the interface, soliciting help for selection, or partnering with scholarly projects (Garrett 2002).

Sustainability

In essence, all of these models come down to sustainability. Institutional models often are highly useful to particular communities, but are not sustainable because they are very expensive compared to commercial products of similar scope, and such projects are usually dependent on the energy of a single faculty member. It would be impossible to build a universal digital library using multimillion dollar grants to create scholarly editions of every single book. Likewise, commercially produced databases are unsustainable because the subscription fees they charge are unaffordable by the universities that require them. As a result, projects like Google Books are filling the void. Models like the TCP could certainly work with a Google library (Martin 2008). The key is making any model of electronic resource sustainable. In order for a project to be sustainable it has to have enough money; in order to have enough money there needs to be a large enough audience to support a project monetarily; in order for there to be a large enough audience, there has to be a broad enough range of material to support such an audience; in order to create so broad a range of material, there needs to be a standardized procedure for creating it; in order to create a standardized procedure, one has to sacrifice some of the editorial work available in many scholarly projects. TCP has been very successful in most of these factors, though it still struggles with how to get greater support among libraries and the scholarly community.

One of the main problems all digital libraries face is money. It is important that all projects realize how expensive a digital library is to create. The figures from TCP show that to complete 41,000 texts (approximately 20% of the entire collection in EEBO, Evans, and ECCO) will cost approximately $13 million. For TCP to create full texts for the entire collection of roughly 300,000 texts would cost over $100 million. These figures also do not count the ongoing costs of maintenance and preservation, which will likely need to be borne by institutions in the future. Though TCP's costs are perhaps not applicable to all types of digital libraries, they indicate that the cost of creating an electronic collection is higher than any grant, single institution, or combination thereof is likely to be able to generate. Digital libraries of the future will need to generate large amounts of capital and will probably need to seek it among multiple institutions and from the commercial sector. TCP is just one way of doing this.

The EEBO collection is unique in that it contains nearly every book published between 1470 and 1700. Therefore it is of use not just to literary scholars but also to historians, legal scholars, and many others in all disciplines of the humanities. As a community we need to look for broad ranges of material that will be useful to large numbers of people. Google has already done this for a large number of books. Yet, it seems unlikely that they will be able to digitize the vast amount of rare book and manuscript material available. What are some efficient ways of digitizing this material collaboratively and in large enough quantities to create a sustainable audience? TCP may provide some answers here, for one of its successes has been the standardized workflows it uses. All of the staff at the Universities of Michigan, Oxford, and Toronto, the National Library of Wales, and other projects that cooperate with TCP, adhere to the same principles of text creation. There is a standard way TCP creates text, a common philosophy under which we operate, and a standard editorial policy used for all texts. These are working documents not meant to produce a standard *per se*. Rather, they are constantly evolving ways of thinking as staff at the TCP find new problems.

The key to these constant struggles between collaboration and centralization, or standardization and meeting individual needs, has been TCP's desire to seek a middle ground between seemingly opposed and entrenched positions. Many scholarly projects seek to create a highly edited and tagged corpus of material for a specific group of scholarly users. Though these projects unquestionably offer the best for scholars in those disciplines, they cost a great deal of money and produce a very small number of titles. TCP on the other hand produces many more texts than smaller projects like it have done. Though it is true that TCP texts are produced to a much lower standard of metadata and, therefore, are less useful to scholars than a highly tagged text would be, TCP does not aim to be a project useful only to particular groups within the humanities community. Rather the project seeks to provide a foundation for other groups to build upon. The foundation is the basic structural tagging TCP provides, the largely accurate transcriptions, and the standards-based text all done to a particular and overt philosophy.

Conclusion

In the digital world, there seems to be a divergence of opinion between the commercial and non-profit worlds about how to create content and how to create sustainable publishing. Large electronic publishing operations like Google are digitizing content on a massive scale with the hope of making money from advertising, selling chapters in print, or otherwise commercializing small pieces of content for niche markets. For a large corporation, the considerable investment needed for mass digitization would seem to be returned by the potential long-tail income from selling advertising and print-on-demand services to a large number of niche markets. For non-profit organizations, however, and particularly universities, publishing models tend to focus on small niche markets and make investments in digitizing small amounts of material (manuscripts, collections of books); the cost of doing this far outweighs the potential income they may generate. Since all universities are grappling with economic downturn, shrinking budgets, and increasing costs, it no longer seems likely that they will be able to sustain investment on this scale. Nonetheless, universities, unlike large corporations, have an important mandate to disseminate information, which by its very nature is of negligible market value, though it may be of extremely high intellectual value. How do we deal with these issues which seem to be pulling universities in two directions?

The Text Creation Partnership is just one possible model that attempts to balance these competing forces. It has sought to maintain a middle way by which Open and Closed Access can work together and in which commercial and academic interests can be promoted side by side. If nothing else, it serves as an example of how the library, scholarly, and publishing communities can come together in order to find common solutions. No scholarly project will ever match the size of a commercial database, and no commercial database will ever have the editorial apparatus of a scholarly project. Grant funded scholarly projects and other similar Open Access projects serve their purposes, and commercial databases serve theirs. In the wake of increasing pressure from the commercial world, it is essential that the academic community comes together to create models that satisfy the needs of as many constituents as possible. In many ways, what we are discussing is how to create an entirely new infrastructure for scholarship in the electronic world. Though that is too broad a question for just one essay, it is hoped that by looking at one particular project, it will be possible to contribute in the creation of a solution.

WORKS CITED

Garrett, Jeffrey. 2002. Casting a Wide Net: The Early English Books Project Meets at Northwestern. *College & Research Libraries News* 63, no. 2 (February): 117–19.

Guthrie, Kevin, Rebecca Griffiths, and Nancy Maron. 2008. Sustainability and Revenue Models for Online Academic Resources. May. http://www.jisc.ac.uk/media/documents/themes/eresources/sca_ithaka_sustainability_report-final.pdf.

Martin, Shawn. 2008. To Google or Not to Google, That Is the Question: Supplementing Google Book Search to Make It More Useful for Scholarship. *Journal of Library Administration* 47, no. 1 & 2: 141–50.

Sandler, Mark. 2004. New Uses for the World's Oldest Books: Democratizing Access to Historic Corpora. *Association of Research Libraries (ARL) Bimonthly Report* 232 (February): 4-6.

Suber, Peter. 2007. Open Access Overview. http://www.earlham.edu/~peters/fos/overview.htm.

Unsworth, John. 2006. "Our Cultural Commonwealth": The Report of the American Council of Learned Societies Commission on Cyberinfrastructure for the Humanities and Social Sciences. http://www.acls.org/uploadedFiles/Publications/Programs/Our_Cultural_Commonwealth.pdf.

From Edition to Experience:
Feeling the Way towards User-Focussed Interfaces

Paul Vetch

King's College London

paul.vetch@kcl.ac.uk

A significant impact of technology on traditional academic practice has been its tendency to force us to critically re-evaluate that practice. The process of creating digital editions is forcing us to confront the question of what is an edition, and from a much higher altitude than might normally be the case since we now consider not only the question of the content but also the form of the edition: the manner and nature of its presentation. Bound up with this is the question of affordance (what we will allow the user to do), which is a consideration scarcely, if at all, applicable to a traditional print edition. This additional dimension was inherent to the advent of hypertext, but the question of affordance, considered in the context of the Internet as it is today, rather than in its nascent form in the early 1990s, is very much more suggestive. Whilst users have always to some extent been the architects of their own experiences on the Internet, increasingly this is true in a more significant, and yet a more subtle, way. Dynamic, complex applications now routinely permit users to customize their experience of a website by altering the form as well as the content of what they see.

I will argue that the visual and functional design and implementation of the Web interface for a scholarly digital edition are deserving of greater significance than has previously been the case and are fundamental to the materiality of the Web as a publishing medium. (I use "scholarly digital edition" in the broadest possible sense, beyond the "textual edition" *per se*.) I shall suggest that the phenomenon of editable and mutable Web interfaces (relatively recent when seen in the context of the history of humanities computing) makes the user's interaction with any digital publication more nuanced than previously, and that the creation of electronic scholarly resources and the interfaces that give them expression must therefore be critically re-evaluated. We must attend to the changing expectations and habits of users, based on their increasing exposure to, and experience of, different idioms of Web publication. In part, my aim here is to try to explore exactly what it means to be user-focussed now. This is a pragmatic assessment grounded in the mechanics of building Web interfaces, from the point of view of the

ISBN 978–0–86698–021–0 (online)   ISBN 978–0–86698–449–2 (print)

New Technologies in Medieval and Renaissance Studies 2 (2010) 171–184

latest technologies and approaches involved and of the ways in which users respond to them. I report below on a recent body of user-needs analyses
specifically designed to test this. I cannot engage here with the substantial
body of critical work furthering the conception of the digital edition itself,
although I acknowledge its importance and relevance in the context of what
follows (Sutherland 2008).

One of my starting points for this analysis stems from development work and
follow-up research that John Bradley and I carried out (Bradley and Vetch
2007) for the Online Chopin Variorum Edition (OCVE). A surprising outcome
of this work, which included a prototype tool for Web-based annotation, was
the way that the tool we built was used. This was a case where an interaction model and usage paradigm emerged that was quite different from what
was designed or envisaged. The tool intended for end users was used by
the project's scholarly team as a pragmatic means of attaching a granular,
highly specific critical commentary to particular points in the musical scores
that the project published online. Although this was a pilot project, never
meaningfully used outside the immediate project team, this unexpected use
of our tool gave the scholarly apparatus the same conceptual status as annotations added by members of the public. This showed that the practical
consideration of being able to annotate the source material atomically (by
attaching notes to the precise point(s) in the music to which they referred)
was compelling enough for the musicology scholars that the status of the
apparatus—in effect, just another set of user-contributed content and not
specially privileged—was of little or no concern. Two interrelated questions
arising from this fall firmly within the philosophy of User Centred Design
(UCD). The first is "how can we better understand our users and build interfaces that satisfy their needs?" and the second, "how can we better integrate
and align digital publications and tools with the way our users carry out their
research?"

Scholarly interfaces: The status quo

In many ways digital editions have changed little in the modes of engagement they offer to their users. Whilst our understanding and use of the underlying technologies for markup and textual fidelity, storage, text-mining,
data modelling and classification have considerably evolved since the early
days of SGML corpora on CD-ROM, our ambitions for the form and display
of digital editions have, in relative terms, progressed modestly. There have
been, however, two key shifts: firstly in the constantly changing conceptions
of what a digital edition should be and do, in large part catalysed by the

steady transition of digital editions to publication online; and secondly, in attempts to align the design of digital publications more closely to the practice
and process of scholarly research. So far, we have tended to see developments along these lines expressed in two ways: the ability to *control* what
is visible, and in the provision of *tools*. Users are able to choose their own
perspective (albeit within predefined parameters), for example, by showing
or hiding different texts, and selecting from different editorial views of texts
(including the hiding of overt editorial apparatus), effectively giving them a
degree of editorial control or responsibility by allowing them to privilege a
certain reading path. See, for illustration of this, the Online Chopin Variorum
Edition and Woolf Online.

Tools typically allow users to do more of their work online or within the
context of the resource itself, making the process of using a digital resource
more natural, and better orientating a resource towards use in a pedagogic
context. Examples might include the ability to annotate (see for example
British History Online or the Digital Image Archive of Medieval Music),
"lightbox" functionality that allows close viewing of images without leaving
current page (see the Shahnama Collection), the ability to save search queries and results (see the Clergy of the Church of England Database), and more
broadly the provision of a richer set of contextual (and contextually sensitive) secondary material. The trend is towards devolution of responsibility to
the end users by giving them the ability to create customized reading paths,
together with the provision of functionality designed to make the scholarly
publication more useful or convenient within its immediate context. These
developments represent significant progress from the early days of digital
publishing, but they do not constitute a deep engagement with the possibilities afforded by the second generation Web. In popular culture, a digital
edition is simply an electronic surrogate of an existing object (where edition
means version), or a "remediation" (Bolter and Grusin 1999). As has been
extensively argued elsewhere, scholarly digital editions have yet fundamentally to break away from this model of surrogacy.

Part of the problem may be that many of the vexed characteristics of Web
2.0 entail issues that affect all modes of academic discourse: copyright pro-
tection and intellectual property, authorship/anonymity/credit, credibility,
and stability. And yet, it is also clear that many of the newer modes of interaction that we see expressed on the Web have a transformative potential for
the way we actually carry out research. Instant publication, always-available
taxonomies and reference tools, and Web-based version control offer modes
of scholarly interaction bounded only by the imagination. This transforma-

tive potential is already being realized by scholars who are technically aware enough to perceive it and confident enough in the technology and their own competence to want to experiment. Thus change is happening only on a personal level, not an institutional or disciplinary one.

The near-anarchy of the second generation Web as a publishing environment seems to be a particularly hostile environment for scholarship and in many ways represents the antithesis of long-established practice. A Web 2.0 resource is often mutable and ephemeral, may be experimental (or indeed expendable), and its functionality and the associated terminology (such as wiki, blog, and mash-up) consciously evokes associations of anti-intellectualism and populism. Andrew Keen famously put forward the specious idea that learned resources are devalued by the participation and the contribution of amateurs and non-specialists (Keen 2007). An even more pressing consideration is sustainability. Full adoption of new approaches for creating Web interfaces means buying into the use of edgier, more labour-intensive and potentially more burdensome development techniques as we attempt to squeeze every last drop of functionality from the Web browsers that deliver them, often at the expense of existing standards, such as they are. It is fair to say we do not yet know what the long-term implications of this will be for Web-based scholarly resources.

The second generation Web

The development of the Internet as a publishing environment over the course of the last five years has taken almost all parties by surprise, not least end users. As a result, our understanding of exactly how communication works on the Internet, and the subtleties of human computer interaction involving rich Internet applications, has struggled to keep up. What were once rigid parameters for Web publication—as determined primarily by the capabilities of user agents, and by the design of HTTP, HTML, and associated early standards—have come to constitute an ever-weakening barrier to development and creativity that, almost incredibly, flourishes despite these dated technical foundations, and sees Web users routinely exposed to new modes and moments of interaction on the Web. The term Web 2.0 has come to embody not simply the technical approaches that have enabled this new dimension of Web usage (which is of course the sense for which it was originally coined), but also, in a much broader and often an unhelpfully nebulous way, it has come to denote the concomitant changes in usage paradigms. These are often implicitly codified in terms of polar opposition to what has gone before: the fluid, dynamic, open, free-form, empowering, and personal are set against now pejorative terms such as static, closed, institutional, and read-only.

The Internet today represents at once a uniquely volatile, highly creative and experimental development environment. New resources spring up which become animate and vital only when people use them; without sufficient attention, they wither and die unnoticed. Standards have been pushed to their absolute limits as the Web has continued to seep out of its originally well-defined domain, hungry for the richer, more expressive heritage of capabilities (including user interface metaphors and conventions) known to us from the Graphical User Interface (GUI) operating environments packaged with operating systems.

Technology accelerating the pace of change

The building blocks for creating richer Web interfaces are well-established, as evidenced by the increasing prevalence of JavaScript on the client side, and development toolkits using Asynchronous JavaScript and XML (Ajax), which works on the client and server to pull or push data to or from a Web page without the page being conspicuously reloaded. Since about 2006, thanks both to major industry players such as Google and Yahoo, and also the Web developer community at large, developers have had extensive access to what are called JavaScript frameworks, which assist in the development of complex interactions for Web pages. Use of such a framework greatly simplifies development and promotes reliability across different Web browsers, and their rapid uptake has largely contributed to the explosion of richer interfaces on the Internet.

Indeed, one of the most notable trends here has been an emphasis on simplicity and abstraction. Many of the JavaScript frameworks (notably JQuery and *Prototype*) have developed in the form of metalanguages or configuration languages of a sort, the syntax of which serves to divorce cause and effect by hiding the programmatic heavy lifting from the Web developer. This means that it is now quite practical for a traditional Web designer or developer—typically conversant in the languages used to encode and style Web pages, such as (X)HTML and CSS, but not programming languages such as JavaScript—to begin incorporating into their work quite radically different modes of engagement, far beyond the simple interaction inherent to hypertext. Equally, now that JavaScript, as a component of Ajax, connects Web interface and server in a fluid way, the task of working with it also falls within the purview of server-side programmers and developers.

As a result of this effort to standardize JavaScript usage, it is tantalizingly simple to add powerful (or just plain fun) functionality to a Web application. More than ever before the impulse to enhance functionality is too compelling for developers to resist. But back-end programmers and Web developers too are seldom skilled interaction designers, and the child in the sweetshop can quickly become a bull in a china shop. Donald Norman rightly predicted a period of over-enthusiasm in this regard, and his comments accurately characterize the state of Web interfaces today in which "everything shimmers, where panels shrink and expand, where you will never know whether to left click, right click, or center click" (Norman 2006, 71). Operating system GUIs are now in their 20th or 30th generation, and their complex Human Computer Interaction (HCI) gestures have arisen out of years of research, development, refinement, and feedback from users. Complex Web 2.0 applications have typically made clumsy borrowings from these established and accepted conventions and they interpret them poorly because browsers were simply not designed to be vehicles for some of the things we are making them do. The result is that the gestures we ask users to perform become in essence meta-metaphors: a set of movements that users are familiar with performing in different contexts but which involve slightly different actions and produce slightly different results in each case. Whilst some Web applications have made good use of techniques such as drag and drop or zooming via the mouse wheel, the similarity between actions performed inside and outside the context of a Web browser can become a source of confusion and frustration for end users (Bradley and Vetch 2007).

As the point of interconnection between our experiences online and our personal computing microcosm, Web browsers have shown themselves to be poorly equipped to support the kinds of environment that developers are striving to create. Web browser development is slower and more complex than Web application development, so this is not surprising. The most recent browser enhancements show the continued development of the Web as a melting pot for a variety of practices rather than favouring a particular set of clear improvements. The Firefox Web browser—upgraded every month or two for the past few years—has concentrated development effort on the support for its extension (or, Add-on) mechanism, giving developers the ability to add the functionality that they choose. The innovative and progressive WebKit application framework (the basis for a number of popular browsers, including Apple's Safari) has focused, at a much lower level, on a rewrite of its JavaScript engine, primarily for reasons of performance; this is an overt acknowledgement of newly increased importance and prevalence of Java-Script in Web application development.

These decisions reveal that the browser developers and designers have a much less clear (and certainly a less deterministic) stance on what exactly a Web browser is for than was formerly the case. The focus is now on privileging the improvement of the browser as an adaptable and robust development environment. Notable too is the fact that these concessions benefit advanced users and Web developers—those spearheading the changing nature of the Web—more than they do average Web users. One long-term study of the way in which users interact with Web pages and browsers shows that the extension facility in Firefox is proving too demanding for most users and is therefore not commonly used (Weinreich et al. 2008). Improvements in JavaScript promise tangible benefits for developers in the shorter term, but not necessarily for end users. One possible exception here is accessibility: browsers are slowly becoming better at handling the inherent statelessness of complex JavaScript applications and the departures from established convention this approach can entail, most often manifested, to date, in a broken "back" button, or when creating bookmarks.

Usability and the end-user experience

The Internet experience, enriched by the technologies I have described, is more potent and fluid than it used to be. But it is beset by a paucity of conventions, the immaturity of its design models for interaction, and a dearth of solid research. The result is that despite these technologies it is a good deal harder to build a successful Web publication now than it has been in the past. We continue to make assumptions about our users' behaviour, partly as a conceit to make the design of an application—which must operate within finite parameters and within fixed dimensions—a realistic and manageable process. Typically these assumptions form the basis for the design of a set of predetermined encounters, which might comprise a combination of a series of fixed perspectives of data on the screen, and an interaction model that determines the way in which the user can move between those perspectives and modify them. Each of these encounters is typically arrived at by a process of visual design (expedited with wireframe diagrams or storyboards) and interpreted by developers into a representation of action possibilities. This is transmitted over the Internet to a client browser or other user agent, where the act of displaying the page may remove or obscure some of these action possibilities, depending upon the capabilities and age of the browser. Here the action possibilities are finally delivered for interpretation by end users, who may not recognize all of the actions available to them, depending on their competence and experience with the Internet at large.

Jakob Nielsen predictably complained that early Web 2.0 websites were "neglecting some of the principles of good design and usability" (Nielsen 2007). Those principles are his ten usability heuristics (Nielsen 1994), which have remained largely unchanged and unchallenged since first articulated and form a cornerstone for inspecting and assessing the usability of websites. Nielsen commented: "The idea of community, user generated content and more dynamic web pages are not inherently bad in the same way, they should be secondary to the primary things sites should get right" (Nielsen 2007). Nielsen qualified his comments by distinguishing social networking sites as somehow "other," but the popularity of newer websites—in many cases predicated solely on the capabilities flagged by Nielsen as secondary—casts the usefulness of his heuristics as the sole measure of efficacy into doubt.

The body of research investigating usability in second generation Web applications is notably small, however one recent study at Lancaster University set out "to explore social networking sites such as Facebook in order to understand their recent success and popularity" (Hart et al. 2008, 471). Their methodology was to test Facebook against Nielsen's heuristics, capturing how users were engaging with it and their perspectives on their experiences. Their findings reveal that despite scoring poorly in a heuristic evaluation, Facebook was perceived by 85% of the test participants be easy or very easy to use, which result is borne out by the focus group I report on below. Users enjoy Facebook in spite of its numerous failings according to the Nielsen guidelines, and the authors infer a need for "more holistic approach, with ... new design guidelines to support the modern day web experience" (Hart et al. 2008, 474). These new design guidelines remain undefined, but this conclusion gestures towards a very significant shift in thinking about how websites communicate with users. This shift is oriented toward the experiential: in other words, giving equal consideration to both the mode of engagement and the moment of encounter. Sure enough other work in HCI is beginning to explore the significance of aesthetic, hedonic, and ludic factors in our relationship with websites (Van Schaik and Ling 2008).

In the present context, the work reported by Hart et al. has to be qualified by attention to the peculiar nature of Facebook, use of which is a leisure activity in its own right. Nevertheless this example highlights a number of the aspects of current Web interface development:

1) In the past, usability definitions have been predicated upon the existence of an identifiable and clear purpose in the user. This is no longer a given because the tools and possibilities offered to users (those subject to usability inspection) may never have existed before and may therefore constitute a set of activities that a user might never even have anticipated performing. Formal usability heuristics focussed on a set of expected atomic behaviours are inappropriate here.

2) How users feel about what they are doing is at least as important as the processes they perform. The experience at the moment of the encounter may be more important to the user than the efficacy of the mode of engagement.

Despite the absence of a holistic approach to designing websites, creativity in Web development and user experience grows apace. For now, best practice requires that we be guided by the success and failure of interfaces developed by others, often for quite different purposes or audiences, and that the design processes employed in interface design remain largely unchanged.

Feeling the way forward: Out of the Wings

Out of the Wings (more formally known as Spanish and Spanish American Theatres in Translation) is a three-year research project funded by the United Kingdom's Arts and Humanities Research Council (AHRC) from 2008 to 2011. The aim is to provide a website offering an unprecedented breadth of information on Spanish and Spanish American theatre, including contextual materials such as play synopses, sample translation, performance histories, and production notes. A secondary goal is to create and provide via the Web a human resource database, giving comprehensive information about translators, writers, key practitioners, and scholars. The project does not aim to reproduce play texts or sources; its goal is to bring together a body of dynamic paratextual material designed to stimulate new studies and performances of well-known play texts, and to raise the profile of those outside the traditional canon of Hispanic Studies.

The project's subtitle makes claims to the ambition of creating a Virtual Research Environment, and a stated aim is the investigation and development of approaches that will allow for dialogic rather than one-way knowledge transfer, "with the intention of creating a self-sustaining and constantly renewing resource," as stated in the Case for Support. The project was born of a realisation of the potential for newer, Web 2.0 modes of interaction, encompassing the continued growth of the performance histories and production notes data and the growth of the human resources database to its logical conclusion as the basis for a community of practice.

The project team is acutely aware of the risks associated with this sort of approach, especially regarding the scholarly credibility of research disseminated on a website in the context of material added by end users, and the difficulty of assessing whether it is viable to rely on such a user community to sustain the resource in the long term. As a first step towards understanding how best to manage these risks, a User Centred Design approach was adopted. A programme of user-needs analyses was organized to coincide with the launch of the project in September 2008, the data gathered from which is available on the project website. Two activities took place. The first was a focus group of eight participants chosen to represent the likely user constituency for the resource, and the second was a broader survey questionnaire distributed to attendees of the launch. The focus group participants brought with them a combination of perspectives, in several cases combining roles as theatre professionals (actors, dramaturgs, and a director), translators, academics, and representatives of the publishing industry. All of the participants thought of themselves as competent, experienced users of the Web for research, although there were no self-declared experts or advanced Web users within the group.

Our aims were firstly to gain a better understanding of the information-seeking behaviour of those interested in Spanish and Spanish American theatre, and secondly to test the level of experience with, and prevailing attitudes towards, Web 2.0 concepts and trends. The questionnaire collected data on the exposure to and awareness of specific Web 2.0 technologies and gauged reactions to a set of attitude statements concerning potential features for the eventual Spanish Theatres website. The exercise revealed that in almost all cases, and as a general principle, users had developed a well-defined tendency to treat Internet-derived information with suspicion, and this suspicion was heightened where user-contributed content was present. Reasons for this included a general perception of Web-derived material as untrustworthy as well as specific cases from past experience where users had seen that data was incomplete or inaccurate, giving the impression that a website was unreliable.

Participants were alive to the risks of what one called the Wikipedia syndrome, in which a resource is corrupted with falsehoods either out of malice or ignorance. Although generally participants agreed that academic websites were creditable as sources, there was fear that an academic institution being sponsor or creator of a Web resource would confer a spurious air of reliability, as respondents had seen happen with other projects. An overriding concern was the lack of peer review, and for one user this was tellingly a process that needed to take place "outside of the parameters of Internet technology." Despite these objections, participants appreciated the value of user-contributed data for the Spanish Theatres project, given its very clear emphasis on bringing obscure plays into the mainstream and promoting new performances and interpretations that could be recorded on the site to make it a living archive of performance history and critical practice. Participants were aware of the problem of sustainability and grasped the benefits and risks of the user-contribution model from this point of view.

The focus group participants gravitated towards a solution based on a compromise between the academic imprimatur and user input. Although there was debate about how user input might be moderated and validated, the importance of this diminished if such content was detached from the website data itself, but nevertheless visible in mutual context. Indeed, the apposition of peer-reviewed articles with user-inputted material was seen as helpful. The model sketched out by the participants was in essence a combination of a blog commenting mechanism, allowing for free text and links, and a more fully featured (but essentially context-less) traditional threaded forum including the ability to upload documents and audio-visual media. When prompted to think about their motivation for contributing material to the website, participants identified self-interest as well as altruism, since it may serve to retain an individual's work for later consultation.

There was a high degree of interest expressed for website features that would passively expose interconnections or potential lines of further enquiry, and make the underlying data more accessible. Participants expressed the view that the search mechanism should privilege simplicity and speed, and be highly forgiving, allowing for the entry of terms in Spanish or English without needing to be told. They felt also that searching ought also to be tolerant of spelling mistakes, with the British Library catalogue cited as an example of good practice. The serendipity created by auto-generated recommendations or suggestions was familiar to users from other contexts (such as the bookseller Amazon, but in a more directly relevant way at dictionary.com) and considered desirable, and users imagined seeing passive suggestions of other information related by formal metadata (author, translation status, availability of original text), by string similarity, and according to the usage patterns of other users.

Participants thought that the opportunities afforded them by Web technologies lay in approaches that would help them to traverse large bodies of information efficiently and enable them to see connections within data at a macroscopic level, rather than in providing tools that would allow them to examine data and sift it in microscopic detail. In large part, users seemed to expect this behaviour because it mirrored their experience elsewhere on the Web. This was further indicated by the notable lack of enthusiasm for tools or functions that would allow users actively to customize their experience of the resource, for example by choosing or hiding the information they saw. One user preferred simple websites because they "absolve you from the chore *of organising* a page." This is an area in which Web developers and end users have clearly parted company in recent years.

A way forward: Recruiting the second generation Web for scholarship

Many of the theories advanced on the status and nature of the digital scholarly edition are, I believe, either not engaging with the facts or are premised on a tacit assumption that the medium itself and its delivery mechanisms are more or less stable. This is almost entirely the reverse of the truth: the Web, as a delivery mechanism, is a complex system relying upon components and processes whose technical bases continue to evolve and are, in some cases, in a state of near radical flux. Use of the Internet is now ubiquitous, not least as an established pastime and leisure activity, and the capabilities of users grow and adapt as they are exposed to an increasingly diverse and imaginative set of websites. The success stories amongst the current generation of popular Web applications have almost invariably created the very needs they serve, firstly by the mere fact of their existence and secondly as a function of their popularity. This is a pattern illustrative of a very curious form of reciprocal altruism, and numerous arguments have been advanced as to why this might come about (Carr 2006; Weiss 2006). Equally however this is a pattern which begins with huge numbers of visitors; online scholarly publications (at least as we conceive of them for the moment) simply have no chance of achieving the critical mass of users that sustains resources such as Wikipedia.

Finding a way forward for scholarly publication requires us to better understand the medium itself, and this means developing a more sensitive conception of how and from where our user constituency draws its cues as to the status and credibility of a Web publication, and how its experiences on the Web at large inform its expectations. With this understanding in place, we will be better placed to strike an appropriate balance along the dual axes of what is possible versus what is desirable and of what is useful versus what is necessary. Digital publications should then evolve into an expression of this nuanced and informed understanding. It should also be clear that even when these precautions are taken, there can be no guarantee of success on the second generation Web. We need seriously to reconcile ourselves to the possibility that online publication, as an inherently risky activity, needs to be allowed to fail from time to time. This in turn means thinking of digital editions not as deliverables or outputs like monographs, but rather in terms more of process than product. This will allow for the possibility of failure as well as for the possibility of an (in theory) endlessly expendable resource, and recognising the value of what we, as creators (or initiators) of online scholarly publications, and our users, gain from the experience.

WORKS CITED

Bolter, J. David, and Richard A Grusin. 1999. *Remediation: Understanding New Media.* Cambridge, MA: MIT Press.

Bradley, John, and Paul Vetch. 2007. Supporting Annotation as a Scholarly Tool: Experiences from the Online Chopin Variorum Edition. *Literary and Linguistic Computing* 22, no. 2: 225–42.

Carr, Nicholas. 2006. Sharecropping the long tail. Blog. *Rough Type.* December 19. http://www.roughtype.com/archives/2006/12/sharecropping_t.php.

Hart, Jennefer, Charlene Ridley, Faisal Taher, Corina Sas, and Alan Dix. 2008. Exploring the Facebook Experience: A New Approach to Usability. In *The Association for Computing Machinery (ACM) International Conference Proceedings* 358: 471–74.

Keen, Andrew. 2007. *The Cult of the Amateur: How Today's Internet Is Killing Our Culture and Assaulting Our Economy.* London: Nicholas Brealey.

Nielsen, Jakob. 1994. Heuristic Evaluation. In *Usability Inspection Methods*, ed. Jakob Nielsen and Robert L. Mack, 25–62. New York: Wiley.

_____ 2007. Web 2.0 [is] "Neglecting Good Design." Interview. May 14. http://news.bbc.co.uk/1/hi/technology/6653119.stm.

Norman, Donald. 2006. Emotionally Centred Design. *Interactions* 13, no. 3 (June): 53–71.

Sutherland, Kathryn. 2008. Being Critical: Paper-Based Editing and the Digital Environment. In *Text Editing, Print and the Digital World*, ed. Marilyn Deegan, 13–25. Digital Research in the Humanities. Aldershot: Ashgate.

Van Schaik, Paul, and Jonathan Ling. 2008. Modelling User Experience with Web Sites: Usability, Hedonic Value, Beauty and Goodness. *Interacting With Computers* 20, no. 3 (May): 419–32.

Weinreich, Harald, Hartmut Obendorf, Eelco Herder, and Matthias Mayer. 2008. Not Quite the Average: An Empirical Study of Web Use. *Association for Computing Machinery Transactions on the Web* 2, no. 1 (February): Article 5.

Weiss, Taly. 2006. Free Riding is Taking Place at Web 2.0. Blog. *Trendspotting*. December 27. http://www.trendsspotting.com/blog/?p=1.

The Book of English:
Towards Digital Intertextuality and a Second-Generation Digital Library

Martin Mueller
Northwestern University
martinmueller@northwestern.edu

In this essay I make a case for a project that consists of three distinct but overlapping components. The first is an English Diachronic Digital Annotated Corpus (EDDAC), in which

> 1) each individual text is an accurate transcription of an edition of some standing, is explicit about its provenance, and wherever possible is linked to a digital facsimile of its print source;
>
> 2) the texts exist in the public domain, which in practice and for the foreseeable future limits such a corpus to texts published between 1473, the date of William Caxton's *Recuyell of the Historyes of Troye*, the first printed book in English, and James Joyce's *Ulysses* (1922), which barely precedes the copyright cut-off date of 1923;
>
> 3) the texts are designed as intereditions, meaning that they will support a high level of digital intertextuality so that any subset of texts from this archive can be readily compared with any subset or the whole archive for a variety of literary, linguistic, historical, philosophical, or rhetorical purposes, whether directly or through the metadata associated with them. In practice this involves treating the texts as a linguistic corpus that adds part-of-speech tagging and consistent structural encoding to the traditional bibliographical metadata for a text.

Think of such a corpus as a Book of English or cultural genome, a metaphor to which I will return from a variety of perspectives. Between 5,000 and 10,000 texts would constitute a sufficient corpus to begin reaping the benefits of digital intertextuality.

The second component is a scholarly user community that is actively engaged in the task of building and keeping this corpus. User contributors should be textkeepers. I coin this term on the analogy of housekeeping as an activity that goes on all the time in a humble, invisible, but essential man-

ISBN 978-0-86698-021-0 (online)   ISBN 978-0-86698-449-2 (print)
New Technologies in Medieval and Renaissance Studies 2 (2010) 185–204

ner. Distributed collaborative data curation (DCDC) is a more technical name for this component. Any inquiry is constrained by the quality of the data on which it rests. It is a formidable task to build and maintain a large diachronic and fully intertextual corpus sufficiently complex and accurate to meet high scholarly standards. Who has a greater stake in the quality of the data than the scholars whose work depends on them? We are here in the world of Wiki-nomics or crowdsourcing. Central to collaborative digital data curation is the idea that beyond the assembly of an initial corpus the scope and direction of further growth will result from the choices of users who want to add this or that text for this or that purpose. User-driven growth will provide the best direction over time.

The third component is consortial activity by academic libraries to provide the logistical and technical framework for EDDAC and DCDC. This framework will also support the analysis tools needed to explore the textual resources created by a diachronic and fully intertextual digital corpus. This will blur the traditionally clear distinction between libraries and publishers and calls for substantial renegotiations of the implicit contracts that have governed the relationships of librarians and their patrons. Librarians are comfortable with the motto "More books for more readers." But with digital technology libraries need to think about enhanced as well as extended access. It is one thing to grow by extending access to more materials and more readers. It is another to grow by enhancing access to the materials you have. When S. R. Ranganathan formulated the fifth and final law of library science as "The Library is a growing organism," I take it that he had both means of growing in mind (Ranganathan 1931).

Extended access uses digital technology in an emulatory mode as a new way of bringing more books to more readers. Enhanced access aims at enabling more sophisticated analyses of available materials. Enhanced access blurs the distinction between catalogue information about the book and infor-mation in the book. With regard to the primary sources that constitute the evidentiary basis for text-centric scholarship, the concept of the finding aid will increasingly involve tools that go beyond the catalogue record of a given book and help users look inside the book or across many books. Extended and enhanced access are not in conflict, and the digital library of the fu-ture must deal with both. But it would be a mistake not to enhance anything until everything has been extended. Indeed, doing more with the stuff we have may sometimes pay off more handsomely than getting more stuff to do things with.

The scope of EDDAC

As a corpus of fully interoperable primary texts, EDDAC should allow scholars to use digital texts and tools without constraint. The model here is the open-stack library in which researchers walk among shelves and are free to choose and analyze any combination of books for any purpose, subject only to the constraints of human feet, hands, and eyes. The chief obstacles to exploring the affordances of digital texts in a single docuverse are legal rather than technical. The original intent of copyright legislation was clearly to protect intellectual property rights for a shorter than a longer time. Recent legislation has gone the other way (Darnton 2009). For the foreseeable future, the benefits of full digital intertextuality will not be available to literary scholars whose work is anchored in literary texts since the 1920s, because commercially available digital texts are typically tied to particular access tools that severely constrain their use outside of the parameters envisaged by the vendor.

But half a loaf is better than none, especially if it is large in its own right. More than half of the colleagues and graduate students in my not untypical department of English have their scholarly centre of gravity in texts before 1923. A comprehensive version of EDDAC would constitute a basic research tool for approximately half the faculty in Anglophone Literary Studies and cognate disciplines at research universities. For pedagogical work, the percentage is probably lower. The intertextual affordances of EDDAC reach far beyond Literary Studies. The traditional range of the world of letters includes texts that lend themselves to forms of rhetorical, linguistic, philosophical, historical, political, social, or cultural analysis across a wide range of disciplines. It might be instructive to use JSTOR as the basis for a study that looks at this range of texts and asks how many primary texts before 1923 have been cited more than twice in the secondary literature of the last fifty years. The result would probably identify a core group of texts and authors measured in the low thousands. It is a reasonable assumption that a Book of English, consisting of such an initial core collection and supplemented over time by user-contributed texts would meet important needs of a global scholarly community well into the middle of this century. Whether anybody thereafter will read anything written before 2000 is a question upon which future scholars will vote with their feet.

Another way of measuring an initial size of EDDAC points in a similar direction. Consider a collection of 1,001 stories from the Philip Sidney's *Arcadia* to James Joyce's *Ulysses*. How often would this collection fail you if you wanted to follow up references from scholarly articles? Now consider other genres, taking a broad view of the world of letters. How many books would it take to construct a library that covers other genres at the same density that 1,001 texts achieve for fiction from the late 1500s to the early 1900s? A collection of 10,000 books would include all the memorable and quite a few not so memorable texts. 10,000 intereditions would surely amount to a resource sufficiently comprehensive for many scholarly purposes. There is, however, one caveat. In any collection selected by one person, no matter how thoughtfully, there will always be books that are missing when the collection is applied to another person's project. From my perspective therefore a successful EDDAC will need two components:

> 1) enough texts to make digital intertextuality a working reality for me;
> 2) a procedure that lets me add additional texts I need, preferably in a manner that will be helpful to others as well.

Growth beyond the size required for an initial seed corpus should be driven by the needs of particular users who care enough to spend some of their own time and energy to add to the collection.

The Life Sciences provide a useful model. Evolutionary biologists carefully extract DNA sequences from specimens and contribute them to GenBank, an annotated collection of all publicly available DNA sequences. GenBank is part of the International Nucleotide Sequence Database Collaboration. In this enterprise, the immense phenotypical variety of life is reduced to systematic description at the level of the genotype. It is a Book of Nature, written in a four-letter alphabet, with collaboration and reduction as both the cause and cost of scientific insight. The DNA sequences individual researchers contribute in a standardized format acquire much of their meaning from their incorporation into a large gene bank that support different forms of contextualization and analysis. One by one, the contributions of hundreds or thousands of biologists enrich the query potential of this resource. The Book of Nature and the Book of English, the biological and the cultural genome, both support exercises in digital intertextuality of a kind beyond the dreams of earlier scholars and scientists.

Good-enough intereditions

People often talk about digitization as if it were one thing, but its affordances vary with the purposes of the user. In a project described elsewhere in this collection, Robert Whalen is engaged in a digital edition of the manuscripts of George Herbert, a small but exquisite corpus. He asks why in one version of given poem a particular word is capitalized and whether the choice was the poet's or the printer's. He uses the affordances of the digital medium to draw the reader's attention to the minutiae of intratextual variance. Like other scholarly editors who have chafed under the constraints of a print-based *apparatus criticus*, he is delighted by a digital tool that makes readers see complex textual relationships. At the other end of the scale, there is Google Books and the Hathi Trust with its slogan "There is an elephant in the library." Here you are in a world of search engines that will find a needle in the haystack of millions of books and billions of other documents. The benefits and constraints of data curation in these two environments are entirely different. The digital intertextuality of which I speak sits somewhere between the microscopic scale of intratextual variance and the global scale of Google Books. The objects are books from the past that are thought to be worth remembering. The purpose is to use digital technology to make these books talk to one another and to you. Literary scholarship is largely a matter of an endless conversation about the relationships of past authors to one another and to us, and like Michael Oakeshott's ship of state it has "neither starting-place nor appointed destination" (Oakeshott 1962, 127).

How can digital technology further this conversation and what standards of data curation are appropriate to such an enterprise? This question divides into two parts. What standards of data curation are appropriate to a particular text considered by itself, and what is required to maximize its query potential in a docuverse of intertextual inquiry? As for the first, a digital text must be a good enough. I borrow the term from Donald Winnicott's idea of a good-enough mother, defining a level that is dangerous to drop below, while rising above it may for many purposes not add a whole lot. A good-enough edition is first of all an orthographically accurate transcription of a print source of some standing. It must be explicit about its provenance, and it must be citable.

From the perspective of a critical scholarly edition these are very modest goals, but they are typically not met by texts in Project Gutenberg, which are orthographically clean but more often than not bibliographically opaque. They are typically met by digital texts that have been encoded by projects housed at the Universities of Michigan, Virginia, Indiana, and North Carolina on the basis of the Guidelines for Best Encoding Practices (Digital Library Federation 2004). Yet for intertextual inquiry texts from these collections are typically not easy to compare with one another. This does not matter so much for human readers, who are used to negotiating a great deal of stylistic and typographical variance and read everything on the level playing field of their understanding. But if you want to explore the power of "machine-actionable" texts (Crane, Seales, and Terras 2009), encoding practices in different projects create hurdles that machines stumble over although human readers manage them effortlessly. A simple thing like the treatment of hyphenated words at the end of a line or page is a good example of the difference between human and machine in that regard.

From a theoretical perspective, it is possible to imagine a set of tools so smart and comprehensive that they can take in arbitrary textual data and on-the-fly perform the curatorial tasks that will guarantee a high plateau of digital intertextuality. Such tools would combine the smart but slow skills of human readers with the fast but dumb routines of computers. In practice, this is still utopian. The variety of typographical and text encoding practices is such that the construction of an adequate case logic for all kinds of texts is not an achievable goal. In any collection of digitized texts there will be cases that do not yield to algorithmic treatment of any kind but require some human editorial intervention.

There are two choices. Either you take texts as they come, model them at the most primitive level as sequences of spellings, and see what you can do on that minimal level of interoperability. Or you move texts through curatorial processes that raise them to a plateau that supports more complex forms of analysis. While data curation differs from traditional scholarly editing in many ways, both involve intrinsically labour-intensive procedures. It takes ingenuity and patience of one kind to write and test the scripts that do the algorithmic part of data curation. It takes ingenuity and patience of another kind to remedy the cases that resist algorithmic treatment. Will the labour justify itself over time by the insights supported by the data in a new and enhanced format? Martin West and his students at Oxford spent years on the Teubner edition of the *Iliad*, which in its detail of textual witnesses and *testimonia* from later sources is much superior to any previous edition (West 1998). This does little for the average reader of Homer in Greek, but a scholarly cost/benefit calculus runs differently. There may be lessons here for making similar calculations in the field of digital data curation.

Data curation to maximize digital intertextuality

The card catalogue of a library is the guarantor of intertextuality in a world of printed books. The catalogue defines the book as an object and assigns it a place in a hierarchy of other objects. "Object" is a big word in digital discourse. Programmers may speak of a book object or a page object. Why do they not just say book or page? The answer is that a book on a shelf is just a thing. But a catalogued book is a book object that is clearly defined through a set of relationships. Scholars read books, but without the book objects that are created and maintained through the cataloguer's activity, their work would grind to a halt. When computers came into general use in the 1960s, it was both an exciting and a difficult achievement to convert the catalogue records of large library—a million books or more—into digital objects. Difficult because it strained the storage capabilities of the computers of the time. Exciting because it held out the promise of much more sophisticated manipulation of bibliographical data. Today it is possible to extend the cataloguing of books to the word level. Think of EDDAC as a library of word objects with something like a MARC record for each of them. A billion word objects, or word occurrences, with catalogue records attached to them is a much smaller programming task today than cataloguing a million books was fifty years ago.

The transformation of texts into catalogues of word objects has been a centrepiece of the subdiscipline of corpus linguistics. The linguists call it annotation. It can be done automatically with tolerable levels of accuracy (~97%), and it transforms the opening words of *Emma* into something like

> Emma_*name* Woodhouse_*name*, handsome_*adj*, clever_*adj*, and_*conj* rich_*adj*

This does not tell human readers anything they do not know already, but that is not the point. A tedious process of explication injects some rudiments of readerly knowledge into the text so that the machine acquires a very pale simulacrum of human understanding. More importantly, it acquires powers that humans lack. If you have a large body of annotated texts the machine can at lightning speed retrieve all cases of three successive adjectives in a row. If each file searched by the machine is associated with metadata about its author, date, genre, and so on, the machine will dutifully report those associations. In almost the twinkling of an eye you have the materials for the analysis of the three-adjective-rule on which Jane Austen consciously drew in the opening sentence of her novel and which she expected her readers to recognize. If there is an interesting story to be told about who uses three adjectives in what combinations and where, it is a story that, given a sufficiently large corpus, has moved within the grasp of a bright undergraduate.

Linguists, who are interested in low-level linguistic phenomena for their own sake, discovered the query potential of linguistically annotated corpora fifty years ago, and invested an extraordinary amount of data curation in the original Brown corpus of a million words of American English (Francis and Kucera 1979). Literary scholars and other humanists typically do not share this interest. On the other hand, there is very often an interesting path from low-level observation of verbal usage to larger thematic or narrative patterns. Thus a linguistically annotated corpus is a powerful resource for many scholars who would not describe themselves as linguistically or philologically oriented. Linguistic annotation of a particularly comprehensive kind underwrites most of the affordances of digital intertextuality. The German project DDD (DeutschDiachronDigital) makes this point very well (Lüdeling, Poschenrieder, and Faulstich 2004). Linguistic annotation creates a descriptive framework that lets you describe word objects, the molecular components of a text, in a metalanguage that bridges orthographical or morphological variance due to differences in time, place, genre, social status, or other factors. The point is not to erase, but to articulate difference: words, phrases, sentences become comparable across large data sets. Readers do this for the few texts they can hold in their memory. Machines can help readers extend their memory in new and powerful ways.

EDDAC thus is a digital library of specially curated texts that are catalogued at the highest level of the book object and the lowest level of the word object. It is much harder to extend such cataloguing to the internal structural articulation of a text. You can successfully model just about any text as a sequence of sentences, but beyond the level of the sentence, the variance of internal structure among texts poses almost insuperable challenges to a structural metalanguage, with the exception of plays having conventional divisions into speeches, scenes, and acts.

A prototype of EDDAC: The text corpus of the MONK Project

A fairly substantial prototype of EDDAC exists in the corpus of some 2,500 linguistically annotated texts by some 800 British and American authors from the early sixteenth to the early twentieth century (~150 million words) that were prepared from existing digital texts for the MONK Project. The source files were drawn from a variety of archives. Two thirds of them came from the Text Creation Partnership (TCP), which will eventually grow to a public domain collection of approximately 40,000 British and American texts published before 1800. The texts were converted to a Text Encoding Initiative (TEI) format that follows the new P5 standard. They were then tokenized, lemmatized, and morphosyntactically tagged. Although the source texts for the MONK project originated in very similar shops (in Michigan, Virginia, Indiana, and North Carolina), their conversion to a common format turned out to be a non-trivial task. While different projects made sensible decisions about how to do this or that they paid little attention to the needs of users who wanted to mix texts from different collections. The problems involved in such mixing are trivial if the uses of the digital text stay limited to looking up words and reading bits of text. But problems mount quickly if you want a machine to perform complex or iterative searches across arbitrarily chosen texts from different collections. Little things like the soft hyphens mentioned above can become major hurdles.

The conversion to a shared TEI P5 format was the work of Brian Pytlik Zillig and Stephen Ramsay at the University of Nebraska. The name of the format, TEI-Analytics, was chosen to draw attention to the goal of creating intereditions that will be amenable to the analytics or routines that computers are good at and that help human analysts make sense of much larger data sets than they could master by reading alone. The conversion of different text archives into a common TEI P5 interchange format is similar in spirit to the *Kernkodierung* or baseline encoding of the German Textgrid project. Textgrid aims at creating a distributed environment in which scholars can produce digital editions. Each of these editions uses markup to realize its particular goals, but the markup can be reduced to a baseline encoding that makes the texts in Textgrid interoperable. This is a particularly good example of reconciling the different perspectives of intratextual and intertextual analysis. There is much to be said for an environment in which different projects pursue their special needs on a high plateau of shared baseline encoding. The higher that plateau the higher and more granular the potential for intertextual analysis. In practice, the implementation of this principle means agreeing to do a lot of little things in the same way.

Linguistic annotation in the MONK Project was done with MorphAdorner, a Natural Language Processing (NLP) toolkit developed by Phil Burns at Northwestern University. MorphAdorner works with a tagset that can describe morphosyntactic phenomena from late Middle English (such as Chaucer) to the present. In addition to providing a part-of-speech tag for every word token, it also maps the spelling or surface form of each token to a standard spelling and to a lemma. Lemmatization in MorphAdorner takes a lumping rather than splitting approach and is similar to the hyperlemma used by TextGrid. The modern form of a broadly defined lemma bundles diachronic and dialectal variance. Thus the form *sote* in the first line of the *Canterbury*

Tales (more often spelled *swote* in Chaucer) is lemmatized as *sweet*, so a search for *sweet* will retrieve this dialectal variant.

Adding more texts to EDDAC

The operations that have been performed on 1,800 texts can be readily extended to any or all of the 40,000 texts in the final TCP collections. Thus one can claim that for texts prior to 1800, a version of EDDAC already exists or can be easily created. Until about 2015, access to TCP texts is limited to institutions that funded their creation through subscriptions, but within a decade they will pass into the public domain. In the interim they are available to the large community of scholars at the major research universities in the English-speaking world. For texts from 1800 on, if the texts do not already exist in a reliable TEI format, the best choice is to work with texts created with Optical Character Recognition (OCR) by Google Books, the Open Content Alliance, or similar sources. OCR has been much improved in recent years. It is superior in several ways to manual keyboarding because it retains the layout of the page block and makes it much easier to align the digital text with its facsimile image. The digital facsimile communicates the look and feel of the original in ways that no transcription can, and it will always allow scholars to check on the accuracy of transcriptions derived from it. On the other hand, texts created with OCR still require a lot of orthographic clean-up to serve as good-enough diplomatic editions of their sources.

The layout of a printed page is full of implicit metadata that readers tacitly process. There is now good software that transforms this layout into a kind of whitespace-XML from which you can derive a TEI-format through a combination of algorithmic processing and manual editing. Current experiments at the University of Illinois and Northwestern University suggest that you can create good-enough intereditions in reasonable time with editorial assistance from readers who are literate, have an interest in the book, and are willing to pick up modest technical skills of digital editing. Many undergraduate English majors meet those criteria. The German TextGrid project is built around the idea of a platform that supports distributed editing and the sharing of results in a common corpus.

In extending EDDAC beyond 1800, there are good reasons for focusing first on 1,001 novels as a project that can stand on its own but can also be part of a larger enterprise. Substantial portions of these 1,001 novels are already digitized because fiction before 1800 will be adequately covered by TCP and because, notwithstanding some important exception, much of nineteenth-

century American fiction exists in digital versions from which appropriate
intereditions can be easily produced with the routines developed in the
MONK project. What is missing is nineteenth-century British fiction and
early-twentieth-century fiction from both sides of the Atlantic. Coverage
of those areas with 500 texts would go a long way towards creating a quite
robust module of fiction in EDDAC. And if EDDAC never proceeds beyond that
initial module, a digital annotated corpus of 1,001 (or more) public domain
novels in English will be a useful resource for many scholars. Because fiction
is the genre most widely read by readers at very different levels of sophis-
tication and because from some technical perspectives novels are relatively
straightforward texts, fiction makes a good guinea pig for distributed and
collaborative data curation.

Textkeeping, or distributed collaborative data curation

Over the past two decades thousands of texts have been encoded by volunteers for Project Gutenberg. The Distributed Proofreaders Foundation has
very effectively channeled the desires of many individuals who care about
orthographic accuracy (Distributed Proofreaders 2009). The disregard of
Project Gutenberg for provenance issues and accurate bibliographical description rules out most of the texts as candidates for good-enough editions
in EDDAC. But the project is a remarkable testimony to the cumulative power
of the work of many hands. Can the energies and passions of scholars be har-
nessed to a similar enterprise so that, as in the case of life scientists and their
gene banks, textual data can be curated by the scholars and critics who have
the greatest long-term interest in having data of sufficient quality? Textual
data curation takes at least three different forms:

1) the creation of new digital editions
2) the correction of errors in existing editions
3) the adding of additional layers of encoding or annotation to existing
digital texts

With regard to these three different forms of activity, it is necessary to re-
think the opposition of mechanical and manual routines. I exaggerate only
a little if I say that textual projects tend to be located at the two extremes
of a range. There is the boutique project in which scholars lavish unlimited
attention on the details of a text important to them, and there is the institutional project, typically housed in libraries, where the staff shudder at the
thought of manually intervening in a text, rely on automated workflows, and

are willing to live with a level of textual error that no self-respecting teacher would tolerate in a basic composition class.

In a human editorial task such as proofreading there are three stages:

1) finding the passage that needs attention
2) deciding what needs to be done
3) recording what you have decided to do

Of a minute's editorial labour, five seconds might be given over to the actual exercise of human judgment and the remainder on making the change and reporting on what you have done. Can we build systems in which we drive down the time cost of human editorial labour and employ human judgment more effectively and also more consistently? The answer is yes, although it is not easy and involves considerable up-front costs. Consider the 25,000 Early English Books Online (EEBO) books transcribed so far by TCP. They are a remarkable achievement, but they are full of errors. There are several million words where the transcriber could not identify one or more letters. There are countless examples of words that are wrongly joined or split. Sometimes paragraphs or whole pages are missing because they were missing in the microfilm on which the transcription is based. Passages in certain foreign languages such as Greek or Hebrew were not initially transcribed and appear as marked lacunae. The EEBO texts include millions of untagged French or Latin words. These are things that can and should be fixed, and they are best fixed by people who use the texts and care enough about them.

If the texts are not used in the first place, there is no virtue in fixing them. If they are fixed as they are used, users collectively decide priorities as they go along. If the texts are linguistically annotated, as they are in the MONK Project, every word is a word object with a known address to which various kinds of new annotation can be attached without overwriting the text itself. When in reading such a text I come across an incomplete word, I can fix it in a few seconds. If I care enough about a text, I might look for all its lacunae and fix them. What I can do with this text someone else can do with another. Data curation can be the work of many hands at many times in many places. There are two fundamental requirements for this to happen, and both of them are well within reach of current technology. Firstly, there needs to be a stable framework of Internet accessible data that makes it really easy for users to contribute in a casual mode. Secondly, corrections or additions by users should never overwrite the source text but should be submissions that are subject to editorial review, which could include automatic voting procedures. The community of potential contributors to such an enterprise is large, diverse, and global. It begins in the high schools, where thousands of high school students in the world could do a little textkeeping here or there with non-trivial cumulative results. At the other end of the demographic spectrum there are the millions of educated retired people who can be recruited to the task of doing something useful for a book or author they care about. In the middle, there is a world of teachers and scholars who can perhaps be coaxed into contributing something, however busy they claim to be. We are all a little like Chaucer's Sergeant of the Law: "Nowher so bisy a man as he ther nas, | And yet he semed bisier than he was."

If we think of the tasks of textkeeping from the perspective of the volunteers who do it, the aim is a framework in which the volunteers can also do things for themselves while doing things that are helpful to others. It may therefore be productive to think of the software environment as a general framework for annotation. The correction of an orthographic error, a missing word, or the like is easily modelled as an annotation. Think of an annotation as a bundle of key-value pairs including a userID, a time stamp, the wordID that is the target of an annotation, the annotation type, which might be "correct-Spelling" or "addNote," and finally the suggested correction itself. Such a framework for annotation is more than what is needed for the specific tasks of error correction. But it may well be more effective in recruiting volunteers because it embeds their textkeeping in other forms of interacting with the text. These other forms have their own value for many scholarly, pedagogical, and recreational purposes. A proper framework for digital data curation is both more controlled and more spontaneous than manual editorial work. It is more spontaneous because it allows for casual work along the way. It is more controlled because the forms of user intervention are more specified. Above all, the system is much better than any human at keeping consistent records of who did what, when, and where.

It is a more complex task to create a properly structured digital edition of, say, Charles Dickens's *Bleak House* from the digital facsimile and OCR text of the first edition of 1853. The task is not as easily broken down into atomic acts that can be done in any order, as is the case with proofreading or morphosyntactic error correction. It does not rely on skills that come with being an educated reader, but requires some knowledge of markup languages, and it has to be done as a single project. But current experiments at Northwestern University and the University of Illinois suggest that with a proper framework and good documentation we can turn scholars with few technical skills into good enough digital editors of texts that they care about sufficiently to spend a few days of their life on. It may be harder than Googling, but it is a lot easier than learning how to play the violin.

Automatically applied linguistic annotation has an error rate of ~3%. Whether such errors are ever worth fixing is a nice question. Generally speaking, the tolerance of users for morphosyntactic errors will be much higher than for orthographic errors. Orthographic errors are always visible, while morphosyntactic errors will typically be hidden even from users who take advantage of such tagging. From an analytical perspective, an error rate of 3% is unlikely to make much difference for the quantitative operations that linguistic annotation typically enables. Part-of-speech tagging errors are distributed unevenly across texts and cluster in typical errors. The flipside of such clustering is that we can target errors if users care enough about them. If a text is modelled as a sequence of word objects with metadata, we can create a tabular or vertical representation of the text in which every data row consists of the word and the unique ID, lemma, part-of-speech tag, and forty characters before and after. Managed in a database environment, this type of concordance provides very flexible ways of grouping data and makes it possible to identify and correct errors.

Error is endless. In a corpus of any size there will always be a need for text-keeping that consists of the humble tasks of getting it right. But there are ways of adding value to EDDAC that go beyond correcting mistakes, and they do not have to wait until the last error has been corrected. As an example, I discuss the opportunities for identifying spoken language. The spoken language of the past is largely a mystery to us. We have no direct records of spoken language from before the age of Thomas Edison. Extensive documentation of the way people actually talk has been with us for less than a century, so what we know about the speech of earlier ages is largely an extrapolation from its written representations. From comparing the dialogue of movie scripts with the transcripts of what people actually say we know that the differences are very large. Still, the written representations of spoken language are better than nothing, and they are all we have. There are many research scenarios for which it is helpful to distinguish between spoken and narrated text, whether or not the written-spoken is used to form hypotheses about the real-spoken. The distinction between speech and narration is an important part of much fiction. In most novels before 1900 the distinction is clearly marked by typographical indicators. In fact, the distinction between spoken and narrated language is probably the only typographical distinction that readers expect to find in a conventional novel.

Through a combination of automatic routines and manual review and correction it is possible to tag spoken language with <said> tags. From some experiments, I conclude that for a novel of ordinary complexity, this can be done in less than two hours per novel. In a second step, it is also possible—though more time-consuming—to identify speakers, as in a play, or to classify them by sex or social status. The utility of that procedure was demonstrated by John Burrows in his study of the different speech habits of Jane Austen's characters (Burrows 1987). But even without this additional granularity, the coarse binary division into speech and narrative is useful for many purposes. Reasonably comprehensive and accurate encoding of spoken language in a Book of English creates at least a diachronic record of how writers thought people talked. That is in itself a useful thing.

EDDAC, digital intertextuality, and the role of the library

EDDAC is about enhancing rather than extending access, about doing more with the books you already have rather than adding more books. Doing more involves activities that go beyond reading or simple cross-collection searches for character strings with or without secondary constraints, such as a search for *love* near *death* in texts with dates between 1589 and 1612. It is useful to keep in mind that working with a corpus like EDDAC differs in its goals and in many of its procedures from the Web-based look-ups that let us quickly get a little knowledge of things we know nothing about. It is also a different thing from the digital techniques that help us keep up with a growing secondary literature. Googling has become an invaluable tool in scholarship as in everyday life, but it is a shallow tool when compared with the iterative and patient routines that are a prerequisite for successful work with text corpora. Franco Moretti's phrase "distant reading" is a useful way of highlighting ways in which digitally assisted text analysis differs from traditional close reading (Moretti 2005). But such reading may pay close attention to microscopic details and trace their patterns across very large textual spaces. Opposing "distant" to "close" reading may be less productive than seeing the distinctive features of digital reading in a constant shuttling between the very close and the very distant.

Here are some search scenarios that illustrate the "more" that is afforded by enhanced access:

   ★ You choose a set of texts and look for other texts that are like it in terms of lexical or syntactic habits.

★ You select a group of texts, say several hundred sermons between 1500 and 1800, and see whether the distribution of lexical or syntactic phenomena divides them into groups that are useful for subsequent analysis.

★ You look at lexical differences between two novelists and try to filter out differences that arise from the fact that one uses more dialogue than the other.

★ You take a syntactic pattern like "the king's daughter," gather instances across a collection of texts, and visualize the results by a graph in which the owner ("king") appears as a "nucleus" defined by the "rays" of his possessions (among them his daughter).

★ You extract names of people and places from a group of texts and look for patterns in their distribution by genre, region, or date.

★ You define a subcorpus, say novels by George Eliot, and ask what words are disproportionately common or rare in that subcorpus when compared with some other corpus, say novels written by others during her life span.

★ You take a word or a concept defined by a basket of words and track its frequency over time in different text categories defined by the intersection of genre, and sex or origin of author.

★ You take a word in different texts and explore the ways in which its use is inflected by other words that recur near it, or the "company it keeps" (Firth 1968, 179).

★ You look for phrases of varying length that are shared between one work and another and use them as point of departure for allusive relationships, which is intertextuality in a very traditional sense.

These are all search scenarios that are currently supported by programs like MONK, Philologic, WordHoard, or visualization projects like Many Eyes. They depend on familiar techniques in statistics, corpus linguistics, and bio-informatics, with names like supervised/unsupervised classification, log likelihood statistics, collocation analysis, named entity extraction, or sequence analysis.

While all these search scenarios are available somewhere, it is not the case that they are available in a single environment where they can be used by literary scholars with average technical skills on a wide variety of texts, including texts they might want to add to an already existing archive. Who should build such an environment, maintain it, and provide guidance to literary scholars and other humanists whose relationship with digital technology is

as yet insecure? The most obvious and in some ways quite traditional institutional framework for EDDAC is a university library or a group of libraries
acting in a consortial manner. A librarian might at this point object that the
enhancement envisaged in EDDAC are really the reader's responsibility and
that the library's responsibilities have been fully met by making digital texts
available. That is a serious argument, but it can be countered by drawing
attention to the peculiar role that primary texts play in humanities scholarship. Scientists encounter the primary objects of their attention in their
laboratories, which nowadays contain much more complex and expensive
tools than the nineteenth-century chemist's Bunsen burner. The scientist's
library holds the secondary literature, or just literature, about their field.
Primary data in the sciences may be held in laboratories, but increasingly
they are held in library-like environments that share costs and increase the
circulation and analysis of data. GenBank, mentioned above, is a prime example.

By analogy EDDAC is a cultural genome or annotated collection of many
important publicly available texts. Annotation here refers not to critical
commentary but the standardized identification of words, or text molecules,
making the texts machine actionable and allowing scholars to gather and
organize textual data for analysis and integration at a higher level. This is
another step in the allographic journey of texts: a migration from scrolls, co-
dices, and printed books into a digital world that supports all the affordances
of these previous technologies but adds new forms of contextualization and
analysis. What is the appropriate institutional framework for such a cultural
genome? The offices of individual literary scholars will not support a network of collaborative exploration of shared data beyond small communities.
Neither will departments of English, separately or together: their administra-
tive, financial, and technical infrastructure is simply not suited to such
tasks. The best answer to the question is the library, and this answer derives
fairly directly from the traditional role that libraries have played as keepers
and mediators of the primary data of literary studies. The answer becomes
more obvious once you free yourself from the idea that digitized books are
somehow more technological than printed books: the written word has
always already been technologized. If you go into a rare book library, you
would not be surprised to see an old printing press that was in its day a high-
tech tool. The habits and practices of the rare book library in fact set useful
precedents for the work required for EDDAC. Rare book libraries are about
highly curated data. Their achievements have rested on close cooperation
between scholars and librarians and on the conviction that in any large li-

brary there will always be special data that require and justify high levels of data curation.

Digital data curation involves not only metadata that describe an object at the item level, say as a manuscript, but also derivative data structures that may be many times the size of the original object. A morphosyntactically tagged text is a derivative data structure. An even clearer example is sequence alignment, which depends on the prior existence of an annotated corpus. In this technique, common in bio-informatics and plagiarism detection, we ignore the 100–200 most common function words, which account for at least half of the words in a text, map the surface forms of the remaining content words to their lemmata and look for repeated lemma strings or n-grams of variable length. When a new text is added to the collection, an initial algorithm checks for matching n-grams and keeps track of them. The resultant derivative data structure of repeated n-grams weaves a web of intertextual echoes made up of literal and fuzzy string matches. Mark Olsen and his collaborators have used this technique to model the relationship of Charles Diderot's *Encylopédie* to its sources (Horton and Olsen 2009). Sequence alignment is a conceptually simple but computationally intensive procedure. If used across a large data set like EDDAC, it is a powerful way of leveraging the analytical potential of the underlying textual data.

Can we distinguish clearly between content and tools? Their fluid boundaries are further dissolved by digital technology. Curated data typically add layers of information created by tools, and these layers may be extracted, aggregated, and used to create additional data structure. If we follow this way of thinking, the distinction between tools and content eventually disappears: content is layers of value added with the help of tools. It then becomes a pragmatic decision whether to deposit the output of a particular tool as a new layer of content or whether to produce it on demand. Consider the act of cataloguing a book. What value is added by the activities that end with sticking a label with a call number on a book? Does the content of the book change? If you engage in the thought experiment of uncataloguing a million-book collection and scattering the books at random across the floors of the stacks, you recognize the act of cataloguing surrounds the original content layers of a book with a new layer that takes the physical form of the books next to it. The catalogue is a very powerful tool and shapes the knowledge space within which books circulate. Librarians have a deep and honourable reluctance to come between readers and their books. But the truth is that the librarian's work always comes between the readers and their books. A library is an instrumentarium in which a hierarchy of tools adds value to the single book, which is itself a tool to begin with.

Enhanced access to primary digital texts may be understood as a way of extending the findings aids of the catalogue to move below the item level into the digital object itself. The techniques may be new, but the questions are not. "Could you help me find passages in Shakespeare's *Hamlet* that echo earlier plays or are echoed in later plays?" is a proper question addressed to a reference librarian, although she would be hard put to answer it. It is a kind of question that is readily answered by EDDAC with an appropriate analytical instrumentarium and user-friendly interface. The primary texts of Anglophone literatures make up a relatively small percentage of all the books in their library catalogue ranges, and the percentage drops further if you discount virtually identical items. As these primary texts migrate into the digital sphere, we need to think of them as existing in a digital labora-tory in which scholars can take advantage of their digital affordances. If you do not care for the scientific metaphor think of the digital laboratory as a kind of kitchen, perhaps a witch's kitchen. Even in a predigital world, schol-arly reading and writing were forms of cooking in which texts were sliced or diced, kneaded and rolled, boiled, steamed, baked, or roasted. In a digital kitchen it is not enough to have the repositories of pantry, refrigerator, and freezer. And you need a few more tools than a microwave oven.

WORKS CITED

Burrows, J. F. 1987. *Computation into Criticism: A Study of Jane Austen's Novels and an Experiment in Method.* Oxford: Clarendon Press.

Crane, Gregory, Brent Seales, and Melissa Terras. 2009. Cyberinfrastructure for Classical Philology. *Digital Humanities Quarterly* 3, no. 1: Changing the Center of Gravity: Transforming Classical Studies Through Cyberinfrastructure (Winter). http://www.digitalhumanities.org/dhq/vol/3/1/000023.html.

Darnton, Robert. 2009. Google and the Future of Books. *New York Review of Books*, February 12.

Digital Library Federation. 2004. TEI Text Encoding in Libraries Guidelines for Best Encoding Practices. Text. December 7. http://www.diglib.org/standards/tei.htm.

Distributed Proofreaders. 2009. Front Page News and Developments. http://www.pgdp.net/c/.

Firth, J. R. 1968. *Selected Papers of J. R. Firth, 1952–59.* Ed. Frank Robert Palmer. Longmans' Linguistics Library. London: Longmans.

Francis, W. N., and H. Kucera. Brown Corpus Manual of Information to Accompany a Standard Corpus of Present-Day Edited American English, for use with Digital Computers. Revised edition 1979. http://icame.uib.no/brown/bcm.html.

Horton, Russell, and Mark Olsen. 2009. 'Sequence Alignment, Shared Services, and Digital Humanities': Project Bamboo Workshop, Tucson, Arizona, January 2009. http://docs.google.com/present/view?id=ddj2s2rb_197 sfrrrtf7&skipauth=true.

Lüdeling, Anke, Thorwald Poschenrieder, and Lukas Faulstich. 2004. Deutschdiachrondigital — Ein Diachrones Korpus des Deutschen. *Jahrbuch für Computerphilologie* 6: 119–36.

Moretti, Franco. 2005. *Graphs, Maps, Trees: Abstract Models for a Literary History.* London: Verso.

Oakeshott, Michael. 1962. *Rationalism in Politics, and Other Essays.* London: Methuen.

Ranganathan, S. R. 1931. *The Five Laws of Library Science.* Madras: Madras Library Association. http://dlist.sir.arizona.edu/1220/.

West, M. L., ed. 1998. *Homeri Ilias.* Bibliotheca scriptorum Graecorum et Romanorum Teubneriana. Stutgardiae: Teubner.

Afterword

John Lavagnino
King's College London
John.Lavagnino@kcl.ac.uk

The essays about digital publishing and English literary studies in this volume make one thing especially clear: Ted Nelson was right. Nelson and other
prophets of hypertext who were prominent in the early 1990s looked like
figures from the distant past by the end of that decade, when the big news
about the Web was all focussed on making money and Internet Explorer had
become dominant (Bolter 1991; Joyce 1995; Landow 1992). What began as a
strange non-proprietary academic product, the Internet, was expected to
develop into something much more like television, with large corporations
running the show and much less scattered activity of unorganized citizens.
To say that the Web needed to become something written by everyone, that
it would change reading, writing, and thinking, that it was not just for shop-
ping was not the conventional wisdom of the period. Michael Joyce's essay
"New Stories for New Readers" is one trace of how that phase of the Web
looked to someone from the hypertext world (Joyce 1998).

Ten years into the twenty-first century there are features of the online environment that were not anticipated in the 1990s, the most important being
the way that searching became a central feature and the normal first step.
In early hypertext discussions, searching has only a minor role, and the assumption is that you'd always prefer to follow links where possible. But most
major developments since the rise of search, of AltaVista and then Google,
have been moving us back towards the classical hypertext idea: blogs, social networking, micro-blogging, amazing phenomena like Wikipedia, are
all about broad individual involvement and not just a continuation of the
ways of older media systems. In Nelson's version of the hypertext vision, the
system was not a place where you went to do a few specific functions (word
processing, email), but the place where all text lived; everyone was a writer
and not just a reader, and extensive explicit linking was going to replace the
informal references of traditional writing, which had no power to get you
quickly to the material in question (Nelson 1981, chapter 2). That idea still
looked utopian even ten years ago; today it is the natural assumption that all
new writing *could* be online, that it is a choice and not a necessity when other

ISBN 978-0-86698-021-0 (online)   ISBN 978-0-86698-449-2 (print)
New Technologies in Medieval and Renaissance Studies 2 (2010) 205–214

modes of publication are used. Web resources that only make sense online, that cannot be downloaded in any meaningful way but are dynamic networks that you explore, now flourish and go far beyond their 1990s precursors. The extinction of some kinds of publication, such as newspapers, begins to seem possible.

The fulfilment of Nelson's vision depended in part on getting a significant bulk of the world's existing collection of text into digital form. That looked like an impossible dream in 1990, though not in digital-humanities circles; it was in that year that Steven J. DeRose published, on the Humanist discussion list, an estimate of the cost of digitizing all thirty million books in the U.S. Library of Congress, the first attempt I know of to work out what it would take. His figure was $41 million (DeRose 1990). In 2007 one published estimate for the cost of the Google Books operation was $5 million for the first million books (Hafner 2007); another, extrapolating from the experience of Google Books and other large-scale efforts, estimated the Library of Congress task at $300 million (Kahle 2009). DeRose's was an excellent estimate for an era that had seen no projects yet on that scale; though there are many problems with mass digitization today, we now know that it is practical and that the sums of money are, as Brewster Kahle points out, not enormous compared to our total annual spending on libraries.

We can say, then, that today we have the pieces in hand for a version of Nelson's vision: a working hypertext system that many people use for reading and writing, and a large digital library. Creators of digital scholarly editions are no longer proposing technical experiments and impossible social developments; we have a substantial infrastructure to build on and no longer need to argue about the very idea of the computer as a literary machine. And Peter Shillingsburg expresses well a sentiment many now share, that the digital age gives us a position from which we can see what the printed book was; we have a better perspective on the social organizations of publishing as well. But such understanding does not answer all our questions about what to do and how. The essays in this collection are particularly strong on four key issues in the field today: the nature of the resources we need, sustainability and funding, the identity of the humanities scholar in this new world, and broadening our ideas of what digital editions should be and do.

As has long been clear to those in the field, the digital library adequate for literary study needs to be something far beyond the Google Books model. The present volume's essays make clear the great variety of editorial approaches that we require, much beyond the normal methodological range of digital libraries. In particular, reproducing and analyzing manuscript texts remains an insufficiently explored task: Robert Whalen's essay makes clear the attention to detail and to the protean forms of literature that are necessary. His project is at one end of the digital-text spectrum represented in this volume, from work focussed on many aspects of a few texts to work focussed on many texts reduced to a few aspects: most often, to the pictures and the transcribed words.

The first kind of work, carefully edited and encoded, usually involving canonical works like George Herbert's poetry, has the strongest resemblance to traditional scholarly editing. The second kind, more what we usually think of as the digital library, is exemplified by the huge Early English Books Online (EEBO) corpus described by Shawn Martin, and at its extreme gives us a complete collection of all printed material for one place and period; this too has its version in traditional scholarship, in large-scale series such as Jacques-Paul Migne's *Patrologia Latina*. That series, and the microfilm series that preceded EEBO, have been important sources for early digital-library work, though we have also seen entirely new digital projects of the same scope, such as the project to assemble the larger canon described by Martin Mueller. The influence especially of EEBO, in the decade that it has been available, shows how powerful the effect of such a large corpus can be, even without special analytic tools. The alert scholar will recognize the use of EEBO, Google Books, and other resources behind many recent articles that never cite them directly. But even in newer projects like Mueller's, this phase of digitization has been greatly dependent on earlier scholarly projects that surveyed large regions of the print world, so that the basic work of enumerative bibliography has been done already.

EEBO has its roots in a series of microfilm facsimiles of early English books; the microfilm series was based on the Short Title Catalogues of A. W. Pollard and G. R. Redgrave and Donald Wing. Similarly, the Chadwyck-Healey Literature Online collection depended on *The New Cambridge Bibliography of English Literature* and other reference works to guide its selection. None of these microfilm and digital resources claimed to have done *new* bibliographical work. The resources built without the benefit of such bibliographical research have a lot of problems. Geoffrey Nunberg has described the many problems with the metadata behind Google Books, and it is easy for any user to collect further examples: its many errors in dates, authors, and every other detail about books, an impediment in particular to any research that goes beyond finding individual items and tries to use the collection as a corpus (Nunberg 2009). Some think it matters little because you can eventually work out what it was you were looking at, by your own efforts and consultation of printed sources; but it skews the large-scale studies that are one point of this sort of collection.

These resources are also derived entirely from the printed record. But the manuscript world is considerably larger and its importance to scholarship has only increased in the last century. Steven May estimates that there are at least 200 times more works surviving in manuscript than in print for the early-modern period in England (May 2010, 100). Every year, more pages of material are classified by the United States government than are acquired in print by major research libraries; and no doubt the unclassified and non-governmental manuscript world is vastly larger (Galison 2004). While historians take the use of archives very seriously, many literary scholars find it easy to avoid them, though in general the use of manuscript material in historical and literary research greatly increased in the second half of the twentieth century. The expansion of scholarly attention beyond the canonical and official also demands a broader range of sources, to tease out the things that were rarely said or mentioned. Looking at manuscripts still matters (Burke 2007; Ezell 2008). As scholarship has made a strong shift in the historicist direction in the last few decades, a shift towards more study of manuscripts is unavoidable.

But the manuscript world, and this tendency in scholarship, are little reflected in the new resources, in part because manuscripts are much less amenable to the high-volume and largely mechanical production systems that have been used for digitizing print. So a project like Robert Whalen's that directs keen attention to a few manuscripts is doing the groundwork for what needs to happen in the future, in the way that the laborious digitization from the 1960s through the 1980s of individual books did the foundational work for digital libraries. We need further initiatives to start bringing the richness of the manuscript world into the digital realm: we have opened up a wide range of printed sources that had been neglected, but still ignore almost everything that was not printed.

The essays by Ian Lancashire and Murray McGillivray gesture in the direction of a quite different project that repeatedly returns and whose time may eventually come: the making of digital text representations with far more ambitious goals, seeking to say what the text actually means. The gap that is always observed between the concerns of digital text production (or scholarly editing) and what literary critics are talking about could vanish if we had such texts; we would also be much closer to another idea that keeps returning, that of a really scientific literary criticism, one with rigorous statement of theories and facts rather than the haphazard accumulations we are accustomed to. A typical response to the idea from others in literary studies is that we do not know enough about literature or how it works to create such representations; a typical response from the scientific world would be that the difficulty makes it a good area of research and we ought to start trying things out. We will surely see more work in this direction, but it may be a long time before it converges with the rest of literary studies.

Even if we stick to the kind of projects described by the other contributors, we do not yet know how to pay for it all and keep it going, which is an issue that Paul Vetch and Peter Robinson explore and that everybody has in mind. Though the ephemerality of some editions derives from the fragility and novelty of the infrastructure, it is also a reflection of grant-funding priorities, in which long projects are prohibited and nothing matters once the deliverables are completed; to conduct a project that takes many years and survives for many further years after that is to go against the intention of this system. There have been kinds of research funding in the past that had other intentions: the British Academy was once more able and willing to fund projects that were expected to take a long time. And outside the humanities the idea that there are short-term projects and long-term infrastructure is common; nobody builds particle accelerators and telescopes and then plans on using them for less than five years. But in the second half of the twentieth century, when we started getting some grant funding in the humanities for projects and not just individual leave, we did not happen to get this other part of the science funding model.

The deeper problem, in the view of many humanities scholars, is that there is not enough money around. Of course there is actually quite a lot of money around; the Higher Education Funding Council for England distributed £7.5 billion (~$12.2 billion) in 2008–2009 to universities and colleges, and £1.5 billion (~$2.4 billion) was specifically for research. But the money is mostly not available directly for specific pieces of research, and instead there is a largely indirect system that is best at supporting small bits of work rather than large projects. (Even this system has a more clarity than many other worlds: as Clay Shirky observed [2009], it is odd that news reporting from Iraq should be supported by the advertising budgets of department stores, but that is what traditional newspaper arrangements amount to.) The money is mostly there, but is already committed in various ways that are hard to shift. Our thinking is more generally constrained by the idea that our ways of doing and publishing research are fixed; it is, of course, easy to make proposals for how it could all be better, but hard to get there, and we have to be grateful to those who struggle in the current climate to create examples of what is possible. Many of the projects discussed in this volume would do best in a system that provided for large investments in infrastructure, but it is quite difficult to get such a system started.

We can imagine that these editions might happen by getting away from centralizing, grant-funded projects and making more use of the time and imagination of many individuals in their scattered moments of research time. Brewster Kahle's discussion of mass digitization compared the cost of the total digital library with the much larger annual cost of running existing libraries; his point was not that we should shut down those libraries but that a small fraction of each library's budget would be enough to fund the digitization effort. But his idea of having each library do a bit does not work as a way for this to happen: it does not allow for the substantial costs of management and coordination of the whole, if what we want in the end is a unified system and not islands of information scattered everywhere. A similar problem exists for us in the worlds of history and literary studies: a large amount of money in effect goes to support scholarship every year, which theoretically could be used to build up digital infrastructure, but we do not have a mechanism in place to direct small individual efforts towards that goal. This approach, as also described here by Peter Robinson, does nevertheless have the advantage of suggesting a way to proceed that is compatible with the current system, rather than requiring a complete change of system. As Shawn Martin explains very well, there is a complex array of funding models behind scholarly publishing today, and we cannot expect to see these transformed into a narrow and unified channel; we will surely continue to do best with more rather than fewer models.

However funded, the large project creates unfamiliar roles for humanists. There are pockets of teamwork and close collaboration in the humanities, but it is remote from traditional training and rarely figures in evocations of the ideals of the humanities. The idea of developing areas of scholarship in a systematic way, involving large numbers of people doing coordinated work pointing in a single direction, is essential to the framework behind infrastructural development in the sciences, and distasteful to many in the humanities. And the small project raises the identity question in other ways, as that approach in the digital humanities requires scholars to develop unusual kinds of expertise. Alan Galey and Robert Whalen explore the questions that digital editing raises about the identity of humanities scholars: are we still doing the same sort of thing Erasmus did? To most humanists the field's concern with such things as data encoding and software seems wholly alien; but by now there is also a substantial tradition of work with that focus, and to those just now becoming scholars it seems natural. Methods that looked dauntingly technical to people in other sections of the scholarly world have been current in scholarly editing for some time; the rise of digital techniques only continues that tendency.

The possibility of a transformation in our very idea of what scholarly editors do and what scholarly editions are has always been part of the world of digital editions. For Peter Robinson getting away from the edition that is a shrine to an individual's judgment is a benefit, whereas for Peter Shillingsburg it is a divergence from the proper role of editions and editors. Among scholars generally a decrease in the individual authority of publications is unwelcome: in surveys scholars are shown to not greatly esteem blogs and social-networking systems (Harley et al. 2008). Many prominent academic blogs are much more about scholarly news than scholarly research, which is to say that they are mostly about administration rather than scholarship. The focus on the identifiable role of individuals remains strong in the academic world, and in its procedures for hiring and payment, even in more collaborative disciplines; the diffusion of authority that some editorial thinking now encourages is an idea most scholars have not caught up with yet. Important scientific discoveries have often been reported in very brief papers; important developments in the humanities very often seem to require much more writing.

The strongest impetus towards collaboration and shared authority in some areas of literary scholarship may simply be the weight of accumulated scholarship. There is an evident strain in publications that must cover wide areas of learning. A volume in the Arden Shakespeare or a similar series must deal with textual scholarship, literary criticism, performance criticism, and history, and the recent prevalence of co-edited volumes indicates the creep towards a division of labour. Despite all these worries, the world of digital scholarly editions today has breadth and openness far beyond what is visible in many fields of literary scholarship. This is a change from the 1990s, when the field had a great deal of excitement but also too much certainty about what digital scholarly editions had to be. Early pioneers had lucid explanations and arguments: we could present more texts and more about their relationships, and overcome the restrictions of print publishing. As has repeatedly happened in the world of scholarly editing, the results of that archivally focussed line of work have proven of interest to many other scholarly editors but often not to the larger scholarly public, or to the general public.

With time the significance of some unusual initiatives became clearer, such as the *Blake Archive* with its strong visual focus, extending to indexing that focussed on the elements of Blake's pictures, and a comparative lack of stress on matters that are strictly textual. Some recent survey articles focus not on digital editions as such but on resources like the *Blake Archive* that in diverse ways have gone beyond the framework of traditional scholarly editing, notably in incorporating many materials beyond the texts to be edited and in adding to that digital tools for working with the material (Palmer 2004; Crane, Bamman, and Jones 2007). Even within the world of scholarly editing there are more models available than is usually recognized. In 1996 W. Speed Hill listed eight kinds—documentary reprints, copy-text editions, genealogical editions, multiple-version editions, socialized editions, hypertext editions, genetic editions, and facsimile editions—and there is more exploration of the digital world to be done in every one of these directions (Hill 1996).

Within the present volume, Peter Robinson and Paul Vetch in different ways describe efforts to think anew about editions of literature in modern languages. And Martin Mueller indicates the potential of computer-assisted analysis, which would produce a very different way of working in literary studies. But of the contributors to this volume, Jeff Smith is best at suggesting in detail how different things could be in the end and how much our activity may change, as he discusses how writing itself might happen differently. This is the general direction that Mueller, Robinson, and Vetch are thinking about, but in Smith's case with the emphasis moved from resources we might build and draw upon to the way we write new texts. That direction is the one least explored in current research. For humanities scholars, today's digital world is full of resources but with largely traditional approaches to writing and publishing, in which digital publication is typically limited to reproductions of printed pages or forms such as blogs that can be seen as marginal.

The prophets of hypertext anticipated vast transformations in thought; the essays in this volume are more tactful than to suggest anything like that. But they already assume as background an environment that would have sounded like an impossible fantasy in 1990, in which the digital world does affect every aspect of scholarship. One gets the sense that people do not read those classics by Ted Nelson, J. David Bolter, Michael Joyce, or George P. Landow much now; probably because they were right. Much remains to be done, but we have actually come very far already.

WORKS CITED

Bolter, J. David. 1991. *Writing Space: The Computer, Hypertext, and the History of Writing.* Hillsdale, NJ: Lawrence Erlbaum Associates.

Burke, Victoria. 2007. Let's Get Physical: Bibliography, Codicology, and Seventeenth-Century Women's Manuscripts. *Literature Compass* 4, no. 6 (September): 1667–682.

Crane, Gregory, David Bamman, and Alison Jones. 2007. ePhilology: When the Books Talk to Their Readers. In *A Companion to Digital Literary Studies*, ed. Susan Schriebmann and Ray Siemens, 29–64. Malden, MA: Blackwell.

DeRose, Steven J. 1990. Paper versus Electronic Documents. *Humanist*, March 16.

Ezell, Margaret J. M. 2008. The Laughing Tortoise: Speculations on Manuscript Sources and Women's Book History. *English Literary Renaissance* 38, no. 2 (May): 331–55.

Galison, Peter. 2004. Removing Knowledge. *Critical Inquiry* 31, no. 1 (Autumn): 229–43.

Hafner, Katie. 2007. History, Digitized (and Abridged). *New York Times*, March 10.

Harley, Diane, Sarah Earl-Novell, Sophie Krzys Acord, Lawrence Shannon, and C. Judson King. 2008. Center for Studies in Higher Education Draft Interim Report: Assessing the Future Landscape of Scholarly Communication. University of California at Berkeley. http://cshe.berkeley.edu/publications/publications.php?id=300.

Hill, W. Speed. 1996. Where We Are and How We Got Here: Editing after Poststructuralism. *Shakespeare Studies* 24: 38–46.

Joyce, Michael. 1995. *Of Two Minds: Hypertext Pedagogy and Poetics.* Studies in Literature and Science. Ann Arbor: University of Michigan Press.

_____ 1998. New Stories for New Readers: Contour, Coherence and Constructive Hypertext. In *Page to Screen: Taking Literacy into the Electronic Era*, ed. Ilana Snyder, 163–82. London: Routledge.

Kahle, Brewster. 2009. Economics of Book Digitization. *Open Content Alliance Blog.* March 22. http://www.opencontentalliance.org/2009/03/22/economics-of-book-digitization/.

Landow, George P. 1992. *Hypertext: The Convergence of Contemporary Critical Theory and Technology.* Baltimore: Johns Hopkins University Press.

May, Steven W. 2010. All of the Above: The Importance of Multiple Editions of Manuscripts. *Literature Compass* 7.2: 95-101.

Nelson, Ted. 1981. *Literary Machines 93.1.* Swarthmore PA: Ted Nelson.

Nunberg, Geoffrey. 2009. Google's Book Search: A Disaster for Scholars. *Chronicle of Higher Education*, August 31.

Palmer, Carole L. 2004. Thematic Research Collections. In *A Companion to Digital Humanities*, ed. Susan Schreibman, Ray Siemens, and John Unsworth, 348–66. Blackwell Companions to Literature and Culture. Oxford: Blackwell.

Shirky, Clay. 2009. Newspapers and Thinking the Unthinkable. March 13. http://www.shirky.com/weblog/2009/03/newspapers-and-thinking-the-unthinkable/.

Contributors

Gabriel Egan is the author of *Shakespeare and Marx* (2004), *Green Shakespeare* (2006), and *The Edinburgh Critical Guide to Shakespeare* (2007). He co-edits the journals *Theatre Notebook* (for the Society for Theatre Research) and *Shakespeare* (for the British Shakespeare Association). His latest book, a history of the theory and practice of editing Shakespeare in the twentieth century called *The Struggle for Shakespeare's Text: Twentieth-Century Editorial Theory and Practice*, is published by Cambridge University Press.

Alan Galey is Assistant Professor in the Faculty of Information at the University of Toronto, where he also teaches in the collaborative program in Book History and Print Culture. His research focuses on intersections between textual scholarship and digital technologies, especially in the context of theories of the archive and the history of scholarly editing. He has published on these topics articles in journals such as *Early Modern Literary Studies*, *Archiv für das Studium der neueren Sprachen und Literaturen*, and *College Literature*, and co-edited special issues of *Shakespeare* ("Reinventing Digital Shakespeare") and *TEXT Technology* ("Digital Humanities and the Networked Citizen"). His contribution to this volume is part of a research project titled *Archive and Interface in Digital Textual Studies: From Cultural History to Critical Design* (supported by a Standard Research Grant from the Social Sciences and Humanities Research Council of Canada).

Ian Lancashire, Professor of English at the University of Toronto, and Fellow of the Royal Society of Canada, is author of *Two Tudor Interludes* (1980), *Dramatic Texts and Records of Britain* (1984), *The Humanities Computing Yearbook* (1991), and *Forgetful Muses: Reading the Author in the Text* (forthcoming); and co-author of *Using TACT with Electronic Texts* (1996). He has edited *Teaching Literature and Language Online* (forthcoming) as well as the Web-based databases *Representative Poetry Online* (1994–) and *Lexicons of Early Modern English* (2006–). As founding director of the Centre for Computing in the Humanities at Toronto (1985–96), he attended the first meeting of Text Encoding Initiative (TEI) at Vassar College in November 1987. He served as the Modern Language Association's representative to TEI for half a dozen years afterwards. His non-TEI recommendations for encoding old-spelling editions of early English Renaissance texts were adopted by the Internet Shakespeare Editions. Although in the early 1980s he used COCOA encoding practices and after 1997 preferred database technology, his Lexical Analysis Centre funded by the Text Analysis Portal for Research (TAPoR) eventually joined the TEI consortium.

John Lavagnino studied physics at Harvard University and American literature at Brandeis University, where he wrote his dissertation on Vladimir Nabokov. He has worked in atmospheric science at the Smithsonian Astrophysical Observatory and in electronic publishing for numerous organizations; he is now Reader in Digital Humanities at King's College London, where he teaches both in the Centre for Computing in the Humanities and in the Department of English. His major field of research has been in scholarly editing; he and Gary Taylor were general editors of the Oxford University Press edition of Thomas Middleton's collected works, published in 2007. The edition was awarded the Modern Language Association's Prize for a Distinguished Scholarly Edition in 2009. He is currently working with Peter Beal and Henry Woudhuysen on the digital Catalogue of English Literary Manuscripts 1450–1700, funded by a major grant from the UK's Arts and Humanities Research Council; this online publication will reprint and expand Beal's *Index of English Literary Manuscripts* covering the same period.

Shawn Martin is Scholarly Communication Librarian at the Van Pelt Library of the University of Pennsylvania. He has a BA in history from Ohio State University and an MA in history from the College of William and Mary. He has worked for several years in digital libraries including the Digital Library Project at the Colonial Williamsburg Foundation, the Ohio Memory Project at the Ohio Historical Society, and, most recently, the Text Creation Partnership at the University of Michigan. Shawn is also active in several library and scholarly associations and serves as the Executive Director of the American Association for History and Computing.

Murray McGillivray teaches Old and Middle English language and literature and humanities computing at the University of Calgary. His current digital projects include an electronic edition of the *Sir Gawain and the Green Knight* manuscript and the Online Corpus of Old English Poetry.

Martin Mueller is Professor of English and Classics at Northwestern University. His books include *Children of Oedipus and Other Essays on the Imitation of Greek Tragedy, 1550–1800* and a monograph on *The Iliad*, of which a thoroughly revised edition was recently published in the Bristol Classical Paperbacks (2009). He is the general editor of WordHoard, an application for the close reading and scholarly analysis of deeply tagged texts.

Peter Robinson is co-director of the Institute for Textual Scholarship and Electronic Editing at the University of Birmingham. He started experiments with the text of the *Canterbury Tales* in the late 1980s, when he was at Oxford. He is the developer of Collate and the Anastasia publishing system. His main research interests are: the study of large textual traditions and the developments of new tools for electronic analysis and publication. Peter pioneered the use of phylogenetic software applied to the study of large textual traditions, which is now being used by many scholars interested in the relationships between different witnesses of a text. He has worked closely with Prue Shaw on the editions of Dante's *Commedia* and *Monarchia*. Peter has been working with the Institute for New Testament Textual Research on the 28th edition of Erwin Nestle and Kurt Aland's Greek New Testament and a Digital Nestle-Aland edition. He is the founder of Scholarly Digital Editions and he is currently working on EDITION, a tool to produce electronic editions.

Peter Shillingsburg holds the Svaglic Chair in Textual Studies at Loyola University Chicago. He is author of *Scholarly Editing in the Computer Age*, *Resisting Texts*, and *From Gutenberg To Google*.

Jeff Smith is a computer scientist specializing in creativity enhancement for multimedia tools. After earning a Bachelor of Mathematics from the University of Waterloo, Jeff spent fifteen years in industry before returning to academia where he is currently completing a PhD in computer science at the University of Saskatchewan. In addition to his media and creativity research, Smith is also actively engaged in interdisciplinary outreach. He has co-authored a number of papers on literary analysis, medieval studies, astronomy, collaboration theory, and epidemiology, and he serves on the boards of a number of community arts and social service agencies across Canada.

Paul Vetch is a Research Fellow and Project Manager at the Centre for Computing in the Humanities (CCH) at King's College London, where he is a Co-Investigator or technical research director of nine major projects with funding from the Andrew W. Mellon Foundation, AHRC, JISC, Leverhulme Trust, British Academy, and UK Heritage Lottery Fund. His management responsibilities also include strategic oversight of CCH's substantial server and storage infrastructure. Paul's research and teaching interests lie in Web application interface design and implementation, user engagement and communication strategy, Web usability, and accessibility, and he has overall responsibility for interfaces across all CCH research projects (well over fifty to date). He has spoken widely on the specific interface design challenges and creative opportunities posed by complex, Web-based projects in the digital humanities.

In addition, Paul has acted as a consultant on a number of high profile Web publication projects for a range of cultural heritage and third sector clients including the National Theatre, the ICA, and Care International.

Robert Whalen, Associate Professor of English at Northern Michigan University, is editor of *The Digital Temple: A Documentary Edition of George Herbert's English Poems* (University of Virginia Press, forthcoming) and author of *The Poetry of Immanence: Sacrament in Donne and Herbert* (University of Toronto Press, 2002) as well as articles on Renaissance literature and humanities computing. With others at the Maryland Institute for Technology in the Humanities he is a developer of the Versioning Machine software, and he is a National Endowment for the Humanities Research Fellow 2009–2010.